FRONT-END DEVELOPMENT WITH ASP.NET CORE, ANGULAR, AND BOOTSTRAP

Front-end Development with ASP.NET Core, Angular, and Bootstrap

Front-end Development with ASP.NET Core, Angular, and Bootstrap

Simone Chiaretta

Front-end Development with ASP.NET Core, Angular, and Bootstrap

Published by
John Wiley & Sons, Inc.
10475 Crosspoint Boulevard
Indianapolis, IN 46256
www.wiley.com

Copyright © 2018 by John Wiley & Sons, Inc., Indianapolis, Indiana

Published simultaneously in Canada

ISBN: 978-1-119-18131-6
ISBN: 978-1-119-24396-0 (ebk)
ISBN: 978-1-119-18140-8 (ebk)

Manufactured in the United States of America

10 9 8 7 6 5 4 3 2 1

For general information on our other products and services please contact our Customer Care Department within the United States at (877) 762-2974, outside the United States at (317) 572-3993 or fax (317) 572-4002.

Wiley publishes in a variety of print and electronic formats and by print-on-demand. Some material included with standard print versions of this book may not be included in e-books or in print-on-demand. If this book refers to media such as a CD or DVD that is not included in the version you purchased, you may download this material at http://booksupport.wiley.com. For more information about Wiley products, visit www.wiley.com.

Library of Congress Control Number: 2018930062

For Signe, for the support over the project

ABOUT THE AUTHOR

SIMONE CHIARETTA (Brussels, Belgium) is a web architect and developer who enjoys sharing his development experiences and more than 20 years' worth of knowledge on web development with ASP.NET and other web technologies. He has been a Microsoft MVP for ASP.NET for eight years, has authored several books about ASP.NET MVC (*Beginning ASP.NET MVC 1.0* and *What's New in ASP.NET MVC 2?*, both published by Wrox, and *OWIN Succinctly* and *ASP.NET Core Succinctly*, published by Syncfusion), and has contributed to online developer portals (like Simple Talk). Simone also co-founded the Italian ALT.NET usergroup ugialt.NET and is the co-organizer of many conferences in Milan, including the widely appreciated Web.NET European Conference in 2012.

You can read Simone's thoughts and development tips on his blog: `http://codeclimber.net.nz`.

When not writing code and blog posts and taking part in the worldwide .NET community, Simone likes to play with Arduino, drones, and underwater robots, and he is training to complete his first Ironman in 2018. He is one of the many expats living and working in the capital of Europe, Brussels, where he is leading the team that develops the public web site of the Council of the European Union, one of the ruling bodies of the European Union.

ABOUT THE TECHNICAL EDITOR

UGO LATTANZI is a Microsoft-certified ASP.NET MVP who specializes in enterprise application development with a focus on web applications, service-oriented applications, and environments where scalability is a top priority. He is highly skilled in technologies such as ASP.NET MVC, NodeJS, Azure, and more. He is currently the Chief Software Architect for Technogym, and he formerly has served as a technical manager for MTV and has been a consultant for some of the largest companies in Italy. He also has enjoyed an active role in the tech community, serving as a technical writer, editor, and speaker for numerous conferences, book publishers, newspapers, webcasts, and forums. He's also the co-owner of the Web.NET European Conference located in Milan.

CREDITS

ACKNOWLEDGMENTS

I WANT TO START BY THANKING MY GIRLFRIEND SIGNE, for her support and for putting up with the many hours that this project took from my free time. This book would have not been possible without her support and blessing.

Then I would like to thank the editorial group at Wiley/Wrox. To Jim Minatel for helping draft the original idea behind the book and getting started with the project, and to Kelly Talbot, who without any shadow of a doubt did an amazing job with the copyediting of the manuscript and improving the language and readability of the book, and who kept pushing me and motivating me during the various rewrites that this book needed due to fundamental changes in the technologies covered.

And also a great thank you to Ugo Lattanzi, the technical editor, who helped catch some technical flaws and overall helped a lot with the quality of the book.

Besides the people directly involved in the writing of the book, I also want to thank the ASP.NET team, first for creating such a great framework, and also for helping me out in the early stages to understand where the framework was going. In particular I want to thank Bertrand Le Roy, Scott Hunter, and Scott Hanselman for providing me with up-to-date details about the upcoming releases.

A special thanks goes to Mads Kristensen for writing the preface and for always helping me out with questions about integration of front-end features into Visual Studio 2017.

I also want to thank Jason Imison for his help in better understanding the role of OmniSharp inside VS Code and to Juri Strumpflohner, for helping me out with some Angular-related matters.

Finally, I also have to thank my coworkers and manager Gunter for their support and review of the manuscript.

CONTENTS

FOREWORD

The web becomes an increasingly capable platform with each new browser release. Tomorrow's new features become available to early adopters while yesterday's stabilize for mass adoption. This ever-growing toolbox of HTML, CSS, and JavaScript capabilities seems to be accelerating and shows no signs of slowing down. In fact, it's growing so fast that specialized tooling is required to take advantage of these new features—tooling such as WebPack and Gulp.

The amount of knowledge required to build modern browser applications is illustrated by the new job title "front-end engineer"—a term that didn't exist just a few years ago.

In addition to the advances in the web platform, the server-side technologies powering the web are evolving as well. To provide the best experience for both end-users and web developers, the server-side platform must be ultra-fast, secure, cross-platform, and cloud scalable, and it must have great tooling.

Most web applications consist of client-side code running in the browser and server-side code running on one or more servers. To be a proficient web developer, it is necessary to know *enough* of both client and server technologies, and that is a big challenge. Because how much is *enough*, and how much time should we devote to continuously learning?

One way to make it easier for ourselves is to choose the right set of frameworks and tools to build our applications upon. Frameworks are useful because they usually wrap complex platform features into easy-to-use components, so web developers can focus on writing their applications' logic instead of all the plumbing needed to work with the browser or server platforms.

Choosing the right frameworks is important. The options are many, but there are a few that have shown to be particularly well-suited for building modern web applications. ASP.NET Core as the application framework for the server and Angular for the client is a great combination. Bootstrap makes sure the app looks good in all browsers and on all types of devices.

Simone has done a great job showing how these frameworks complement each other and how tooling provides a solid development experience. In the fast-moving world of web development, it is good that we have books like this to give us a pragmatic approach to building web applications using the latest and greatest in both client and server technologies.

MADS KRISTENSEN

INTRODUCTION

There was a time when "backend" and "front-end" developers were doing pretty different work. Backend developers were writing code to render web pages, using some server-side language; front-end developers were programming some interactivity using JavaScript and making the web pages look beautiful with CSS.

A few years ago, with the arrival of SPAs (Single Page Applications), JavaScript was not only used to add "some" interactivity, but was used to build the application itself. The skill-set of the so-called backend developers had to expand to include all the tools that were typical of front-developers, such as specific JavaScript frameworks and some basic understanding of CSS.

The goal of this book is to explain the tools in "front-end" developers' toolbox and how to use them effectively in combination with ASP.NET Core MVC.

WHY WEB DEVELOPMENT REQUIRES POLYGLOT DEVELOPERS

In everyday life, a polyglot is a person who knows and is able to use several languages. They are not necessarily bilingual (or multi-lingual), but they can use their second or third or fourth language with a good level of proficiency.

With that definition in mind, what is a polyglot developer? It's a developer who knows more than one (programming) language or framework and uses them within the scope of the same application.

From the beginning of IT industry, applications were mainly written in one language. I personally started with C, then moved to Visual Basic, landed on Cold Fusion, used JavaScript at its early stages (both on the client and the server), did a bit of Java, and finally landed on the .NET platform, but only one at a time.

It was the time of the big enterprise frameworks, when vendors tried to squeeze into their language or platforms all the possible features that an application might need. You probably remember when Microsoft tried to shield web developers from the actual languages of the web, HTML and JavaScript, introducing ASP.NET WebForms and the ASP.NET Ajax Framework. And if you look back at your personal experience in the IT industry, you'll probably find many other similar examples.

But lately a new trend has appeared, which has gone in the opposite direction. The IT industry understands that maybe some languages are more suitable than others for specific tasks, and instead of trying to force everything on top of one single language, applications are being written in multiple languages. We are entering the era of the polyglot developer.

Now that we share the same definition of a polyglot developer, let's see what the benefits of being one are.

The Right Tool for the Job

The first and probably most important benefit of being a polyglot is being able to choose the right tool for the job without having to compromise because your language or framework of choice doesn't support a given feature.

For example, by using the Microsoft AJAX Framework, you are limited by the functionalities it provides, while by directly using JavaScript you have all the flexibility provided by the language.

And I'm confident you will agree with me that as a web developer you have to know HTML, but nevertheless using the design surface of Visual Studio, you can build web applications just by dragging elements from the toolbox. Obviously, you do not have the same level of control as when crafting your HTML code directly.

So, to a certain degree, every web developer is already a polyglot developer.

The integration of SASS into Visual Studio 2015 is another example. A few years ago the Ruby community came up with the idea of a preprocessor for CSS styles. Instead of creating a .NET version of SASS, Microsoft decided to integrate the original version into its IDE, and SASS was the right tool for preprocessing CSS styles.

Cross Pollination

A second benefit of knowing multiple languages or frameworks is that you can take inspiration from what vendors and open-source communities are doing in other languages, and when you cannot just use it, you can adapt it or make a version specific to your own.

A very good example of this is ASP.NET MVC. About 10 years ago, the popular language of the moment was Ruby, thanks to its simple web framework, Ruby on Rails, built on top of the Model View Controller pattern. The .NET developer community took inspiration from it and started building .NET web frameworks also based on the MVC pattern. This led to Microsoft building the ASP.NET MVC framework that is one of the main topics of this book.

Growing Your Comfort Zone

Using several languages and frameworks brings an additional, if not technical, benefit: It forces you to step out of your existing comfort zone, making you more adaptable and breaking the potential boredom of always following the same routine. Not surprisingly, many developers are hesitant to experiment with new things and prefer the comfort of using the tools, frameworks, and language they know best, even if doing so gives them less flexibility and control. But if you are reading this book, you are probably not one of them. So, through the rest of the book, prepare to learn new languages and frameworks that originated outside of the Microsoft .NET space. In the beginning, you'll be stepping out of your comfort zone. By the time you are done, you'll find that your comfort zone has become even larger and more rewarding.

WHO THIS BOOK IS FOR

The audience of this book is web developers who have knowledge of ASP.NET MVC, either with the latest version or with previous versions of the framework, and who want to start using the tools and frameworks that are popular in the front-end development world. Additionally, this book can serve as a guide for developers who are already adopting some of the front-end tools and frameworks but want to make a more efficient use of them via the integrations that have been introduced with Visual Studio 2017.

WHAT THIS BOOK COVERS

This book is about front-end development with ASP.NET Core MVC. Together with giving an overview of the latest framework from Microsoft, it also covers some of the most popular frond-end frameworks and tools, like Angular, Bootstrap, Nuget, Bower, webpack, Gulp, and Azure.

In addition to the frameworks, the book shows the new front-end development-oriented features of Visual Studio 2017 but also how to develop an ASP.NET Core MVC application without it, using instead standard developers' text-editors like Visual Studio Code on Mac OS X.

This is not a beginners' book, so I assume that you know the basics of HTML, JavaScript, and CSS, that you know C# or VB.NET (keep in mind that all samples will be in C#), and that you have already worked with ASP.NET MVC and WebAPI.

HOW THIS BOOK IS STRUCTURED

If you still haven't decided whether this it the right book for you, in this section I'm briefly going to explain how the book is structured and the content of each chapter.

➤ **Chapter 1, "What's New in ASP.NET Core MVC":** The first chapter covers all the new features and the new approach to development brought to the table with ASP.NET Core and ASP.NET Core MVC and in general with .NET 2017. This chapter can be used as a refresher for those who already know the latest version of ASP.NET MVC or as a concise introduction for those who haven't seen it yet.

➤ **Chapter 2, "The Front-End Developer Toolset":** This chapter starts to explore the world of front-end developers, introducing the categories of tools they use and describing the top players in each category of tools and frameworks.

➤ **Chapter 3, "Angular in a Nutshell":** The third chapter introduces Angular, the JavaScript framework from Google, explaining its main concepts and the new Angular tools that came with Visual Studio 2017.

➤ **Chapter 4, "Bootstrap in a Nutshell":** The fourth chapter introduces the CSS framework from Twitter, Bootstrap, and shows how to use it to build responsive websites. The chapter also talks about Less, a CSS pre-processing language, and its integration with Visual Studio 2017.

➤ **Chapter 5, "Managing Dependencies with NuGet and Bower":** Managing all those components, both front-end and server-side, can be very painful, but luckily there are a few component managers that make it very easy. You can use NuGet to manage .NET server-side dependencies and Bower to handle them on the client-side. The fifth chapter explains how to use them, alone and in combination with Visual Studio 2017, and also how to package your libraries for sharing within your company or with the rest of the world.

➤ **Chapter 6, "Building Your Application with Gulp and webpack":** The sixth chapter is about Gulp and webpack, two build systems that can be programmed with JavaScript. Their integration with Visual Studio 2017 is also explained in this chapter, together with some common recipes used in ASP.NET development.

➤ **Chapter 7, "Deploying ASP.NET Core":** Once the application is ready, it's time for the deployment. This chapter uses Azure to show how to implement a continuous deployment flow that integrates testing, build, and deployment.

➤ **Chapter 8, "Developing Outside of Windows":** One of the main features of the .NET Core stack is that it can also run on Linux and Mac. Microsoft built a cross-platform IDE, but there are other options too. In this chapter you'll see how to do all your ASP.NET development on a Mac.

➤ **Chapter 9, "Putting It All Together":** The last chapter of the book puts together all the concepts and goes through all the steps required to build a modern, responsive website, with integration with third-party services and authentication via oAuth.

WHAT YOU NEED TO USE THIS BOOK

The book has lot of samples, so the best way to experience it is to try them yourself on your computer. In order to do so, you'll need either Windows 7, 8, or 10 and you'll need Visual Studio 2017 Community edition.

ASP.NET Core MVC can also be developed on any text editor on Windows, Mac OS X, or Linux. Microsoft also developed a cross-platform text editor called Visual Studio Code. You will also need it in order to follow along in Chapter 8 about developing outside of Windows. You can use any of the other compatible text editors, but the commands used and screenshots will be different from the ones used with Visual Studio Code.

The source code for the samples is available for download from the Wrox website at `www.wiley.com/go/frontenddevelopmentasp.netmvc6`.

CONVENTIONS

To help you get the most from the text and keep track of what's happening, we've used a number of conventions throughout the book.

> **WARNING** *Warnings hold important, not-to-be-forgotten information that is directly relevant to the surrounding text.*

> **NOTE** *Notes indicates notes, tips, hints, tricks, or asides to the current discussion.*

As for styles in the text:

➤ We *highlight* new terms and important words when we introduce them.

➤ We show keyboard strokes like this: Ctrl+A.

➤ We show file names, URLs, and code within the text like so: `persistence.properties`.

We present code in two different ways:

```
We use a monofont type with no highlighting for most code examples.
We use bold to emphasize code that is particularly important in the present context
or to show changes from a previous code snippet.
```

SOURCE CODE

As you work through the examples in this book, you may choose either to type in all the code manually, or to use the source code files that accompany the book. All the source code used in this book is available for download at `www.wrox.com`. Specifically for this book, the code download is on the Download Code tab at:

`www.wiley.com/go/frontenddevelopmentasp.netmvc6`

You can also search for the book at `www.wrox.com` by ISBN (the ISBN for this book is 978-1-119-18131-6) to find the code. And a complete list of code downloads for all current Wrox books is available at `www.wrox.com/dynamic/books/download.aspx`.

Most of the code on `www.wrox.com` is compressed in a .ZIP, .RAR archive, or similar archive format appropriate to the platform. Once you download the code, just decompress it with an appropriate compression tool.

> **NOTE** *Because many books have similar titles, you may find it easiest to search by ISBN; this book's ISBN is 978-1-119-18131-6.*

ERRATA

We make every effort to ensure that there are no errors in the text or in the code. However, no one is perfect, and mistakes do occur. If you find an error in one of our books, like a spelling mistake or faulty piece of code, we would be very grateful for your feedback. By sending in errata, you may save another reader hours of frustration, and at the same time, you will be helping us provide even higher quality information.

To find the errata page for this book, go to `www.wiley.com/go/frontenddevelopmentasp.netmvc6` And click the Errata link. On this page you can view all errata that has been submitted for this book and posted by Wrox editors.

If you don't spot "your" error on the Book Errata page, go to `www.wrox.com/contact/techsupport.shtml` and complete the form there to send us the error you have found. We'll check the information and, if appropriate, post a message to the book's errata page and fix the problem in subsequent editions of the book.

Front-end Development with ASP.NET Core, Angular, and Bootstrap

1

What's New in ASP.NET Core MVC

The year 2016 is a historical milestone for Microsoft's .NET web stack, as it is the year in which Microsoft released .NET Core, a complete open-source and cross-platform framework for building applications and services. It includes ASP.NET Core and a reworked MVC framework.

This first chapter is a brief introduction to ASP.NET Core. It can be used either as a refresher if you already have experience with this new framework or as a teaser and summary if you haven't seen anything yet.

GETTING THE NAMES RIGHT

Before delving into the new framework, it is important to get all the names and version numbers right, as for the untrained eye it can otherwise seem just a big mess.

ASP.NET Core

ASP.NET Core was released in 2016. It is a full rewrite of ASP.NET, completely open-source, cross-platform, and developed without the burden of backward compatibility. Notable features are a new execution environment, a new project and dependency management system, and a new web framework called ASP.NET Core MVC that unifies the programming model of both ASP.NET MVC and WebAPI. The rest of this chapter is mainly focused on all the features of ASP.NET Core.

.NET Core

ASP.NET Core can run on the standard .NET framework (from version 4.5 onward), but in order to be cross-platform it needed the CLR to be cross-platform as well. That's why .NET Core was released. .NET Core is a small, cloud-optimized, and modular implementation of .NET, consisting of the CoreCLR runtime and .NET Core libraries. The peculiarity is that this runtime is made of many components that can be installed separately depending on the necessary features, can be updated individually, and are bin-deployable so that different applications can run on different versions without affecting each other. And, of course, it can run on OSX and Linux.

.NET Core also provides a command-line interface (referred to as .NET CLI) that is used by both tools and end users to interact with the .NET Core SDK.

Visual Studio Code

Visual Studio Code is the cross-platform text editor developed by Microsoft for building ASP.NET Core applications (and many other frameworks and languages) without the full-fledged Visual Studio. It can also be used on OSX and Linux.

Visual Studio 2017

Visual Studio 2017 introduces a completely renewed installation procedure based on "workloads" to better tailor it to users' needs. One of these workloads, the ASP.NET one, includes integration with the most popular front-end tools and frameworks. This book covers them further in the upcoming chapters.

Versions Covered in this Book

I hope that now the version and naming madness is a bit clearer. This book covers Visual Studio 2017, ASP.NET Core (and ASP.NET Core MVC), and .NET Core, but it will not cover anything that is related to the full framework. At the end of the book, Visual Studio Code is also covered.

Figure 1-1 shows how all these components relate to each other.

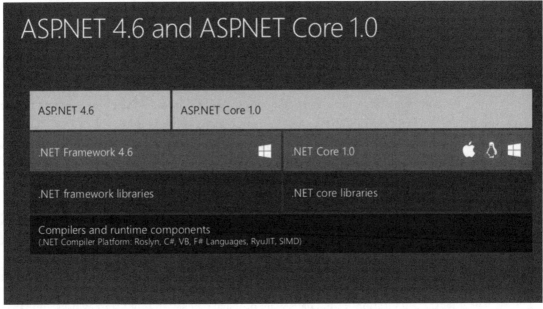

FIGURE 1-1: Diagram of the new .NET stack

A BRIEF HISTORY OF THE MICROSOFT .NET WEB STACK

Before diving into the new features of ASP.NET Core and ASP.NET Core MVC, I think it is important to look back at the evolution of the .NET web stack and the reasons why we arrived at ASP .NET Core and .NET Core.

ASP.NET Web Forms

In 2001, Microsoft released the .NET framework and its first web framework: ASP.NET Web Forms. It was developed for two types of users:

➤ Developers who had experience with classic ASP and were already building dynamic web sites mixing HTML and server-side code in Jscript. They were also used to interacting with the underlying HTTP connection and web server via abstractions provided by the core objects.

➤ Developers who were coming from the traditional WinForm application development. They didn't know anything about HTML or the web and were used to building applications by dragging UI components on a design surface.

Web Forms were designed to cater to both types of developers. Web Forms provided the abstractions to deal with HTTP and web server objects and introduced the concept of server-side events to hide the stateless nature of the web, using the ViewState. The result was a very successful, feature-rich web framework with a very approachable programming model.

It had its limitations though:

➤ All the core web abstractions were delivered within the System.Web library, and all the other web features depended on it.

➤ Because it was based on a design-time programming model, ASP.NET, the .NET framework and also Visual Studio were intimately tied. For this reason, ASP.NET had to follow the release cycle of the other products, meaning that years passed between major releases.

➤ ASP.NET only worked with Microsoft's web server, Internet Information Services (IIS).

➤ Unit testing was almost impossible and only achievable using libraries that changed the way Web Forms worked.

ASP.NET MVC

For a few years these limitations didn't cause any problems, but with other frameworks and languages pushing the evolution of web development, Microsoft started to struggle to follow their faster pace. They were all very small and focused components assembled and updated as needed, while ASP.NET was a huge monolithic framework that was difficult to update.

The problem was not only a matter of release cycles. The development style also was changing. Hiding and abstracting away the complexities of HTTP and HTML markup helped a lot of WinForm developers to become web developers, but after more than five years of experience, developers wanted more control, especially over the markup rendered on pages.

In order to solve these two problems, in 2008 the ASP.NET team developed the ASP.NET MVC framework, based on the Model-View-Controller design pattern, which was also used by many of the popular frameworks at the time. This pattern allowed a cleaner and better separation of business and presentation logic, and, by removing the server-side UI components, it gave complete control of the HTML markup to developers. Furthermore, instead of being included inside the .NET framework, it was released out of band, making faster and more frequent releases possible.

Although the ASP.NET MVC framework solved most of the problems of Web Forms, it still depended on IIS and the web abstracting library System.Web. This means that it was still not possible to have a web framework that was totally independent from the larger .NET framework.

ASP.NET Web API

Fast-forward a few years, and new paradigm for building web applications started to become widespread. These were the so-called single page applications (SPAs). Basically, instead of interconnected, server-generated, data-driven pages, applications were becoming mostly static pages where data was displayed interacting with the server via Ajax calls to web services or Web APIs. Also, many services started releasing APIs for mobile apps or third-party apps to interact with their data.

Another web framework was released to adapt better to these new scenarios: ASP.NET Web API. The ASP.NET team also took this opportunity to build an even more modular component model, finally ditching System.Web and creating a web framework that could live its own life independently from the rest of ASP.NET and the larger .NET framework. A big role was also played by the introduction of NuGet, Microsoft's package distribution system, making it possible to deliver all these components to developers in a managed and sustainable way. One additional advantage of the break-up from System.Web was the capability to not depend on IIS anymore and to run inside custom hosts and possibly other web servers.

OWIN and Katana

ASP.NET MVC and ASP.NET Web API solved all the shortcomings of the original ASP.NET, but, as often happens, they created new ones. With the availability of lightweight hosts and the proliferation of modular frameworks, there was the real risk that application developers would need separate processes to handle all the aspects of modern applications.

In order to respond to this risk even before it became a real problem, a group of developers, taking inspiration from Rack for Ruby and partially from Node.js, came out with a specification to standardize the way frameworks and other additional components can be managed from a central hosting process. This specification is called OWIN, which stands for Open Web Interface for .NET. OWIN defines the interface that components, be they full-fledged frameworks or just small filters, have to implement in order to be instantiated and called by the hosting process.

Based on this specification, in 2014 Microsoft released Katana, an OWIN-compliant host and server, and implemented lots of connectors to allow developers to use most of its web frameworks inside Katana.

But some problems persisted. First of all, ASP.NET MVC was still tied to System.Web, so it could not run inside Katana. Also, because all the frameworks were developed at different points in time, they had different programming models. For example, both ASP.NET MVC and Web API supported dependency injection, but differently from each other. This meant that developers using both frameworks in the same application had to configure dependency injection twice, in two different ways.

The Emergence of ASP.NET Core and .NET Core

The ASP.NET team realized that there was only one way to solve all the remaining problems and at the same time make web development on .NET possible outside of Visual Studio and on other platforms. They re-wrote ASP.NET from the ground up and created a new cross-platform .NET runtime that later came to be .NET Core.

.NET CORE

Now that it is probably more clear why ASP.NET Core came to be, it is time to take a better look at .NET Core, the new entry point of this whole new stack. .NET Core is a cross-platform and open-source implementation of the .NET Standard Library, and it is made of a few components:

➤ The .NET Runtime, also known as CoreCLR, which implements the basic functionalities such as JIT Compilation, the base .NET types, garbage collection, and low-level classes

➤ CoreFX, which contains all the APIs defined in the .NET Standard Library, such as Collections, IO, Xml, async, and so on

➤   Tools and language compilers that allow developers to build apps

➤   The dotnet application host, which is used to launch .NET Core applications and the development tools

> **DEFINITION** *The .NET Standard Library is a formal specification of all the .NET APIs that can be used in all .NET runtimes. It basically enhances the CLR specifications (ECMA 335) by also defining all the APIs from the Base Class Library (BCL) that must be implemented by all .NET runtimes. The goal of such a standard is to allow the same application or library to run on different runtimes (from the standard framework to Xamarin and Universal Windows Platform).*

Getting Started with .NET Core

Installing .NET Core on Windows is pretty trivial, as it gets installed by selecting the .NET Core workload when installing Visual Studio 2017. And creating a .NET Core application is just like creating any other application with Visual Studio. Chapter 8 shows how to install .NET Core and develop applications without Visual Studio, also on a Mac, but it is important to understand how .NET Core applications are built because it will it make easier later to do the same without Visual Studio or even on another operating system.

The dotnet Command Line

The most important tool that comes with .NET Core is the dotnet host, which is used to launch .NET Core console applications, including the development tools, via the new .NET command-line interface (CLI). This CLI centralizes all the interactions with the framework and acts as the base layer that all other IDEs, like Visual Studio, use to build applications.

In order to try it out, just open the command prompt, create a new folder, move into this folder, and type dotnet new console. This command creates the skeleton of a new .NET Core console application (Listing 1-1), made of a Program.cs code file and the .csproj project definition file, named as the folder in which the command was launched.

LISTING 1-1: Sample Program.cs file

```
using System;

namespace ConsoleApplication
{
    public class Program
    {
        public static void Main(string[] args)
```

```
        {
            Console.WriteLine("Hello World!");
        }
    }
}
```

The new command can be executed using other arguments to specify the type of project to build: console (the one we used before), web, mvc, webapi, classlib, xunit (for unit testing), and some others that are discussed further in Chapter 8. This is also the structure of all commands of the .NET CLI: dotnet followed by the command name, followed by its arguments.

.NET Core is a modular system, and, unlike the standard .NET framework, these modules have to be included on a one to one basis. These dependencies are defined in the .csproj project file and must be downloaded using another command of the .NET Core CLI: restore. Executing dotnet restore from the command prompt downloads all the dependencies needed by the application. This is needed if you add or remove dependencies while developing, but it's not strictly needed immediately after creating a new application because the new command runs it automatically for you.

Now that all the pieces are ready, the application can be executed by simply typing the command dotnet run. This first builds the application and then invokes it via the dotnet application host.

In fact, this could be done manually as well, first by explicitly using the build command and then by launching the result of the build (which is a DLL with the same name of the folder where the application has been created) using the application host: dotnet bin\Debug\netcoreapp2.0\ consoleapplication.dll (consoleapplication is the name of the folder).

In addition to building and running apps, the dotnet command can also deploy them and create packages for sharing libraries. It can do even more thanks to its extensibility model. These topics are discussed further in Chapter 8.

INTRODUCING ASP.NET CORE

Now that you are armed with a bit of knowledge of .NET Core tooling, you can safely transition to Visual Studio and explore ASP.NET Core.

Overview of the New ASP.NET Core Web Application Project

As with previous version of the framework, you create a new ASP.NET Core application using the command menu File ⇨ New ⇨ Project and then choosing ASP.NET Core Web Application from the .NET Core group of projects.

Here you have several additional options, as shown in Figure 1-2:

➤ **Console App:** This creates a console application like the one in Listing 1-1.

➤ **Class Library:** This is a .NET Core library that can be reused in other projects.

➤ **Unit Test Project:** This is a test project running on the Microsoft MSTest framework.

➤ **xUnit Test Project:** This is another test project, but built using the xUnit OSS test framework.

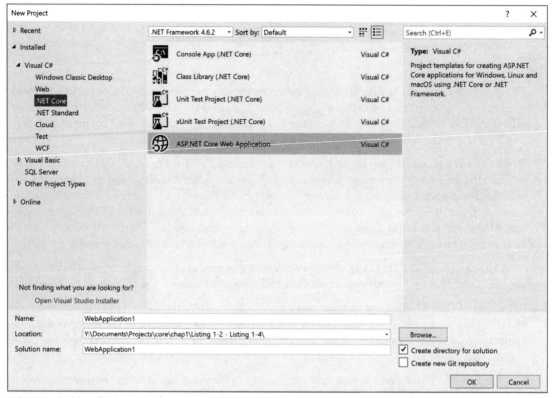

FIGURE 1-2: New Project Window

At this point you get the familiar template selection window (Figure 1-3), which by default gives you three options:

➤   Empty creates an ASP.NET Core project with the bare minimum to get you started.

➤   Web API creates an ASP.NET Core project that contains the dependencies and the skeleton on which to build a REST web application.

➤   Web Application creates a web application built with Razor pages, which is a simpler development paradigm that isn't covered in this book.

➤   Web Application (Model-View-Controller) creates the full-blown project with everything you might need in a web application.

➤   Angular, React.js, and React.js and Redux are project templates used to create single-page applications using these frameworks.

In addition to the authentication type, you can also choose with which version of ASP.NET Core to build the application (ASP.NET Core 1.0, 1.1, or 2.0) and whether to enable support for Docker (this last option is covered in Chapter 7).

For this initial overview, you will select the Web Application (Model-View-Controller) template and proceed through all the pieces of the puzzle.

Figure 1-4 shows the all the files and folders added to the project, and you can see that there are already a lot of changes compared to the traditional ASP.NET project. Apart from the `Controllers` and `Views` folders, all the rest is different.

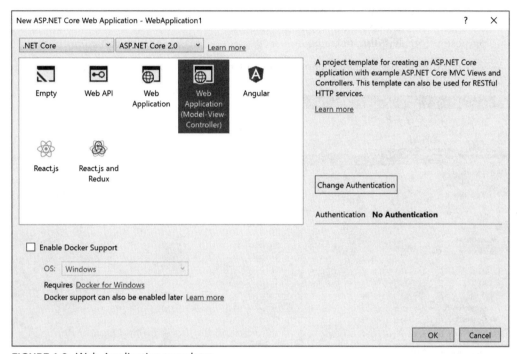

FIGURE 1-3: Web Application templates

Starting from the top, the first new element is the Connected Services node, which contains the list of extensions that connect to a third party remote service.

The next element is a node called Dependencies. This contains all the dependencies the application has, which can be .NET packages (via NuGet), Bower, as shown in Figure 1-4, or NPM if you application needs it.

A reference to Bower appears also later in the tree with the file `bower.json`, which contains the actual configuration of all the dependencies. These dependencies, once downloaded, will be stored in the `lib` folder inside the new `wwwroot` folder.

The next element is the `wwwroot` folder, which is even represented with a different "globe" icon. This is where all the static files of the application, CSS styles, images and JavaScript files, will be.

These files in the root of the project are also new additions:

➤   `appsettings.json` is the new location for storing application settings instead of storing them in the `appsetting` element in the `web.config`.

➤   `bower.json` is the configuration file for Bower dependencies.

➤   `bundleconfig.json` defines the configuration for bundling and minifying JavaScript and CSS files.

➤ Program.cs is where the web application starts. As mentioned earlier, the .NET Core app host can only start console applications, so web projects also need an instance of Program.cs.

➤ Startup.cs is the main entry point for ASP.NET Core web applications. It is used to configure how the application behaves. Thus the Global.asax file, which was used for this purpose before, has disappeared.

➤ web.config disappeared as it's not needed any more.

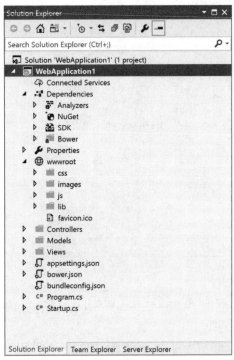

FIGURE 1-4: The elements of the new ASP.NET Core Web Application

Of the many changes introduced in the new project template, some are on the .NET side, like the Startup.cs, and others are in the broader web development sphere, like the introduction of Bower, the capability to include dependencies to NPM, minification, bundling, and the new approach to publishing applications.

Chapter 5 covers Bower and NPM in more detail, while Chapter 6 describes automated builds and publishing. The rest of this chapter is about all the changes introduced to the .NET side of things, starting with the Startup.cs file.

OWIN

In order to understand the new ASP.NET Core execution model and why there is this new Startup .cs file, you have to look at OWIN (Open Web Interface for .NET), the application model by which

ASP.NET Core is inspired. OWIN defines a standard way for application components to interact with each other. The specification is very simple as it basically defines only two elements: the layers of which an application is composed and how these elements communicate.

OWIN Layers

The layers are shown in Figure 1-5. They consist of the following:

➤ **Host:** The host is responsible for starting up the server and managing the process. In ASP .NET Core this role is implemented by the `dotnet` host application or by IIS directly.

➤ **Server:** This is the actual web server, the one that receives HTTP requests and sends back the responses. In ASP.NET Core there are a few implementations available. These include IIS, IIS Express, and Kestrel or WebListener when the application is run within the dotnet host in self-hosting scenarios.

➤ **Middleware:** Middleware is composed of pass-through components that handle all requests before delivering them to the final application. These components make up the execution pipeline of an ASP.NET Core application and can implement anything from simple logging to authentication to a full-blown web framework like ASP.NET MVC.

➤ **Application:** This layer is the code specific to the final application, typically built on top of one of the middleware components, like a web framework.

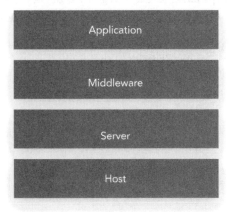

FIGURE 1-5: OWIN Layers

OWIN Communication Interface

In OWIN, all the components that are part of the pipeline communicate with each other by passing a dictionary that contains all information about the request and server state. If you want to make sure all middleware components are compatible, they must implement a delegate function called `AppFunc` (or application delegate):

```
using AppFunc = Func<
    IDictionary<string, object>, // Environment
    Task>; // Done
```

This code basically says that a middleware component must have a method that receives the Environment dictionary and returns a Task with the async operation to be executed.

> **NOTE** *The signature of* AppFunc *is the one defined by the OWIN specifications. While working inside ASP.NET Core, it's rarely used as the .NET Core API provides an easier way to create and register middleware components in the pipeline.*

A Better Look at Middleware

Even if not strictly standardized in the specification yet, OWIN also recommends a way to set up the application and register middleware components in the pipeline by using a builder function. Once registered, middleware components are executed one after the other until the last produces the result of the operation. At this point, middleware is executed in the opposite order until the response is sent back to the user.

An example of a typical application built with middleware might be the one shown in Figure 1-6. The request arrives, is handled by a logging component, is decompressed, passes through authentication, and finally reaches the web framework (for example ASP.NET MVC), which executes the application code. At this point the execution steps back, re-executing any post-processing steps in middleware (for example, recompressing the output or logging the time taken to execute the request) before being sent out to the user.

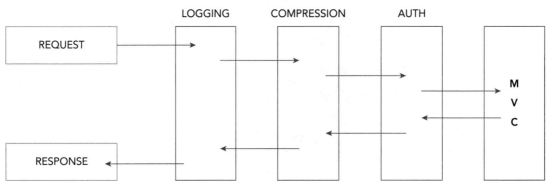

FIGURE 1-6: Execution of middleware

Anatomy of an ASP.NET Core Application

In order to better understand ASP.NET Core and its new approach to web development with .NET, it is worthwhile to create a new ASP.NET Core project. This time you will use the Empty project template to focus just on the minimum sets of files needed to start an ASP.NET Core application.

As shown in Figure 1-7, the project tree in the Solution Explorer is almost empty in comparison to the Web Application project template of Figure 1-4. The only elements needed are the Program.cs and Startup.cs code files.

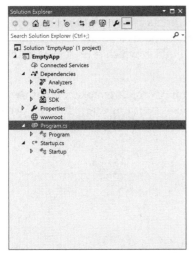

FIGURE 1-7: Empty project template

Host Builder Console Application

An ASP.NET Core application is basically a console application (Listing 1-2) that creates a web server in its Main method.

LISTING 1-2: Program.cs

```
public class Program
{
    public static void Main(string[] args)
    {
        BuildWebHost(args).Run();
    }

    public static IWebHost BuildWebHost(string[] args) =>
        WebHost.CreateDefaultBuilder(args)
            .UseStartup<Startup>()
            .Build();
}
```

The BuildWebHost method is used to create the web application host using the default configuration and by specifying which class to use for the startup (UseStartup<Startup>).

The web host created uses Kestrel as the server, sets it up to integrate with IIS when needed, and specifies all the default configurations for logging and configuration sources.

ASP.NET Core Startup Class

The configuration of the execution pipeline of an ASP.NET Core application is done via the Configure method of the Startup class. At its simplest this method needs a parameter of type IApplicationBuilder to receive an instance of the application builder, which is used to assemble together all middleware components.

Listing 1-3 shows the code of the Startup class created by the empty project template. It has two methods, ConfigureServices and the aforementioned Configure. ConfigureServices is covered later in this chapter, when talking about dependency injection, so you'll focus on the Configure method for the moment.

LISTING 1-3: Startup.cs

```
public class Startup
{
    public void ConfigureServices(IServiceCollection services)
    {
    }

    // This method gets called by the runtime. Use this method to configure the
HTTP request pipeline.
    public void Configure(IApplicationBuilder app, IHostingEnvironment env)
    {

        if (env.IsDevelopment())
        {
            app.UseDeveloperExceptionPage();
        }

        app.Run(async (context) =>
        {
            await context.Response.WriteAsync("Hello World!");
        });
    }
}
```

The important part of Listing 1-3 is the call to the app.Run method. It tells the application to run the delegate function specified in the lambda expression. In this case, this web application will always return the text string "Hello World!".

The Run method is used to configure *terminal* middleware, which doesn't pass the execution to the next component in the pipeline. In Listing 1-3, a specific middleware component is also added, using app.UseDeveloperExceptionPage(). As general rule, third-party middleware usually provides a UseSomething method for facilitating the registration into the pipeline. Another way of adding custom middleware is by calling the `app.Use` method, specifying the application delegate function that should treat the request.

As you might have noticed, in Listing 1-3 the `Configure` method has an additional parameter: `IHostingEnvironment`, which provides information on the hosting environment (including the current `EnvironmentName`). You'll see more about them in a while.

NEW FUNDAMENTAL FEATURES OF ASP.NET CORE

Together with a whole new startup model, ASP.NET Core also gained some features that previously needed third-party components or some custom development:

➤ Easier handling of multiple environments

➤ Built-in dependency injection

➤ A built-in logging framework

➤ A better configuration infrastructure that is both more powerful and easier to set up and use

Environments

One of the basic features available in ASP.NET Core is the structured approach for accessing information about the environment in which the application is running. This deals with understanding whether the environment is development, staging, or production.

This information is available inside the `IHostingEnvironment` parameter passed to the `Configure` method. The current environment can be identified by simply checking its `EnvironmentName` property. For the most common environment names, there are some extension methods that make the process even easier: `IsDevelopment()`, `IsStaging()`, and `IsProduction()`, and you can use `IsEnvironment(envName)` for other more exotic names.

Once you have identified the environment, you can add features to handle different conditions based on the environment. For example, you can enable detailed errors to only be displayed in development and user-friendly messages to only be displayed in production.

If differences between the environments are even more pronounced, ASP.NET Core allows different startup classes or configuration methods per environment. For example, if a class named `StartupDevelopment` exists, this class will be used instead of the standard `Startup` class when the environment is `Development`. Likewise, the `ConfigureDevelopment()` method will be used instead of `Configure()`.

The environment is specified via the environment variable `ASPNETCORE_ENVIRONMENT`, which can be set in many different ways. For example, it can be set via the Windows Control Panel, via batch scripts (especially in servers), or directly from within Visual Studio in the project properties debug section (Figure 1-8).

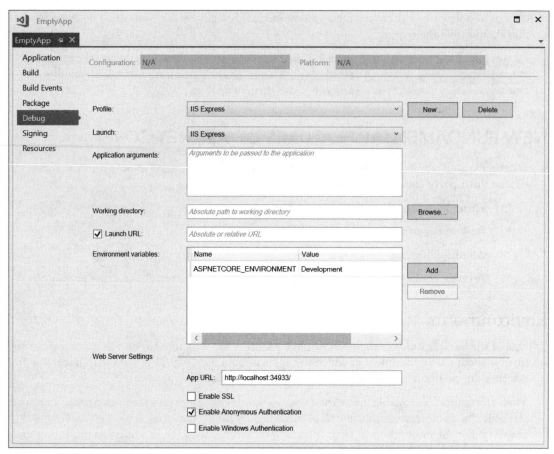

FIGURE 1-8: Project settings

Once set via the GUI, this information is stored in the launchSettings.json file, as shown in Listing 1-4.

LISTING 1-4: LaunchSettings.json

```json
{
  "iisSettings": {
    "windowsAuthentication": false,
    "anonymousAuthentication": true,
    "iisExpress": {
      "applicationUrl": "http://localhost:34933/",
      "sslPort": 0
    }
  },
  "profiles": {
    "IIS Express": {
```

```
        "commandName": "IISExpress",
        "launchBrowser": true,
        "environmentVariables": {
          "ASPNETCORE_ENVIRONMENT": "Development"
        }
      },
      "EmptyApp": {
        "commandName": "Project",
        "launchBrowser": true,
        "environmentVariables": {
          "ASPNETCORE_ENVIRONMENT": "Development"
        },
        "applicationUrl": "http://localhost:34934"
      }
    }
  }
```

Dependency Injection

In the previous ASP.NET framework, the usage of external dependency injection libraries was left to the goodwill of developers. ASP.NET Core not only has built-in support for it, but actually requires its usage in order for applications to work.

What Is Dependency Injection?

Dependency injection (DI) is a pattern used to build loosely coupled systems. Instead of directly instantiating dependencies or accessing static instances, classes get the objects they need somehow from the outside. Typically these classes declare which objects they need by specifying them as parameters of their constructor.

Classes designed following this approach adhere to the Dependency Inversion Principle. It states that:

> A. High-level modules should not depend on low-level modules. Both should depend on abstractions.

> B. Abstractions should not depend on details. Details should depend on abstractions.

ROBERT C. "UNCLE BOB" MARTIN

This also means that these classes should not require concrete objects but just their abstractions, in the form of interfaces.

The problem with systems built in this way is that, at a certain point, the number of objects to create and to "inject" into classes can become unmanageable. To handle this, you have a factory method that can take care of creating all these classes and their associated dependencies. Such a class is called a *container*. Typically containers work by keeping a list of which concrete class they have to instantiate for a given interface. Later when they are asked to create the instance of a class, they look at all its dependencies and create them based on that list. In this way very complex graphs can also be created with just one line of code.

In addition to instantiating classes, these containers, called *Inversion of Control* or *Dependency Injection Containers* (IoC/DI containers), can also manage the lifetime of dependencies, which means that they also know whether they can reuse the same object or they must create another instance every time.

> **NOTE** *This was a very brief introduction to a very wide and complicated topic. There are numerous books on the topic, as well as lots of articles available on the Internet. In particular I suggest the articles from Robert C. "Uncle Bob" Martin or from Martin Fowler.*

Using Dependency Injection in ASP.NET Core

Despite the relative complexity of the concept, using dependency injection in ASP.NET Core is very easy. The configuration of the container is done inside the `ConfigureServices` method of the `Startup` class. The actual container is the `IServiceCollection` variable that is passed to the method as a parameter named `services`. It is to this collection that all dependencies must be added.

There are two types of dependencies: the ones needed for the framework to work and those needed by the application to work. The first type of dependencies is usually configured via extension methods like `AddService`. For example, you can add the services needed to run ASP.NET MVC by calling `services.AddMvc()`, or you can add the database context needed by the Entity Framework using `services.AddDbContext<MyDbContext>(...)`. The second type of dependencies is added by specifying an interface and one concrete type. The concrete type will be instantiated every time the container receives a request for the interface.

The syntax for adding the services depends on the kind of lifetime the service needs:

➤ **Transient** services are created every time they are requested and are typically used for stateless lightweight services. Such services are added using `services.AddTransient<IEmail Sender,EmailSender>()`.

➤ **Scoped** services are created once per web request and are usually used to hold references to repositories, data access classes, or any service that keeps some state that is used for the whole duration of the request. They are registered using `services .AddScoped<IBlogRepository, BlogRepository>()`.

➤ **Singleton** services are created once, the first time they are requested, and later the same instance is reused for all following requests. Singletons are usually used to keep the status of an application throughout all its life. Singletons are registered using `services .AddSingleton<IApplicationCache, ApplicationCache>()`.

A typical `ConfigureServices` method for an ASP.NET Core application can look like the following snippet taken from the default project template when choosing individual user accounts:

```
public void ConfigureServices(IServiceCollection services)
{
    // Add framework services.
    services.AddDbContext<ApplicationDbContext>(options =>
        options.UseSqlServer(Configuration.GetConnectionString
        ("DefaultConnection")));

    services.AddIdentity<ApplicationUser, IdentityRole>()
        .AddEntityFrameworkStores<ApplicationDbContext>()
        .AddDefaultTokenProviders();

    services.AddMvc();

    // Add application services.
    services.AddTransient<IEmailSender, AuthMessageSender>();
    services.AddTransient<ISmsSender, AuthMessageSender>();
}
```

Additionally, a specific instance can be given (and in this case this is what will always be created by the container). For more complex scenarios a factory method can be configured to help the container create instances of specific services.

The usage of the dependencies is even easier. In the constructor of the class, controller, or service, just add a parameter with the type of the dependencies required. A better example is shown later in this chapter when covering the MVC framework.

Logging

ASP.NET Core comes with an integrated logging library with basic providers that write to console and to the debug output already configured as part of the setup of the default web host via the `WebHost.CreateDefaultBuilder` as seen in Listing 1-2.

Logger Instantiation

The logger is injected directly using dependency injection by specifying a parameter of type `ILogger<T>` in the constructor of the controllers or services. The dependency injection framework will provide you with a logger whose category is the full type name (for example `Wrox .FrontendDev.MvcSample.HomeController`).

Writing Log Messages

Writing messages is easily done with the extension methods provided by the built-in logging library.

```
_logger.LogInformation("Reached bottom of pipeline for request {path}", context.
Request.Path)
_logger.LogWarning("File not found")
_logger.LogError("Cannot connect to database")
```

Additional Logging Configuration

The logger is already configured by default with the console and debug providers, but additional providers and configuration can be specified.

All additional configuration must be specified in the `Program.cs` file, when setting up the web host, using the `ConfigureLogging` method.

```
WebHost.CreateDefaultBuilder(args)
    .UseStartup<Startup>()
    .ConfigureLogging((hostingContext, logging)=>
    {
        //Here goes all configuration
    })
    .Build();
```

ASP.NET Core comes with built-in providers to write to the console, the debug window, Trace, Azure App logging, and the Event Log (only on the standard framework), but if needed third-party logging providers like NLog or Serilog can be added as well.

For example, to add another provider like the one that writes to the Windows Event Log, `logging.AddEventLog()` must be called inside the `ConfigureLogging` method.

Another important configuration that must be specified is the log level that you want to write to the log files. This can be done for the whole application using the method `logging.SetMinimumLevel(LogLevel.Warning)`. In this example, only warnings, errors, or critical errors will be logged.

Configuration of the logging level can be more granular, taking into account the logger provider and the category (most of the time the name of the class from which the message originates).

Say for example that you want to send all log messages to the debug provider and in the console logger you are interested in all the messages from your own code but only in warnings or above originating from the ASP.NET Core libraries.

This is configured using *filters*. They can be specified via configuration files, with code, or even with custom functions.

```
The easiest approach is using JSON inside the standard appsettings.json
configuration file:{
  "Logging": {
    "IncludeScopes": false,
    "Debug": {
      "LogLevel": {
        "Default": "Information"
      }
    },
    "Console": {
      "LogLevel": {
        "Microsoft.AspNet.Core": "Warning",
        "MyCode": "Information"
      }
    },
    "LogLevel": {
      "Default": "Warning",
    }
  }
}
```

Something similar can be done by calling the `AddFilter` method in the `ConfigureLogging` method when building the web host:

```
logging.AddFilter<ConsoleLoggerProvider>("Microsoft.AspNet",LogLevel.Warning);
logging.AddFilter<DebugLoggerProvider>("Default",LogLevel.Information);
```

Both methods can be used together, and multiple filters can potentially apply to one single log message. The logging framework applies the following rules to decide which filter to apply:

1. First it selects all the filters that apply to the provider and all the ones that are specified without the provider.

2. Then the categories are evaluated and the most specific is applied. For example `Microsoft .AspNet.Core.Mvc` is more specific than `Microsoft.AspNet.Core`.

3. Finally, if multiple filters are still left, the one specified as last is taken.

Configuration

If you worked with Configuration Settings in the standard ASP.NET framework, you know that it could be very complicated to set up, apart from the simple scenarios.

The new configuration framework supports different sources of settings (XML, JSON, INI, environment variables, command-line arguments, and in-memory collections). It also automatically manages different environments and makes it very easy to create strongly-typed configuration options.

The recommended approach for using the new configuration system is to set it up when building the web host and then read it within your application, either directly or via the new strongly-typed option.

Setting Up the Configuration Sources

Because the `Configuration` class, in its simplest form, is just a key/value collection, the setup process consists of adding the sources from which all these key/value pairs must be read from. The default web host builder already sets it up for you, so you just need to know where the configuration is read from:

➤ The first source of the configuration is the `appsettings.json` file in the root of the project.

➤ Then the configuration is read from a file named `appsettings.{env.EnvironmentName}` `.json`.

➤ The configuration can be read from environment variables.

➤ Finally, there are also the arguments used when launching the application using the `dotnet run` command.

This setup allows the default settings defined in the first `appsettings.json` file to be overwritten in another JSON file whose name depends on the current environment and finally by a possible environment variable set on the server or argument passed to the command-line tool that runs the application. For example, paths to folders or database connection strings can be different in different environments.

Other configuration sources are the in-memory collection source, typically used as the first source, to provide default values for settings, and the Users Secrets source, used to store sensitive information that you don't want committed to a source code repository, like password or authorization tokens.

Reading Values from Configuration

Reading the collection is also easy. Settings are read just by using their key, for example `Configuration["username"]`. If the values are from a source that allows trees of settings, like JSON files, the key is to use a concatenation of all the property names, separated by `:`, starting from the root of the hierarchy.

For example, to read the connection string defined in the setting file of Listing 1-5, the following key should be used: `ConnectionStrings:DefaultConnection`. Sections of the settings can be accessed in a similar way, but instead of using the simple dictionary key approach, the `GetSection` method must be used. For example, `Configuration.GetSection("Logging")` gets the whole subsection related to logging (which can then be passed to the logger providers instead of configuring them by code).

LISTING 1-5: Appsettings.json file of the default project template

```
{
  "ConnectionStrings": {
    "DefaultConnection":
"Server=(localdb)\\mssqllocaldb;Database=aspnet-ConfigSample-c18648e9-6f7a-40e6-
b3f2-12a82e4e92eb;Trusted_Connection=True;MultipleActiveResultSets=true"
  },
  "Logging": {
    "IncludeScopes": false,
    "LogLevel": {
      "Default": "Warning"
    }
  }
}
```

Unfortunately this naive approach works only if you have access directly to the instance of the configuration class (for example, as with the `Startup` class). There are two options to share the configuration with other components. The first is to create a custom service that centralizes the access to configuration, as was done with the standard ASP.NET framework. And second, which is the new and recommended approach, is easier to configure and requires no custom coding. This approach uses `Options`.

Using Strongly-Typed Configuration

Creating strongly-typed configuration options doesn't require much more than creating the actual classes to hold the settings.

For example, say you want to access the following configuration settings.

```
"MySimpleConfiguration": "option from json file",
"MyComplexConfiguration": {
    "Username": "simonech",
    "Age": 42,
    "IsMvp": true
}
```

All you need to do is to create two classes that map the properties in the JSON file one to one, as shown in Listing 1-6.

LISTING 1-6: Options' classes (Configuration\MyOptions.cs)

```
public class MyOptions
{
    public string MySimpleConfiguration { get; set; }
    public MySubOptions MyComplexConfiguration  { get; set;}
}

public class MySubOptions
{
    public string Username { get; set; }
    public int Age { get; set; }
    public bool IsMvp { get; set; }

}
```

All that is left now is to create the binding between the configuration and the classes. This is done via the `ConfigureService` method as shown in following snippet.

```
public void ConfigureServices(IServiceCollection services)
{
  services.AddOptions();
  services.Configure<MyOptions>(Configuration);
}
```

The `AddOptions` method just adds support for injecting options into a controller or service, while the `Configure<TOption>` extension method scans the `Configuration` collection and maps its keys to the properties of the Options classes. If the collection contains keys that do not map, they are simply ignored.

If an option class is just interested in the values of a sub-section, for example `MyComplexConfiguration`, the `Configure<TOption>` extension method can be called by specifying the section to use as the configuration root, similar to what is done when configuring Logging:

```
services.Configure<MySubOptions>(Configuration.GetSection("MyComplexConfiguration"))
```

Now options are ready to be injected into any controller or service that requests them, via its constructor.

Listing 1-7 shows a controller that accesses the option class MySubOptions by simply adding a parameter of type IOptions<MySubOptions> to the constructor. Notice that it is not the actual option class to be injected but an accessor for it, so when using it the Value property needs to be used.

LISTING 1-7: HomeController using options

```
public class HomeController : Controller
{
    private readonly MySubOptions _options;

    public HomeController(IOptions<MySubOptions> optionsAccessor)
    {
        _optionsAccessor = optionsAccessor.Value;
    }

    public IActionResult Index()
    {
        var model = _options;
        return View(model);
    }
}
```

ALTERNATIVES TO IOptions

Using IOptions is the approach recommended by the ASP.NET Core team because it opens the door to other scenarios such as automatic reload of the configuration on change, but some people find this approach a bit too complicated.

Luckily, there are a few other alternatives, one of which is simply passing the configuration to the controllers by registering it directly in the IoC container. Most of the code is similar to what you use with IOptions with the exception of the ConfigureServices method and the Controller.

Instead of enabling the Options framework by calling the AddOptions method, you can directly bind the Configuration object to the strongly-typed class and then register it inside the IoC container.

```
var config = new MySubOptions();
Configuration.GetSection("MyComplexConfiguration").Bind(config);
services.AddSingleton(config);
```

This way the configuration can be used directly by the controller without going through the IOptions interface.

AN OVERVIEW OF SOME ASP.NET CORE MIDDLEWARE

So far the application you built doesn't do a lot of work. It just always renders a text string. But you can add more functionality simply by adding some of the middleware that has been released as part of ASP.NET Core.

Diagnostics

The first additional component you might want to add is available in the package `Microsoft.AspNetCore.Diagnostics`. There is no need to manually add the package because in ASP.NET Core 2.0 all the packages are already included as part of the `Microsoft.AspNetCore.All` metapackage.

It contains a few different components that help with handling errors. The first is the developer exception page, added to the pipeline using `UseDeveloperExceptionPage`, which is a more powerful replacement of the Yellow Page of Death, as it also shows some information on the status of the request, cookies, and headers (Figure 1-9).

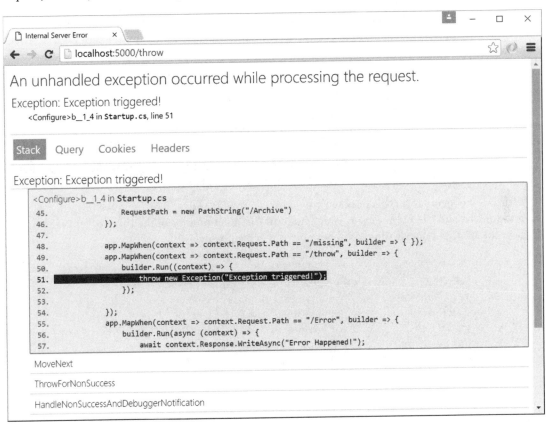

FIGURE 1-9: Developer Exception Page

This page is useful while in development, but such detailed information should never be exposed to the public. The Exception Handler middleware can be used to send users to a different page when an error happens by specifying the path to which the application has to redirect:

```
app.UseExceptionHandler("/Error")
```

If a page doesn't exist, normally the application should return an HTTP 404 status code and a page not found warning, but ASP.NET Core won't do so unless instructed. Luckily, it can be easily done as you just need to add it to the pipeline using `app.UseStatusCodePages()`.

Serving Static Files

HTML, CSS, JavaScript, and images can be served by an ASP.NET Core application by using functionalities of the `Microsoft.AspNetCore.StaticFiles` package and by registering the middleware using `app.UseStaticFiles()`.

This middleware component serves all files under the `wwwroot` folder as if they were in the root path of the application. So the `/wwwroot/index.html` file will be returned when a request for `http://example.com/index.html` arrives. Optionally, other paths can be defined for serving folders outside of `wwwroot`. The following snippet shows how to create another instance of the StaticFile middleware that serves all files under `MyArchive` when requests for the path `http://example.com/archive` arrive.

```
app.UseStaticFiles(new StaticFileOptions()
{
    FileProvider = new PhysicalFileProvider(
        Path.Combine(Directory.GetCurrentDirectory(), @"MyArchive")),
    RequestPath = new PathString("/Archive")
});
```

If you want to have `index.html` files served automatically without specifying their name, another middleware component, `UseDefaultFiles`, must be added before any `UseStaticFiles`.

Other components from this package are `UseDirectoryBrowser`, which allows browsing of files and folders, and `UseFileServer`, which adds all the functionality of the three other components (but for security reasons directory browsing is disabled by default).

> **WARNING** *There are some security considerations. The* `UseStaticFiles` *middleware doesn't perform any check on authorization rules, so all files stored under* `wwwroot` *are publicly accessible. Also, enabling directory browsing is a security risk and should not be done in a production site. If either protection of static assets or directory browsing are needed, it is better to store the files in a folder not accessible from the web and return the results via a controller action using ASP.NET Core MVC.*

Application Frameworks

The most important middleware components are the ones that completely take over the execution and host the code of the application. With ASP.NET Core there are two application frameworks available:

➤ **MVC** is used for building web applications that render HTML and handle user interactions.

➤ **Web API** is used for building RESTful web services that can be consumed by either single-page applications or by native applications on mobile or IoT devices.

These two frameworks share many concepts, and, unlike with the previous versions, the programming model has been unified so that there is almost no difference between the two.

ASP.NET CORE MVC

It might seem strange that a chapter titled "What's New in ASP.NET Core MVC" of a book that's about frontend development with ASP.NET Core MVC doesn't mention MVC almost till the end of the chapter. The reason is that almost all the new features in the updated MVC framework are related to the move from the standard ASP.NET framework to ASP.NET Core. The new startup process, the new OWIN-based execution pipeline, the new hosting model, the built-in configuration, logging, and dependency injection libraries already have been covered.

This last section of the chapter covers the new features that are specific to the MVC framework, starting from the new way of setting it up inside an ASP.NET Core application and how to define the routing table. Later it covers how to use dependency injection in controllers and ends with interesting new features related to views: view components and tag helpers.

Using the MVC Framework inside ASP.NET Core

The easiest way to start an MVC project on ASP.NET Core is to create a new project using the Web Application template. This will set up everything so that you can start right away with writing the code of the application. Most of the wiring up is done inside the Startup class (Listing 1-8).

LISTING 1-8: Startup class for the Web Application template

```
public class Startup
{
    public Startup(IConfigurationRoot configuration)
    {
        Configuration = configuration;
    }

    public IConfigurationRoot Configuration { get; }
```

```
        // This method gets called by the runtime. Use this method to add services to
   the container.
        public void ConfigureServices(IServiceCollection services)
        {
            // Add framework services.
            services.AddMvc();
        }

        // This method gets called by the runtime. Use this method to configure the
   HTTP request pipeline.
        public void Configure(IApplicationBuilder app, IHostingEnvironment env)
        {
            if (env.IsDevelopment())
            {
                app.UseDeveloperExceptionPage();
                app.UseBrowserLink();
            }
            else
            {
                app.UseExceptionHandler("/Home/Error");
            }

            app.UseStaticFiles();

            app.UseMvc(routes =>
            {
                routes.MapRoute(
                    name: "default",
                    template: "{controller=Home}/{action=Index}/{id?}");
            });
        }
    }
```

In addition to what has already been described in previous sections of this chapter (diagnostics, error handling, and serving of static files), the default template adds the Mvc middleware to the pipeline and the Mvc services to the built-in IoC container.

While adding the Mvc middleware, routing is configured as well. In this case the default route is specified. It matches the first segment of an URL to the controller name, the second to the action name, and the third to the argument named id of action method. And if they are not specified, the request will be handled by the action named Index and by the controller named Home.

It doesn't differ from the previous ASP.NET MVC framework. It's just a different way of defining the routing table. Instead of doing it inside the global.asax file, it is done inside the configuration of the middleware.

Using Dependency Injection in Controllers

Dependency injection was covered earlier in this chapter, together with how to add custom services into the built-in container. Now you will take a look at how to use these services inside controllers and action methods.

One of the many reasons for using an abstraction is to make it easy to test the behavior of the application. For example, if an online shop has to display a special message on the first day of spring, you probably don't want to wait till March 21st to make sure that application works correctly. So, in this case, instead of depending directly on the `System.DateTime.Today` property, it would be wiser to wrap it inside an external service so that it can later be replaced with a fake implementation that, for the purpose of testing, always returns March 21st.

This is done by defining the interface, which in this case is very simple, and by implementing it in a concrete class, as is done in Listing 1-9.

LISTING 1-9: IDateService interface and its implementations

```
public interface IDateService
{
    DateTime Today { get; }
}

public class DateService: IDateService
{
    public DateTime Today
    {
        get {
            return DateTime.Today;
        }
    }
}

public class TestDateService : IDateService
{
    public DateTime Today
    {
        get
        {
            return new DateTime(2017, 3, 21);
        }
    }
}
```

Once the interface and the concrete class are ready, the controller must be modified to allow injection into its constructor. Listing 1-10 shows how this is done.

LISTING 1-10: HomeController with constructor injection

```
public class HomeController : Controller
{
    private readonly IDateService _dateService;

    public HomeController(IDateService dateService)
    {
        _dateService = dateService;
    }
```

```
public IActionResult Index()
{
    var today = _dateService.Today;
    if(today.Month==3 && today.Day==21)
        ViewData["Message"] = "Spring has started, enjoy our spring sales!";
    return View();
}
}
```

The last piece needed to tie the service and controller together is the registration of the service into the built-in IoC Container. As previously seen, this is done inside the `ConfigureServices` method, using `services.AddTransient<IDateService, DateService>()`.

Another way of using services inside an action method is via the new `[FromServices]` binding attribute. This is particularly useful if the service is used only inside one specific method and not throughout the entire controller. Listing 1-10 could be rewritten using this new attribute as shown in Listing 1-11.

LISTING 1-11: HomeController with action method parameter injection

```
public class HomeController : Controller
{
    public IActionResult Index([FromServices] IDateService dateService)
    {
        var today = dateService.Today;
        if(today.Month==3 && today.Day==21)
            ViewData["Message"] = "Spring has started, enjoy our spring sales!";
        return View();
    }
}
```

View Components

Now that you have seen the setup procedure and some new features of the controller, you will take a look at what's new on the View side, starting with View Components. They are in a way similar to Partial Views, but they are more powerful and are used in different scenarios.

Partial Views are, as the name suggests, views. They are used to split a complex view into many smaller and reusable parts. They are executed in the context of the view, so they have access to the view model, and being just razor files, they cannot have complicated logic.

View Components, on the other hand, do not have access to the view model but just to the arguments that are passed to it. They are reusable components that encapsulate both backend logic and a razor view. They are therefore made of two parts: the view component class and a razor view. They are used in the same scenarios as Child Actions, which have been removed from the MVC framework in ASP.NET Core, and are reusable portions of pages that also need some logic that might involve querying a database or web services, like sidebars, menus, and so on.

The component class inherits from `ViewComponent` and must implement the method `Invoke` or `InvokeAsync`, which returns `IViewComponentResult`. By convention view component classes are located in a `ViewComponents` folder in the root of the project, and its name must end with `ViewComponent`. Listing 1-12 shows a view component class named `SideBarViewComponent` that shows a list of links that need to appear in all the pages of the site.

LISTING 1-12: ViewComponents\SideBarViewComponent.cs file

```csharp
namespace MvcSample.ViewComponents
{
    public class SideBarViewComponent : ViewComponent
    {
        private readonly ILinkRepository db;
        public SideBarViewComponent(ILinkRepository repository)
        {
            db = repository;
        }

        public IViewComponentResult Invoke (int max = 10)
        {
            var items = db.GetLinks().Take(max);
            return View(items);
        }
    }
}
```

As shown in the example, the view component class can make use of the dependency injection framework just like controllers do (in this case it uses a repository class that returns a list of links).

The view rendered by the view component is just like any other view, so it receives the view model specified in the `View` method, and it is accessible via the `@Model` variable. The only detail to remember is its name. By convention, the view must be `Views\Shared\Components\<ComponentName>\Default.cshtml` (so, in this example it should be `Views\Shared\Components\SideBar\Default.cshtml`), as shown in Listing 1-13.

LISTING 1-13: Views\Shared\Components\SideBar\Default.cshtml

```cshtml
@model IEnumerable<MvcSample.Model.Link>

<h2>Blog Roll</h2>
<ul>
    @foreach (var link in Model)
    {
        <li><a href="@link.Url">@link.Title</a></li>
    }
</ul>
```

Finally, to include the view component into a view, the `@Component.InvokeAsync` method must be called, providing an anonymous class with the parameters for the view component's `Invoke` method.

```
@await Component.InvokeAsync("SideBar", new { max = 5})
```

If you used Child Actions from the previous version you will immediately notice the main difference. The parameters are provided directly by the calling method and are not extrapolated by the route via model binding. This is because view components are not action methods, but are a whole new element that doesn't reuse the standard MVC execution pipeline. An added benefit is that you cannot expose these components by mistake to the web, like you could do with Child Actions if you forgot to specify the `[ChildOnly]` attribute.

Tag Helpers

Tag helpers are a new concept introduced in ASP.NET Core MVC. They are a mash-up of standard HTML tags and Razor HTML helpers, and they take the best part of both of them. Tag helpers look like standard HTML tags, so there is no more switching between writing HTML and C# code. They also have some of the server-side logic of HTML helpers, so, for example, they can read the value of the view model and conditionally add CSS classes.

Using Tag Helpers from ASP.NET Core

For example, take a look at how to write an input textbox for a form. With HTML helpers you would write `@Html.TextBoxFor(m => m.Email)`, while using tag helpers the code is `<input asp-for="Email" />`.The first case is C# code that returns HTML, while the second case is just HTML that is enhanced with some special attribute (`asp-for` in this case).

The advantage becomes more obvious when the HTML tag needs additional attributes (for example if you want to add a specific class or some `data-*` or `aria-*` attributes). With HTML helpers you would need to provide an anonymous object with all the additional attributes, while with tag helpers you write as if you were writing standard static HTML and just add the special attribute.

The differences become apparent by comparing the two syntaxes for a textbox that needs an additional class and for which you want to disable autocomplete. With HTML helpers it is:

```
@Html.TextBoxFor(m=>m.Email, new { @class = "form-control", autocomplete="off" })
```

The same textbox using a tag helper is:

```
<input asp-for="Email" class="form-control" autocomplete="off" />
```

Another added value of using tag helpers is the support inside Visual Studio. Tag helpers get IntelliSense and have a different syntax highlighting.

Figures 1-10 through 1-12 show what happens when you start typing in Visual Studio a tag that could be a tag helper. In the IntelliSense list, you can identify which tags could be tag helpers because of the new icon (the @ sign with < > angular brackets). Once you select the tag, IntelliSense shows all the possible attributes, again identifying the tag helpers with the new icon. Finally, when the attribute is typed as well, Visual Studio recognizes it as a tag helper; it colorizes it differently and also provides IntelliSense for the value of the property `asp-for`.

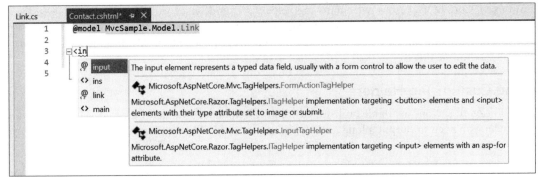

FIGURE 1-10: Identifying which tags can be tag helpers

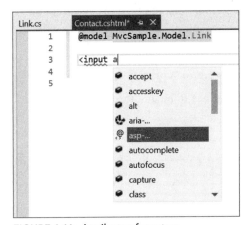

FIGURE 1-11: Attributes for a tag

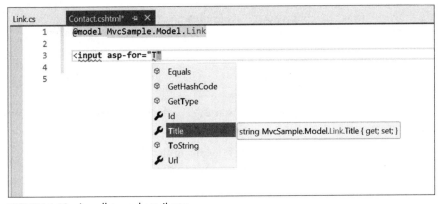

FIGURE 1-12: A well-typed attribute

ASP.NET Core MVC comes with many tag helpers for rendering forms but also for other tasks, such as an `Image` tag helper that can also add a version number to the URL to make sure it is not cached or an `Environment` tag helper for conditionally rendering different HTML fragments depending on which environment it is.

Writing Custom Tag Helpers

In addition to the one available built-in, custom tag helpers can be easily created. They are very useful when you need to output a long and repetitive piece of HTML code that changes very little from one instance to another.

To see how to build a custom tag helper, let's make one that automatically creates an email link by specifying the email address. We'll create something that converts `<email>info@wrox.com</email>` to `<a href="mailto:info@wrox.com">info@wrox.com</a>`.

The tag helper is a class, named `<Helper>TagHelper`, that inherits from `TagHelper` and implements the `Process` or `ProcessAsync` methods.

Those two methods have the two following parameters:

➤   `context` contains the information on the current execution context.

➤   `output` contains a model of the original HTML and has to be modified by the tag helper.

Listing 1-14 shows the full code for the tag helper.

LISTING 1-14: EmailTagHelper.cs

```
public class EmailTagHelper: TagHelper
{
    public override async Task ProcessAsync(TagHelperContext context,
TagHelperOutput output)
    {
        output.TagName = "a";
        var content = await output.GetChildContentAsync();
        output.Attributes.SetAttribute("href", "mailto:"+content.GetContent());
    }
}
```

Let's see what the code does.

The first line replaces the tag name (which in our case is `email`) with the one needed in the HTML code. Since we are generating a link, it must be an a tag.

The second line gets the content of the element. This is done using the `GetChildContentAsync` method, which also takes care of executing any Razor expression present.

Finally, the `href` attribute is set to the previously retrieved string.

Before using the newly created tag helper, we must instruct the framework where to look for tag helpers. This is done in the `_ViewImports.cshtml` file. See Listing 1-15.

LISTING 1-15: _ViewImports.cshtml

```
@using MvcSample
@addTagHelper *, Microsoft.AspNetCore.Mvc.TagHelpers
@addTagHelper "*, MvcSample"
```

The first line is added by the default project and is needed to be able to use the built-in tag helpers, while the second instructs the framework to look for new tag helpers in any class of the project.

Finally we can use the tag helper by typing the following:

```
<email>info@wrox.com</email>
```

In addition to this sample, Chapter 4 shows the code for a tag helper that renders a Bootstrap component.

View Components as Tag Helpers

We've seen how to add a View Component in a razor view by using the `InvokeAsync` method. But starting with ASP.NET Core 1.1, View Components can also be included using the same syntax as tag helpers (and IntelliSense) by appending the prefix `vc`.

With this syntax, the View Component of Listings 1-12 and 1-13 can also be instantiated using `<vc:sidebar max="5"></sidebar>`, and also gets IntelliSense as shown in Figure 1-13.

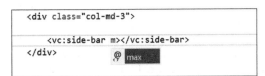

FIGURE 1-13: IntelliSense on View Components

Web API

Unlike previous versions of Web API, with ASP.NET Core, Web API applications reuse all the same features and configurations of MVC ones.

For example, to write an API that returns the list of links used in the side bar of Listing 1-12, you just need to create a controller that adheres to the Web API routing conventions and that specifies the HTTP verbs to which each action responds. See Listing 1-16.

LISTING 1-16: LinksController.cs

```
[Route("api/[controller]")]
public class LinksController : Controller
{
    private readonly ILinkRepository db;
    public LinksController(ILinkRepository repository)
    {
```

```
        db = repository;
    }

    [HttpGet]
    public IEnumerable<Link> Get()
    {
        return db.GetLinks();
    }

    [HttpGet("{id}")]
    public Link Get(int id)
    {
        return db.GetLinks().SingleOrDefault(l=>l.Id==id);
    }
}
```

This controller will respond to HTTP GET requests to the URL /api/Links by returning the list of all links in JSON format, and to /api/Links/4 by returning the link whose id is 4. This behavior is specified by the Route attribute, which configures the name of the API method, and by the HttpGet method, which specifies which action to execute when the API is called with GET.

SUMMARY

ASP.NET Core introduces a new, more modern framework that encourages writing code of good quality thanks to the built-in support for dependency injection and the easy-to-use component model. Together with this better framework, the whole development experience got an overhaul. New command-line-based developer tools make it possible to develop with a lighter IDE, and the introduction of elements typical of the front-end development world like Bower, NPM, and Gulp make the new .NET stack more appealing for developers coming from different backgrounds.

But all these changes also bring new challenges. .NET developers have to evolve and start learning new technologies and get fluent in other languages. The rest of the book covers in detail all these new technologies and languages that are now required in order to be a skilled .NET web developer.

The Front-End Developer Toolset

WHAT'S IN THIS CHAPTER?

➤ The types of tools used in front-end development

➤ The main actors in each type of tool

After the previous chapter's brief overview of what comes with the latest server-side frameworks, ASP.NET Core and ASP.NET Core MVC, this chapter gives you a foundation in front-end development, showing when you need additional tools to get your work done more efficiently.

The chapter covers the following categories of tools:

➤ **JavaScript frameworks:** These frameworks help you build complex web interfaces by bringing to front-end development the best practices that are typical of server-side systems, like the model-view-controller (MVC) pattern, the model-view-view model (MVVM), dependency injection (DI), routing, and many others.

➤ **CSS frameworks:** Developers are generally bad at making web apps look good and consistent. CSS frameworks provide a set of styles and UI components with which you can build web applications that look as if they were created by professional designers. CSS frameworks also help address the issue of responsive design that adapts to multiple resolutions and screen sizes and can also apply complex animations and transitions.

➤ **Package managers:** Systems are becoming more and more a mix and match of different components, many of which depend on other components. Managing all these dependencies and correct versions would be a nightmare if it wasn't for package managers.

➤ **Build systems:** If you are coming from a pure .NET background, you probably have used some build systems already, like NAnt or MSBuild. The front-end development world came out with their own build systems, which are made specifically for managing the build of front-end systems.

➤ **Languages:** These extend beyond C# or VB.NET. Most of the tools from the previous categories are built and must be used with JavaScript or other domain-specific languages (DSL).

This chapter provides an overview of the most popular tools for each of the aforementioned categories, starting with the most fundamental of them, namely the additional languages you need to know.

WROX.COM CODE DOWNLOADS FOR THIS CHAPTER

The wrox.com code downloads for this chapter are found at `www.wrox.com` Search for the book's ISBN (978-1-119-18131-6), and you will find the code in the chapter 2 download and individually named according to the names throughout the chapter.

ADDITIONAL LANGUAGES YOU HAVE TO KNOW

C#, standard client-side JavaScript, and CSS are not the only languages needed for developing web applications the "front-end developer" way. Many of the tools described in this book rely on another version of JavaScript, Node.JS, and other domain-specific languages like Sass/Less and JSON.

Node.js

Node.js isn't actually a language. Node.js is more of a platform for building very fast and scalable network applications. It's built on top of Chrome V8 JavaScript runtime (the same JavaScript engine used inside Google Chrome).

Node.js is an asynchronous event-based framework with non-blocking input/output (I/O), which basically means that applications don't consume CPU cycles when they are waiting for I/O operations (reading from or writing to a data stream, be it a file on a disk, an HTTP connection, standard output, or anything else that "streams" data) or waiting for any other event to happen.

If you have never seen it, Listing 2-1 is the standard "Hello World" example for Node.js. It loads the `http` module, it creates the `server` object by specifying the function that should be executed when a response comes in, and it starts listening for an HTTP connection on port 8080.

LISTING 2-1: Node.js Hello World sample

```
var http = require('http');

var server = http.createServer(function (req, res) {
```

```
        res.writeHead(200, {'Content-Type': 'text/plain'});
        res.end('Hello ASP.NET Core developers!\n');
    });

    server.listen(8080);

    console.log('Server running at http://127.0.0.1:8080/');
```

But I/O is not just related to HTTP. I/O also deals with reading and writing files from disk or memory streams, so Node.js also has been popular for building command-line tools and utilities. The reason I'm mentioning it in an ASP.NET web development book is because the most popular build tools in the "front-end world" are developed with Node.js.

Another reason to use Node.js is because this framework comes with a very useful tool, the Node Package Manager (NPM), that is introduced later in this chapter and covered in more detail in Chapter 5, "Managing Dependencies with NuGet and Bower".

JSON

Strictly speaking, JSON (JavaScript Object Notation) is not a language, but rather a data-interchange format meant to be easily parsed and generated by machine while being easy to read and write for humans. As the name implies, it's essentially the serialization of a JavaScript object. As Listing 2-2 shows, it's an object whose properties are a series of key-value pairs, where the key is always a string, and the value can be either a string/number/Boolean value, another object (enclosed within curly brackets), or an array of values (in square brackets).

LISTING 2-2: JSON data

```
{
  "name":"Simone Chiaretta",
  "age": 42,
  "address": {
    "city":"Brussels",
    "country":"Belgium"
  },
  "hobbies": [
    "triathlon",
    "web development",
    "jigsaw puzzles"
  ],
  "employed": true
}
```

Parsing a JSON text with the JavaScript eval function will put the data structure that is serialized in the file directly into memory. However, that's not recommended as the eval function executes everything, so there can be security issues. JavaScript has a native parsing function, JSON .parse(jsonText), that after validating the text excludes the malicious and possibly security-threatening code, and returns just the "sanitized" data structure.

The opposite operation, writing a JSON text from a JavaScript object, is also natively supported with the function `JSON.stringify(myObject)`.

Given the native support in JavaScript for parsing and writing JSON strings, this format is also used to send data back and forth between clients and servers in single page applications over Ajax calls.

Over time, thanks to the easy human readability, JSON has also started being used as a format for configuration files. In ASP.NET Core projects, the preferred format for configuration files is JSON. In addition to this, all the package managers' configuration files are in JSON format too.

Sass and Less

If you have used CSS you might have noticed that at first it seems like an easy syntax to work with, but if not carefully organized it becomes a maintenance nightmare. If you want to change the color of something, you might have to change it in many different class definitions. Also, to specify the size of boxes, usually you have to do some math to get the right padding, margin, and border size.

To overcome these problems, more than five years ago the Ruby community developed two meta-languages that would then compile to standard CSS: Sass (which stands for Syntactically Awesome Stylesheets) and Less. By adopting this approach they could introduce such concepts as variables, functions, mixins, and nesting and still get a standard CSS file. Sass and Less both started as Ruby tools, but later compilers in other languages were written, so now they can be integrated in any development workflow and IDE, including Visual Studio.

Now you will look at how some of the basic features are implemented in both languages and how they translate to CSS.

First, consider the basic principle of each language, variables.

In Sass variables are identified by the prefix $:

```
$dark-blue: #3bbfce;
#header {
  color: $dark-blue;
}
h2 {
  color: $dark-blue;
}
```

Less uses @ as the prefix:

```
@dark-blue: #3bbfce;

#header {
  color: @dark-blue;
}
h2 {
  color: @dark-blue;
}
```

And they both compile to the following CSS:

```
#header {
  color: #3bbfce;
}
h2 {
  color: #3bbfce;
}
```

Another basic feature is mixins, which basically are more CSS properties that can be included in many classes' definitions. They can also accept parameters.

In Sass the concept of inclusion is very obvious in the syntax. The mixin is defined by the keywork `@mixin` and is used with the keyword `@include`:

```
@mixin menu-border($width: 1px) {
  border-top: dotted $width black;
  border-bottom: solid $width*2 black;
}

#menu {
  @include menu-border
}

#side-menu {
  @include menu-border(2px)
}
```

On the other hand, Less doesn't introduce any new syntax but just repurposes the standard class syntax of CSS, basically allowing classes to be part of other classes:

```
.menu-border(@width: 1px) {
  border-top: dotted @width black;
  border-bottom: solid @width*2 black;
}

#menu {
  .menu-border
}

#side-menu {
  .menu-border(2px)
}
```

Both syntaxes compile to the following lines of code:

```
#menu {
  border-top: dotted 1px black;
  border-bottom: solid 2px black;
}

#side-menu {
  border-top: dotted 2px black;
  border-bottom: solid 4px black;
}
```

Sass is bit more explicit in the syntax, while Less reuses the standard CSS as much as possible, but at the end of the day they are pretty similar, so the choice of which one to use is up to you.

I encourage you to read about the other features on their respective websites and experiment with them to determine which one you like better. But the choice probably boils down to which CSS framework you want to use. Out of the four covered in this chapter, two use Sass (Primer CSS and Material Design Lite) and two use Less (Bootstrap CSS and Semantic UI).

The Future of JavaScript

JavaScript is based on an evolving standard, ECMAScript, which in 2015 reached version 6, often referred to as ES6. This version brings new interesting features, for example, classes (with constructors, getter, setter, and inheritance), modules and a modules loader, the "arrow" syntax (the lambda expressions of C#), and standard data structures like Map, Set, and many others.

Even though the major browsers are implementing ES6 features in their latest versions, older versions do not support them, so it probably will take a while before ES6 can be used in web development. But just as Sass and Less overcame some of the limitations of CSS, there are meta-languages that implement part of these new specifications. One of them is TypeScript.

TypeScript

While waiting for the various JavaScript engines to catch up with ES6 features, Microsoft released TypeScript. It introduces support for classes, modules, and arrow syntax as proposed by ES6 and also other concepts that are currently not available in JavaScript, such as strong typing, interfaces, generics, and more.

But this is not a Microsoft version of JavaScript. Similar to Sass and Less, which compile to standard CSS, TypeScript compiles to standard JavaScript. It also performs static analysis and reports on possible misuses and type errors.

As previously mentioned, one of the features of TypeScript is strong typing. In reality strong typing is just type annotations that are checked at compile time:

```
function add(x: number, y: number): number {
  return x+y;
}

var sum = add(2,3);
var wrongSun = add("hello","world");
```

The first call to the function add is correct. It compiles correctly and when executed it returns the right value.

The second call, on the other hand, is wrong. Although it executes correctly, it won't pass the compilation because the static analysis understands that "hello" is not a number and is not what the function add is expecting.

Listing 2-3 shows how a class with constructor, public methods, private fields, and accessors is defined in TypeScript.

LISTING 2-3: A TypeScript Class

```
class Greeter {
  public greeting: string;
  private _name: string;

  constructor(message: string) {
    this.greeting = message;
  }

  greet() {
    return this.greeting + ", " + this._name+"!";
  }

  get name(): string {
    return this._name;
  }

  set name(newName: string) {
    this._name = newName;
  }
}

let greeter = new Greeter("Hello");
greeter.name="World";

alert(greeter.greet()); //Says "Hello, World!"
```

Here I've shown just a few features, but I encourage you to dive more deeply into TypeScript, as it's the way you'll be writing JavaScript applications in Angular, which becomes much more productive with TypeScript.

JAVASCRIPT FRAMEWORKS

As you would never develop a server-side application by manually handling HTTP requests and responses, you should also not build client-side interactions by directly manipulating the DOM and managing the state of the application in simple JavaScript classes. For this purpose JavaScript application frameworks, such as Angular, React, or others, should be used.

If you have been in this industry for a few years, you might have noticed how quickly JavaScript frameworks rise and fall, some faster than others. The next few sections provide a brief overview of the ones that are popular at the moment and, given their corporate backing and relatively long existence, might be here to stay for still some time.

Angular

The Angular framework is currently maintained by Google together with a community of individual and corporate developers. Angular is a client-side framework built around the idea of extending HTML with new elements called web *components* that add additional behaviors. Components can be either HTML attributes or elements. They have associated templates that render a component's data by using expressions written inside double curly-braces ({{   }}). Listing 2-4 showcases the main components of a basic Angular application using two-way binding. Notice that the application is divided into various files.

LISTING 2-4: Simple Angular application

INDEX.HTML: THE MAIN HTML FILE

```
<!doctype html>
<html>
<head>
  <meta charset="utf-8">
  <title>Hello Angular</title>
  <base href="/">
</head>
<body>
  <app-root>Loading...</app-root>
</body>
</html>
```

MAIN.TS: APPLICATION STARTUP FILE

```
import './polyfills.ts';

import { platformBrowserDynamic } from '@angular/platform-browser-dynamic';
import { enableProdMode } from '@angular/core';
import { AppModule } from './app/app.module';


platformBrowserDynamic().bootstrapModule(AppModule);
```

APP.MODULE.TS: APP MODULE DEFINITION FILE

```
import { BrowserModule } from '@angular/platform-browser';
import { NgModule } from '@angular/core';
import { FormsModule } from '@angular/forms';
import { HttpModule } from '@angular/http';

import { AppComponent } from './app.component';

@NgModule({
  declarations: [
    AppComponent
  ],
  imports: [
    BrowserModule,
    FormsModule,
    HttpModule
  ],
  providers: [],
  bootstrap: [AppComponent]
```

```
})
export class AppModule { }
```

APP.COMPONENT.TS: APP COMPONENT APPLICATION FILE

```typescript
import { Component } from '@angular/core';

@Component({
  selector: 'app-root',
  templateUrl: './app.component.html',
  styleUrls: ['./app.component.css']
})
export class AppComponent {

  public firstName: string = "Simone";
  public lastName: string = "Chiaretta";

 fullName() {
    return `${this.firstName} ${this.lastName}`;
  }


}
```

APP.COMPONENT.HTML: APP COMPONENT TEMPLATE FILE

```html
<form>
  <div>
    <label for="firstName">First name:</label>
    <input name="firstName" [(ngModel)]="firstName">
  </div>
  <div>
    <label for="lastName">Last name:</label>
    <input name="lastName" [(ngModel)]="lastName">
  </div>
</form>

<hr/>
<h1>Hello <span>{{ fullName() }}</span>!</h1>
```

It all starts with the app-root element, which defines the root component from which the boot-strapping of the application will start, defined in the main.ts file. You can then see, split into three files, the app component:

➤   app.module.ts, which, among other things, defines all the components in the application.

➤   app.component.ts, which defines the actual component (which html element, which template, which style) and its behvior.

➤   app.component.html is the template that contains the HTML markup rendered by the component.

Another important directive is [(ngModel)], which binds the form element to properties of the model of the component.

As you have probably noticed, the JavaScript code of the Angular application is written with TypeScript.

There is much more to Angular than just these basic features. There is dependency-injection, templating, routing, modules, testing, and the possibility to define custom directives. The next chapter covers all of these features in detail.

Knockout

Knockout is a JavaScript framework that is particularly popular in the Microsoft developer's world. Originally developed by Microsoft developer Steve Sanderson, this framework implements the model-view-view model pattern. In a certain sense its syntax is pretty similar to Angular, even if it has fewer features and requires a bit more of work to define which properties support two-way databinding and which do not. It also supports templating in order to reuse the same code snippets across the application.

Listing 2-5 shows the same "Hello World" form from the previous section written with Knockout.

LISTING 2-5: Sample application with Knockout

```html
<!doctype html>
<html>
  <head>
    <title>Hello Knockout!</title>
    <script src="knockout-min.js"></script>
  </head>
  <body>
  <div>
    <p>First name: <input data-bind="value: firstName" /></p>
    <p>Last name: <input data-bind="value: lastName" /></p>
      <hr>
    <h1>Hello <span data-bind="text: fullName"></span>!</h1>
    </div>
  </body>

  <script>
  function ViewModel() {
      this.firstName = ko.observable("Simone");
      this.lastName = ko.observable("Chiaretta");

      this.fullName = ko.computed(function() {
          return this.firstName() + " " + this.lastName();
      }, this);
  }

  ko.applyBindings(new ViewModel());
  </script>

</html>
```

The main component in this simple application is in the `ViewModel` function, which defines the properties of the view model with the functions `ko.observable` and `ko.computed`. The first instructs the framework that a given property has to be "observed" and should be considered by the two-way binding mechanism. The second function defines a property that depends on other properties and that is updated whenever they change.

The properties are then bound to the UI with the `data-bind` attribute:

➤   The `value` binding is used in the form's elements. This associates the value of the element with a property in the view model.

➤   The `text` binding is used whenever you want to display the text value of a property of expressions.

The glue between the HTML template and the view model is the last line of code in the sample: `ko.applyBindings(new ViewModel());`.

Knockout has a less steep learning curve than Angular, but it also has limited functionality and its development has recently slowed down. For this reason it won't be covered in more detail in this book. Nevertheless, if you need to build a simpler application and don't require the power (and complexity) of Angular, I recommend that you have a look at the official website and follow the live tutorial.

React

One more JavaScript framework worth mentioning is React. React is developed and maintained by Facebook, and it's a JavaScript library for building user interfaces without aiming at also taking care about the rest of the application. React is based on the concept of self-contained components that render the HTML needed and that can optionally manage their own internal state. See Listing 2-6 for a simple React application. Notice that the code is split in multiple files.

LISTING 2-6: Simple Hello World app with React

INDEX.HTML: THE MAIN HTML FILE

```html
<!doctype html>
<html lang="en">
  <head>
    <title>Hello React!</title>
  </head>
  <body>
    <div id="greet"></div>
  </body>
</html>
```

INDEX.JS: THE APPLICATION STARTUP FILE

```js
import React from 'react';
import ReactDOM from 'react-dom';
import Greeter from './Greeter';

ReactDOM.render(
```

```
    <Greeter firstName="Simone" />,
    document.getElementById('greet')
);
```

GREETER.JS: THE FILE WITH THE COMPONENT

```javascript
import React, { Component } from 'react';

class Greeter extends React.Component {
  constructor(props) {
    super(props);
    this.state = {firstName: props.firstName, lastName: props.lastName};

    this.handleFirstNameChange = this.handleFirstNameChange.bind(this);
    this.handleLastNameChange = this.handleLastNameChange.bind(this);
  }

  handleFirstNameChange(event) {
    this.setState({firstName: event.target.value});
  }

  handleLastNameChange(event) {
    this.setState({lastName: event.target.value});
  }

  render() {
    return (
      <div>
      <form>
        <div>
          <label>
            First name:
            <input type="text" value={this.state.firstName} onChange={this.
handleFirstNameChange} />
          </label>
        </div>
        <div>
          <label>
            Last name:
            <input type="text" value={this.state.lastName} onChange={this.
handleLastNameChange} />
          </label>
        </div>
      </form>
      <hr/>
      <h1>Hello <span>{this.state.firstName} {this.state.lastName}</span>!</h1>
      </div>
    );
  }
}

export default Greeter;
```

As you can see from the example in Listing 2-6, the code is more convoluted than in Knockout but a bit more similar to Angular. It requires, even for small forms like this one, the code to be converted into a component. Even with the help of the "strange" mixed JavaScript/XML syntax called JSX (the one used for the `render` method) that is used to simplify the outputting of HTML elements, React still performs direct DOM manipulation (actually virtual DOM).

React has this syntax because it was designed to handle the dynamic content load of Facebook where data input is a minor part of the interaction and hundreds of elements are dynamically added to pages. In order to do it in the fastest possible way, it had to directly manipulate the DOM, without going through template parsing and two-way binding. If you don't have such a scenario but just a standard data-bound REST application, Angular is probably a better fit.

> **NOTE** *In Listing 2-6 you can see a "strange" syntax at the beginning of the two JavaScript files:* `import * from *`. *This is an ES6 feature that is used to define and import modules. In using the React build tools, this syntax is converted to "standard" JavaScript using the Babel transpiler.*

jQuery

One last notable mention goes to jQuery, probably the most well-known and most used JavaScript library. jQuery is a library that simplifies the selection of HTML elements, DOM manipulation, event handling, animations, and Ajax calls. It does this using an API that abstracts the implementation differences across various browsers. It was first introduced in 2006, when it was common practice to write the same features multiple times to address the differences between browsers.

jQuery is not a full application framework like Angular, Knockout, and React, but it is just a utility library that helps build interactive interfaces in HTML. For this reason this book doesn't contain a more detailed coverage of jQuery.

> **NOTE** *A very concise and effective way to explain the difference between a framework and a library is this: "A framework calls your code, while your code calls a library."*

CSS FRAMEWORKS

Front-end developers and designers hate reinventing the wheel for each project they work on. For this reason, until a few years ago, web designers had their own small home-grown set of CSS classes and HTML snippets that they reused in all their works. In 2010 the development team working on Twitter decided to release their home-grown CSS library for public use. Later other companies and teams did the same, but only very few of them rivaled Bootstrap.

The next sections, after giving an introduction to Bootstrap, also cover GitHub's CSS framework, Primer, the still relatively new but promising Material Design Lite, developed by Google, and Semantic UI, a framework with a more component-oriented approach to CSS.

Bootstrap

The most popular CSS framework is the one originally released as Twitter Blueprint. It was called that because it was developed to bring consistency across the various sites developed at Twitter. Later it was renamed to Bootstrap when it was released as an open-source project in the summer of 2011. It then came to be the most popular library on GitHub, with more than 100,000 stars.

Bootstrap contains a set of CSS- and HTML-based templates for styling forms, elements, buttons, navigation, typography, and a range of other UI components. It also comes with optional JavaScript plugins to add interactivity to components.

Bootstrap is mobile-first, based on a responsive 12-columns grid system for the layout of the components on the screen. As example here is the code for a grid that automatically adapts to the screen size of the device.

```
<div class="row">
  <div class="col-xs-12 col-sm-6 col-md-8">.col-xs-12 .col-sm-6 .col-md-8</div>
  <div class="col-xs-6 col-md-4">.col-xs-6 .col-md-4</div>
</div>
```

This example of a responsive grid displays differently in different sizes:

➤ On a normal desktop the two cells will appear one next to the other, the first using eight columns, the second using four. (Grid behavior for normal sized screens is defined by the classes that start with `col-md-`.)

➤ On a smartphone (or XS screen, identified by the class's prefix `col-xs-`), the first cell will occupy the full width, while the second will go on a new line and use half width.

➤ On a tablet (small screens, identified with `col-sm-`), the first cell will use only six columns, and the second inherits the smaller size definition, so the two cells will occupy half width each.

FIGURE 2-1: Drop down menu with Bootstrap

If you are wondering how the components look, just look at Twitter. The look and feel of an application fully developed with Bootstrap is just like the famous social network. See Figures 2-1 and 2-2.

FIGURE 2-2: Navigation bar

Apart from standard navigation and menus, one interesting component is called "Jumbotron," shown in Figure 2-3. It's meant to be used as the main headline to catch the visitor's attention.

FIGURE 2-3: Jumbotron

Of course you can change the style and build your own theme with the colors of your brand. This can be done by changing some variables in the Bootstrap files and then recompiling the CSS file or by using the Customize Bootstrap download page on the official website.

This was just a brief introduction to this powerful CSS framework, but Chapter 4 goes into more detail.

Bootstrap is not the only CSS framework, as many others have been released (and many have disappeared), especially grid systems. There are three other CSS frameworks that are particularly worth mentioning, the first of which is GitHub's Primer CSS.

Primer CSS

GitHub released its internal design guidelines as an open-source project known as Primer CSS. This framework is not as fully featured as Bootstrap. For example, despite having a grid system, it is not responsive. But if you like the approach of GitHub to UI design, this framework is easy to use and nicely done. It also includes the famous *octicons*. See Figure 2-4.

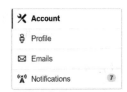

FIGURE 2-4: Navigation with Primer CSS

An interesting component is called "blankslate," which should be used when a content area has no content to show. See Figure 2-5.

FIGURE 2-5: Blankslate component

Since style is pretty much a personal choice, if you are not a big fan of the Twitter or GitHub styles, you might like Google's Material Design Lite.

Material Design Lite

Material Design Lite (MDL) is a CSS framework created by Google to bring the Material Design philosophy to the web. Unlike the Bootstrap and Primer CSS frameworks, Material Design Lite is a combination of CSS and JavaScript where elements' style and classes from the framework are enhanced at runtime by the JavaScript library, which adds additional behaviors to the components. As you can see from the samples of components shown in Figures 2-6 and 2-7, this design is very similar to the look and feel of Android apps.

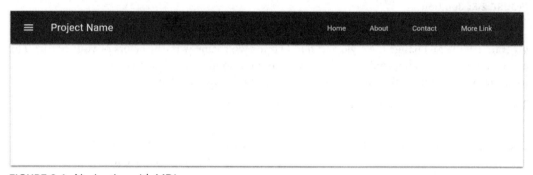

FIGURE 2-6: Navigation with MDL

The official website also provides some templates of websites built with Material Design Lite that can be used as a starting point.

FIGURE 2-7: Buttons with MDL

Semantic UI

One last CSS framework worth mentioning is Semantic UI. As the name implies, it gives to CSS classes names that are easier to understand than those of the other frameworks. For example, to style a button with the primary color, you use `<button class="ui primary button">`.

Semantic UI has its own responsive layout as well, which is designed around a 16-column grid:

```
<div class="ui grid">
  <div class="four wide column"></div>
  <div class="four wide column"></div>
  <div class="four wide column"></div>
  <div class="four wide column"></div>
  <div class="two wide column"></div>
  <div class="eight wide column"></div>
  <div class="six wide column"></div>
</div>
```

This natural language naming is just the tip of the more profound and almost philosophical reasoning that led to the creation of Semantic UI, whose goal is to lower the technical barriers that lie between the concepts of programming and their correlating concepts in human meaning.

Sematic UI comes with a default theme, but additional themes that give the look and feel of Bootstrap, Primer CSS, and Material Design are available.

This book doesn't cover Semantic UI more than what is in this small introduction, but if you are intrigued by its approach, I recommend you have a look at their learning site: `http://learnsemantic.com/`

PACKAGE MANAGERS

With the many components, libraries, and tools needed for developing modern web applications with ASP.NET Core MVC, something is needed to keep everything neatly organized, automating installations and updates and keeping all dependencies in check. This is where package managers come in handy. They download components and tools from official repositories, manage all dependencies, and make it easy to set up a local copy of a project's development environment just by checking it out from the source repository.

This book covers the following package managers:

➤ NuGet, for managing .NET libraries and components

➤ Bower, for JavaScript and CSS frameworks

➤ NPM, for tools and server-side JavaScript libraries

Bower is specifically made for client-side dependencies, but NuGet and NPM can be used for a bit of everything, which is the way they are used in the course of this book.

NuGet

NuGet is the default package manager in .NET and has been integrated into Visual Studio for several versions. With ASP.NET Core, all the references of a project are saved as `PackageReference` in the project definition (`.csproj`) file, as shown in Listing 2-7. Everything, even references to core libraries of the Base Class Library (all grouped inside the Microsoft.AspNet.Core.All metapackage), is retrieved via NuGet packages.

LISTING 2-7: WebApplication.csproj

```
<Project Sdk="Microsoft.NET.Sdk.Web">
  <PropertyGroup>
    <TargetFramework>netcoreapp2.0</TargetFramework>
  </PropertyGroup>
  <ItemGroup>
    <PackageReference Include="Microsoft.AspNetCore.All" Version="2.0.0" />
    <PackageReference Include="Newtonsoft.Json" Version="10.0.3" />
  </ItemGroup>
  <ItemGroup>
    <DotNetCliToolReference
Include="Microsoft.VisualStudio.Web.CodeGeneration.Tools" Version="2.0.0" />
  </ItemGroup>
</Project>
```

Apart from manually adding them to the `.csproj` file, as with the previous version, packages can be installed either via the newly redesigned Package Manager UI (shown in Figure 2-8) or via the package manager console:

```
PM> Install-Package Newtonsoft.Json
```

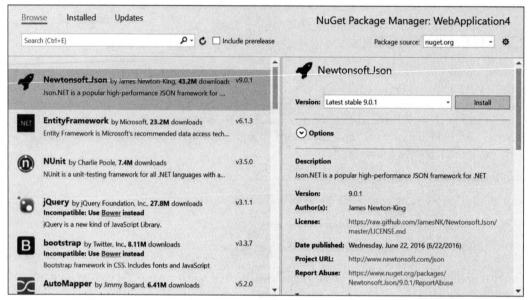

FIGURE 2-8: Package Manager interface in Visual Studio 2017

If you used NuGet in previous versions of ASP.NET, there is a big conceptual difference to take into consideration when using ASP.NET Core. With ASP.NET Core, only server-side dependencies should be referenced and retrieved via NuGet. For client-side dependencies Microsoft decided to rely on another very popular package manager—Bower, which was designed for this purpose.

Bower

Bower is a very simple tool to use. Just as with NuGet, what is needed is to specify in a JSON file called `bower.json` the packages that are referenced in a project, as shown in Listing 2-8.

LISTING 2-8: Bower.json

```json
{
  "name": "asp.net",
  "private": true,
  "dependencies": {
    "bootstrap": "3.3.6",
    "jquery": "2.2.0",
    "jquery-validation": "1.14.0",
```

```
        "jquery-validation-unobtrusive": "3.2.6",
        "jquery-file-upload":"https://github.com/blueimp/jQuery-File-Upload/"
    }
}
```

As you might have noticed in Listing 2-8, the packages can be specified with many notations:

➤ The most common is just to use the package name registered on Bower.io. When referenced this way, Bower will download the whole git repository that was specified when the package was registered.

➤ Another option is to specify directly the git or svn repository from which to download the package.

➤ Finally, also a standard URL can be used. In this case the package will be downloaded from the URL where it is stored (and extracted if the file is an archive).

When you type `bower install` on the console, all the packages are directly downloaded from their location and saved in a folder named `bower_components`. And here Bower stops. How to use them is up to you. You can directly reference the files from their download location, or, as is recommended to keep things tidy, you can copy the needed files (remember that Bower could download the whole git repository) inside your application's folder structure.

NPM

Node Package Manager (NPM) was originally developed to manage Node.js server-side packages, but it later also became popular for distributing command-line tools developed with Node.js. As with the other package managers, NPM downloads the packages that are specified in a manifest file called `package.json` and installs them in a sub-folder of your project called `node_modules`.

Normally packages should be specified in a `dependencies` node, but in the context of an ASP.NET Core project, NPM will be mainly used to install the task runner and its plugins, so in this case they are inside the `devDependencies` node, as shown in Listing 2-9.

LISTING 2-9: package.json

```
{
  "name": "app",
  "version": "1.0.0",
  "private": true,
  "devDependencies": {
    "del": "^2.2.2",
    "gulp": "^3.9.1",
    "gulp-concat": "^2.6.1",
    "gulp-cssmin": "^0.1.7",
    "gulp-htmlmin": "^3.0.0",
    "gulp-uglify": "^2.0.0",
    "merge-stream": "^1.0.1"
  }
}
```

The Folder Structure

To wrap up this section about package managers I want to show how all these references and manifest files look in the Solution Explorer window and on the file system. Essentially each project could have three types of dependencies, which are defined in their respective manifest files:. `csproj` for NuGet server-side references, `bower.json` for Bower client-side components, and `package.json` for the build tools. Figure 2-9 demonstrates where the Solution Explorer shows all the dependencies in the project's tree.

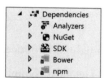

FIGURE 2-9: Dependencies as shown in Solution Explorer

On the underlying file system, the packages are stored in various subfolders: `wwwroot/libs` for Bower components (Visual Studio stores them in a location different from the default one) and `node_modules` for NPM packages. See Figure 2.10.

TASK RUNNERS

Task runners automate the final step of your development workflow: the build and release of the application. This is nothing new in the world of server-side development. You've probably been automating your builds with MSBuild scripts or NAnt tasks for years, but the concept of task runners is pretty new in the front-end world.

At this moment you might be wondering why you should embrace these "new kids on the block." This is a very legitimate question. The main reason is that the task runners made for front-end use are completely server-side language-agnostic. Therefore, they can be used by anyone and thus they have a much larger community, which translates into many more ready-to-use tasks. However, not all your experience is lost. As explained in Chapter 1, the project definition of an ASP.NET Core project is still done with MSBuild, so it can still be used for building applications.

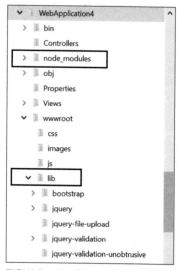

FIGURE 2-10: Dependencies' folders on the file system

> **NOTE** *Recently, a part of the front-end development community, mostly using Linux-based machines or Macs, has stopped using task runners entirely and is using a feature of npm called* npm scripts. *These are just a way to call commands of the operating system, Node.js apps built on purpose to build their app or the development tools that come together with the framework they are using, like one that come with Angular or React.*

The main actor in this category is Gulp. Gulp is code-based and it relies on super-small interconnected plugins instead of stand-alone tasks executed one after the other. If that sounds a bit unclear, Listing 2-10 should help clarify things.

LISTING 2-10: Sample of Gulp configuration file

```
var gulp = require('gulp');
var jshint = require('gulp-jshint');
var concat = require('gulp-concat');
var minifyCss = require('gulp-minify-css');

gulp.task('default', function(done){
  gulp.src('src/**/*.js')
    .pipe(jshint())
    .pipe(concat('bundle.js'))
    .pipe(gulp.dest('dist '))
    .on('end', done);
});

gulp.watch('src/**/*.js', ['default']);
```

It's just code. The task begins by stating which source files it has to process, with gulp.src(). Following that, the operations are plugged one into the other with the pipe(...) function, and finally the resulting file is saved with gulp.dest().

This was a very brief introduction to Gulp, which is described in more detail in Chapter 6.

SUMMARY

Modern web development on the Microsoft technlogcy stack is not just C# and ASP.NET anymore. It is achieved with a mix of different tools and frameworks, each built with the best language for the purpose. This proliferation of additional components adds to the complexity of choosing what to use. This choice is made more difficult due to the volatility and short life of some of them. The upcoming chapters go into more detail about the most popular of those options: Angular and Bootstrap CSS.

3

Angular in a Nutshell

WHAT'S IN THIS CHAPTER?

➤ Understanding the basic concepts of Angular

➤ Building an Angular application

➤ Using AngularJS with ASP.NET MVC Core v1

➤ Discovering Visual Studio 2017 support for Angular

The previous chapter was an introduction to all the frameworks used in front-end development, including Angular.

This chapter goes more deeply into Angular, starting with basic concepts and later approaching more advanced topics. The first part of the chapter relies only on pure client-side JavaScript and can be used with just a simple text editor. The second part of the chapter shows the new integration available within Visual Studio 2017 and how to integrate Angular in ASP.NET Core applications.

Before going into the technical details, I want to stress the fact that Angular is not a "silver bullet." Angular shines when it comes to building CRUD applications, but it is less optimal when heavy DOM manipulation or a very complex GUI are needed. Angular was chosen as the framework for this book because the majority of web applications built with ASP.NET MVC (or in general with any server-side technology) are mostly about data-bound operations and less about complex GUIs.

WROX.COM CODE DOWNLOADS FOR THIS CHAPTER

The wrox.com code downloads for this chapter are found at www.wrox.com Search for the book's ISBN (978-1-119-18131-6), and you will find the code in the chapter 3 download and individually named according to the names throughout the chapter.

ANGULAR CONCEPTS

Angular is a web application framework developed and maintained by Google and the open-source community. The framework has many features, like two-way data-binding, templating, routing, components, dependency injection, and so on. Unfortunately, like all frameworks of its breed, it has a pretty steep learning curve due to the many concepts you have to grasp in order to be fluent in it. Here is a list of the most important Angular concepts:

➤ **Modules:** Containers that group together blocks of functionalities that belong together, like components, directives, services, and so on.

➤ **Components:** Define the behavior of a "portion" of the screen.

➤ **Templates:** HTML files that define how the view for a component is rendered.

➤ **Data binding:** The process that connects a component to its template and allows data and events to flow between them.

➤ **Directives:** Custom attributes that enhance HTML syntax and are used to attach behaviors to specific elements on the page.

➤ **Services:** Reusable functionalities that are independent from the views.

➤ **Dependency injection:** A way to supply dependencies (services most of the time) to classes (other services or components).

➤ **Metadata:** Instructs Angular on how to process a class, whether it's a component, a module, a directive, which services have to be injected, and so on.

Those terms might sound abstract at the moment, but the upcoming pages will make everything more clear, as all of these concepts are used to build a sample single-page application.

ANGULAR VS ANGULARJS

Chances are that you have worked with or at least heard of AngularJS 1.x. Despite the similar name, the Angular covered in this book is a completely new framework, written from scratch and with a different approach. The "old" AngularJS 1.x is a *Model View Controller (MVC)* framework, while Angular is a component-oriented framework.

If you are familiar with AngularJS, not everything is lost. Many of its concepts are still relevant, so learning Angular won't be difficult for you.

Version numbers are different. The new Angular adopts semantic versioning, so every important new feature or breaking change will have a new major version number, similar to how Node.js and Chrome are numbered. The first version, 2.0, was released in September 2016. The latest LTS version, released at the end of March 2017, is 4.0. And the latest stable version is 5.0, released at the end of October 2017. On the other hand, AngularJS versioning went from 1.0 to 1.6 over the seven years since its first release.

Also the reference website is different. Instead of `angularjs.org`, the site for Angular is `angular.io`. See Figure 3-1.

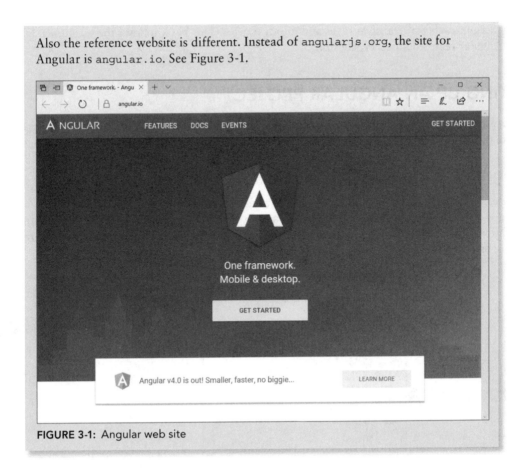

FIGURE 3-1: Angular web site

THE LANGUAGE OF ANGULAR

The title of this section might seem strange: If Angular is a JavaScript framework, isn't it written in JavaScript? The answer is both yes and no.

The modular and component-oriented approach used by Angular requires language features that are available only in ES6. The same functionalites can also be implementend in the "standard" JavaScript supported by most browsers (ECMAScript 5 or ES5) but at the cost of a more complex and cumbersome code.

To avoid complexity and since transpiling to ES5 would have been needed anyway, the Angular team decided to use TypeScript as the language of choice. It includes the features of ES6 that are needed to support the modularity of the framework, but it also adds strong typing (as seen in Chapter 2).

As a developer you can use any of the three versions of JavaScript (ES5, which is the most widely supported version of JavaScript, ES6, which is only supported by most recent browser, or

TypeScript), each with its advantages and disadvantages. This book follows the recommendation of the Angular team and uses TypeScript.

SETTING UP AN ANGULAR PROJECT

There are various ways of writing Angular applications, including using an online editor, starting from the quickstart seed, and using the Angular-CLI tool.

Using an Online Editor

The easiest way to set up an Angular project is to use an online web editing tool like Plunker (https://plnkr.co). See Figure 3-2. It allows you to write code directly in the browser without the additional overhead of setting up the transpiling from TypeScript to JavaScript and the various bundling of all the files.

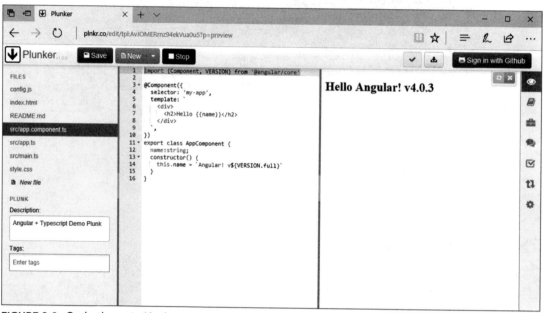

FIGURE 3-2: Code shown in Plunker

This is obviously good only when doing demos or experimenting and trying to understand how things work, as you cannot deploy an application from such sites. They also do the transpiling on the browser, which can become slow when the size of the "demo" is too large.

Starting from the Quickstart Seed

Another solution for setting up an Angular project is to clone onto your machine the quickstart seed project from the Angular team's GitHub repository (`https://github.com/angular/quickstart`). You simply follow the instructions that come in the README file. The download contains the `package.json` file with all the dependencies needed by Angular as well as all scripts needed to build and run the application. Once the application is started with the `npm start` command, you can add and edit files, and the browser will automatically refresh and show the updated result.

Using the Angular-CLI Tool

The last option for setting up an Angular project, and the one that is used in this chapter, is Angular-CLI, the command-line interface tool. As with the dotnet-cli tool discussed in Chapter 1, this tool creates a skeleton of an application, similar to the one in the quickstart.

The tool is installed via NPM with the following command:

```
npm install -g @angular/cli
```

Once the tool is installed, you can create your first Angular application by typing in a command: `ng new my-app`.

This command creates a new folder called `my-app`, adds some the minium needed files to start an Angular application, and automatically starts `npm install` to download all the dependencies.

Once this is complete, move into the `my-app` folder (`cd my-app`) and type the command `ng serve --open` to launch the application in your default browser (Figure 3-3).

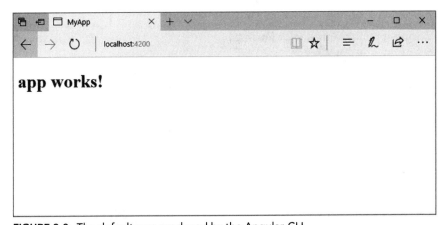

FIGURE 3-3: The default app produced by the Angular-CLI

MORE ABOUT THE ANGULAR-CLI TOOL

The Angular command-line interface tool has many other useful features that can streamline the development of Angular applications. Besides providing the skeleton of the client-side application, it comes preconfigured with the skeleton for running unit tests with the Karma runner and for running end-to-end tests using Protractor. It also provides additional commands for running tests, running code analysis, building a deployable version of the application, and generating new components, services, and classes. All these additional features are beyond the scope of this book, but you can explore more on your own by reading the official documentation at: https://cli.angular.io.

THE STRUCTURE OF AN ANGULAR APP

With the skeleton of a simple application created via the command-line tools, we can now explore the basic components and structure of an Angular application (inside the /src folder).

Application Entry Point

The entry point of this and any other Angular application is the main.ts file (Listing 3-1). Its purpose is to compile the application and to bootstrap its root module (AppModule).

LISTING 3-1: The application's entry point (main.ts)

```
import './polyfills.ts';

import { platformBrowserDynamic } from '@angular/platform-browser-dynamic';
import { enableProdMode } from '@angular/core';
import { environment } from './environments/environment' ;
import { AppModule } from './app/app.module';

if (environment.production) {
  enableProdMode();
}

platformBrowserDynamic().bootstrapModule(AppModule);
```

Root Module

The next file is the inside the app folder and is the one that defines the application's root module: app.module.ts.

What is shown in Listing 3-2 is not just valid for the root module, but also represents the structure of any other Angular module.

LISTING 3-2: Root module (app/app.module.ts)

```
import { BrowserModule } from '@angular/platform-browser';
import { NgModule } from '@angular/core';
import { FormsModule } from '@angular/forms';
import { HttpModule } from '@angular/http';

import { AppComponent } from './app.component';

@NgModule({
  declarations: [
    AppComponent
  ],
  imports: [
    BrowserModule,
    FormsModule,
    HttpModule
  ],
  providers: [],
  bootstrap: [AppComponent]
})
export class AppModule { }
```

The file starts by importing (via the `import` statements) all the JavaScript classes that are referenced inside this class. In this example there are three Angular modules that are going to be used by almost any application (`BrowserModule`, `FormsModule`, and `HttpModule`), one decorator (`NgModule`) that is going to be used to define the application root module, and finally one component (`AppComponent`).

Then there is the actual module definition, the class `AppModule`, decorated by the `@NgModule` decorator, which contains four arrays:

➤ The first is the `declarations` array, which contains all the components belong to this module. In there case there is only one, but as the application evolves, more components will be added.

➤ Then the `imports` array contains all the Angular modules that are going to be used inside this module. This includes both structural modules and as the application evolves custom feature modules. In this example the modules to handle interaction with the browser, to handle HTML forms, and to execute HTTP requests are added.

➤ Third is the empty array `providers`. It is empty because at the moment the application is not using any service, but once we start creating them, they will need to be defined inside this array.

➤ Finally the last array, `bootstrap`, contains the components that have to be created during the application's bootstrapping process. In our example this is the `AppComponent`.

> **NOTE** *Decorators are a feature of TypeScript that are used to add metadata to a class. In Angular there many decorators that are used to specify what kind of Angular element a class represents. Here we have the @NgModule to identify Angular modules, but there is also @Component to indentify components or @Injectable to identify services that can be injected via dependency injection and other modules as well.*

Root Component

The final piece of the puzzle is the root component, AppComponent, defined in the app/app .component.ts file (Listing 3-3).

LISTING 3-3: Root component (app/app.component.ts)

```
import { Component } from '@angular/core';

@Component({
  selector: 'app-root',
  templateUrl: './app.component.html',
  styleUrls: ['./app.component.css']
})
export class AppComponent {
  title = 'app works!';
}
```

Defining the root component (or any other component) is just like defining the root module. It's done with decorator (this time the @Component) and specifying the selector that will be used in the HTML file to include the component, the URL of the view for the component (via the templateUrl property), and the styles specific for this view (with the styleUrls property).

And since a component, unlike a module, has behaviors, the class must do something, in this case just setting the value of the property title. In this example the view of the component is very simple and just displays the title property inside an H1 tag (Listing 3-4).

LISTING 3-4: Root component's template (app/app.component.html)

```
<h1>
  {{title}}
</h1>
```

When templates are so simple, to avoid creating HTML files with just one line of code, the `@Component` decorator provides an additional property called `template` where the full markup of the template can be specified instead of its URL. If both are specified, the inline markup is used:

```
template: `<h1> {{title}} </h1>`
```

The inline markup can also be specified over multiple lines as a multi-line string, enclosing it within backticks (`). Notice that a backtick (`), which is not a single quote ('), is a notation introduced in ECMAScript 2015 (ES6) to allow entering strings over multiple lines in order to keep the HTML more readable.

> **TIP** *Even if pretty uncommon for normal users, the backtick (`) should be somewhat familiar to developers as it is the character used in markdown to format a string as* `code` *when writing comments in various online coding forum like StackOverflow or posting issues on GitHub. On the US keyboard layout, it is at the top left corner of the keyboard. But in other keyboard layouts, like for example Italian, this character doesn't exist and has to be typed using its ASCII code on the numeric keyboard:* `AltGr+96`.

Main HTML Page

The real entry point of the application, which actually starts its boostrapping process, is the main `index.html` page (Listing 3-5).

LISTING 3-5: Index.html

```html
<!doctype html>
<html>
<head>
  <meta charset="utf-8">
  <title>MyApp</title>
  <base href="/">

  <meta name="viewport" content="width=device-width, initial-scale=1">
  <link rel="icon" type="image/x-icon" href="favicon.ico">
</head>
<body>
  <app-root>Loading...</app-root>
</body>
</html>
```

As you can see, the `<app-root>` tag is the same as specified in the `selector` property of the root component. Here is where the bootstrapping process will inject the view rendered by the root component. In this example it is simply `<h1>app works!</h1>`, but, as shown in the rest of the chapter, it can be much more than that.

DATA BINDING

So far the chapter briefly covered four of the eight main concepts of Angular: models, components, templates, and metadata. Listing 3-5 also showed a very simple example of data binding to render a property of a component's model inside the template.

Data Binding is the process that passes data back and forth between components and the view in rendered in the browser. There are four types of Data Binding in Angular:

➤ The first is *interpolation*, which sends data from the component to the browser, rendering it as the content of a HTML tag.

➤ The second is *one-way binding*, which still sends data from the component to the browser, but it assigns the value to an attribute or property of an HTML element.

➤ We then have *event binding*, which sends data from the browser to the component.

➤ Finally, we have *two-way binding* to keep in sync a property of the component with what is rendered in an input element in the browser.

➤ Let's look at each of them individually.

Interpolation

If all you need to do is render the value of property of the model of a component inside the browser as the content of an HTML element, the simplest way of binding is called interpolation. This is done by putting the expression you want to render inside double curly braces {{ ... }}. The content can be just the name of a component's property or a JavaScript expression, for example string concatenation. Listing 3-6 shows both examples.

LISTING 3-6: Example of interpolation (app/app.component.html)

```
<h1>{{title}}</h1>

<p>{{"Hello" + " " + "reader"}}!</p>
```

> **WARNING** *Despite being technically possible, it is better to avoid using expressions inside templates and only use propery names. To keep a good separation of concerns, it is the component that has to do any concatenation or any other type of expression before passing the value to the template.*

One-Way Binding

If instead of displaying a propery as the content of an element you need to pass it to an HTML element's attribute, you need to use a more explicit syntax for the one-way binding. This is done by wrapping the attribute name within square brackets [...] and assigning the value using the property name as if it was a static value.

For example, you can set the value of an input element:

```
<input type="text" [value]="title" />
```

But you are not limited to only elements' attributes. Style properties can also be set:

```
<h1 [style.color]="color" >This is red</h1>
```

With this code, if the property color of the component hold the value "red", that heading will be displayed in red.

Actually, any property of any HTML element can be set via this one-way binding. For example, instead of using interpolation, we could have set the content of the heading by setting the value of its innerText property:

```
<h1 [innerText]="title"></h1>
```

Event binding

To send data (or raise events) from the template to the component, we adopt a similar approach. This time we wrap the name of any valid HTML event with parentheses (...) and assign it to a method of the component. Listing 3-7 shows an example of an event that toggles the color of a header, shown in a component with an inline template.

LISTING 3-7: Event binding (app/app.component.ts)

```
import { Component } from '@angular/core';

@Component({
  selector: 'app-root',
  template: `<h1 [style.color]="color">{{title}}</h1>
  <button (click)="setColor()">Change Color</button>`
})
export class AppComponent {
  title = 'app works!';
  color = "";

  setColor(){
    if(this.color==="")
      this.color="red";
    else
      this.color="";
  }
}
```

COMPARING ONE-WAY AND EVENT BINDING WITH ANGULARJS

If you have used AngularJS, you might have noticed that gone are all the `ng-*` directives like `ng-style`, `ng-src`, and so on. Now it's enough to wrap the name in square brackets. The same is true for the events. There is no need to use the AngularJS `ng-click` event. You can just use any event inside parentheses. This means less code for the team to maintain, fewer possible bugs, and greater ease for developers.

Two-Way Binding

Finally, the most powerful of all bindings, the one that keeps in sync templates and components' models, is two-way binding. This is done using the new syntax `[(ngModel)]`. You just need to apply this directive on the input element you want to bind to, and any changes to the model will automatically reflect on the view, and any changes in the input field will update the property of the component. Listing 3-8 shows an example of two-way data binding.

LISTING 3-8: Two-way binding (app/app.component.ts)

```
import { Component } from '@angular/core';

@Component({
  selector: 'app-root',
  template: `
<h1>{{title}}</h1>
<input type="text" [(ngModel)]="title" />
`
})
export class AppComponent {
  title = 'app works!';
}
```

This notation looks funny at first, but after a while it makes sense. It is basically an event binding inside a one-way binding because you get the model from the component, but you also send it back. This notation is referred to as "football in a box" or "banana in a box" (to help you remember that parentheses go inside the square brackets).

DIRECTIVES

In Angular there are two types of directives. *Structural directives* modify the layout of the page by adding or removing DOM elements. *Attribute directives* change the appearance of an existing elements.

NgIf, NgFor, and NgSwitch are the built-in structural directives, while NgModel, NgStyle, and NgClass are the built-in attribute directives.

Let's see how to use the NgFor directive to iterate an array of objects:

```
<ul>
  <li *ngFor="let item of array">{{item.property}}</li>
</ul>
```

Angular replicates the HTML to which the *ngFor directive is applied (in the case of snippet above, the <li> element) for the items of the array. As soon as new objects are added to the array, the directive automatically adds a copy of the HTML element to the DOM, and when an object is removed, the corresponding element is removed from the DOM as well.

Listing 3-9 shows the *ngFor directive applied to show the top five men of the 2016 Ironman World Championship in Kona, Hawaii. Inside the <li> element, the dot notation is used to access the properties of the item of the repeater.

LISTING 3-9: Using the NgFor directive to display an array of objects

```
import { Component } from '@angular/core';

@Component({
  selector: 'app-root',
  template: `
  <h1>Kona Ironman Top 5 men</h1>
  <ol>
    <li *ngFor="let athlete of athletes">{{athlete.name}} ({{athlete.country}}):
{{athlete.time}}</li>
  </ol>
  `
})
export class AppComponent {
athletes = [
    {name:"Jan Frodeno", country: "DEU", time: "08:06:30"},
    {name:"Sebastian Kienle", country: "DEU", time: "08:10:02"},
    {name:"Patrick Lange", country: "DEU", time: "08:11:14"},
    {name:"Ben Hoffman", country: "USA", time: "08:13:00"},
    {name:"Andi Boecherer", country: "DEU", time: "08:13:25"}
  ];
}
```

SERVICES AND DEPENDECY INJECTION

There are two more important Angular concepts, and they always go together: services and dependency injection.

In Listing 3-9 the list of athletes was hard-coded in the declaration of the component. It is, however, not a realistic example (and not even a very good practice). Normally such a list of items is retrieved from an external source like a call to an HTTP service. Before introducing the dependency to this external resource, let's first set up an external service that will be responsible for retrieving the list of athletes and use dependency injection to pass it to the component.

First the service class must be created. There's nothing special about it. It is just a normal TypeScript class that contains methods that return the data we need. The only peculiarity is that, since it has be injected via dependency injection, it must be decorated with the `@Injectable()` decorator (Listing 3-10).

LISTING 3-10: Athlete Service (app/athlete.service.ts)

```
import { Injectable } from '@angular/core';

@Injectable()
export class AthleteService {
  getAthletes(){
    return [
    {name:"Jan Frodeno", country: "DEU", time: "08:06:30"},
    {name:"Sebastian Kienle", country: "DEU", time: "08:10:02"},
    {name:"Patrick Lange", country: "DEU", time: "08:11:14"},
    {name:"Ben Hoffman", country: "USA", time: "08:13:00"},
    {name:"Andi Boecherer", country: "DEU", time: "08:13:25"}
    ];
  }
}
```

The `component` can be refactored to call the `getAthletes` method in the service, which is injected as the constructor's parameter (Listing 3-11).

LISTING 3-11: Refactored app component (app/app.component.ts)

```
import { Component } from '@angular/core';
import { AthleteService } from './athlete.service';

@Component({
  selector: 'app-root',
  templateUrl: 'app.component.html',
  providers: [AthleteService]
})
export class AppComponent {
  athletes: Array<any>;

  constructor(private athleteService: AthleteService){
    this.athletes=athleteService.getAthletes();
  }
}
```

Highlighted are the main changes to the component class in order to enable the injection:

➤ The constructor declares a parameter of type `AthleteService`.

➤ The decorator has an additional parameter, `providers`, which contains the list of classes that can be injected.

➤ And obviously the class needs to be imported in order to be used.

If a service needs to be used in more components, it's recommended to register it in the `providers` array of the `NgModule`.

We have now covered the main concepts of Angular. Before jumping into how to integrate Angular in an ASP.NET Core application, the upcoming sections show some additional features of Angular like the hierarchy of components, HTTP and array manipulation, and form validation.

> **NOTE** *If you used AngularJS v1, you might have noticed that building a service in Angular is incredibly easier than doing it in AngularJS. All the factories, providers, services, constants, and so on are merged into on type of service, which is just a plain TypeScript class.*

MULTIPLE COMPONENTS

So far we only have worked with the root component of the application, but this is not how things are typically done in more complex applications. More complex applications usually contain more nested components that can also contain other components. This splitting of the application into multiple components results in the need to manage communication between them. This section, building on top of the application introduced in Listing 3-11, covers all these aspects.

So far there is just one component, the root `AppComponent`, which does everything. It renders the title, connects to the service, shows the list, and shows the details of each item. To make it more modular, a better approach is to use the following components:

➤ The `AppComponent` just renders the application title and then included the `AthleteListComponent`

➤ The `AthleteListComponent` connects to the service and shows a list of `AthleteComponents`.

➤ The `AthleteComponent` displays the details of the athlete.

Adding files manually is boring and error-prone, so to make the task easier and less repetitive, we can use the Angular CLI tool.

If you type `ng generate component AthleteList` in the command prompt inside the application folder, the tool will create a new folder, and inside it will add the new component with the name `athlete-list.component.ts` (and all the other files needed for the component). It will also update the root module, `AppModule`, including the newly created component in the list of `declarations` of components used by the module.

So now we can start moving the logic that retrieves and displays the list of athletes from the root component to the `AthleteListComponent`.

Listing 3-12 and Listing 3-13 show the new code for the two components that needed to be changed, the `AthleteListComponent` and the root component. For brevity, the markup is presented inline instead of being in separate files.

LISTING 3-12: AthleteListComponent (app/athlete-list/athlete-list.component.ts)

```
import { Component } from '@angular/core';
import { AthleteService } from '../athlete.service';

@Component({
  selector: 'app-athlete-list',
  template: `
<ol>
   <li *ngFor="let athlete of athletes">{{athlete.name}}
({{athlete.country}}): {{athlete.time}}</li>
   </ol>
   `,
})
export class AthleteListComponent {

  athletes: Array<any>;

  constructor(private athleteService: AthleteService){
    this.athletes=athleteService.getAthletes();
  }

}
```

Listing 3-12 contains exactly the same code that was previously in the root component but with a different selector, now `app-athlete-list`. This is the "tag" that is used by the root component to reference the `AthleteListComponent`.

LISTING 3-13: Root component (app/app.component.ts)

```
import { Component } from '@angular/core';

@Component({
  selector: 'app-root',
  template: `<h1>Kona Ironman Top 5 men</h1>
  <app-athlete-list>Loading athlete list...</app-athlete-list>`
})
export class AppComponent {
}
```

The code is now simpler, and the root component has no actual code but just references the newly created controller in its template. At this point the application behaves the same, but each component serves its own task, achieving a better separation of concerns. But we can bring it a level further and have the markup and logic display the details of an athlete in their own component.

As before, create a new component, called `AthleteComponent`, with the Angular CLI tool.

Previously, the Angular CLI tool created the component in its own folder, with separate files for styles, views, and tests. This is the best practice suggested by the official style guide, but in smaller apps like this example, we can instead put all markup and styles inline and leave the file in the root folder. To do so with Angular CLI tool, you have to specify a few parameters when creating the component:

```
ng g component Athlete --flat=true --inline-template=true --inline-style=true
--spec=false
```

Now, instead of rendering the name and country of the athletes in the list, the `AthleteListComponent` just references the new `AthleteComponent` using its selector `app-athlete`, as seen here:

```
<li *ngFor="let athlete of athletes"><app-athlete></app-athlete></li>
```

But there is a problem here. How do you pass to the child component which athlete to display?

INPUT AND OUTPUT PROPERTIES

To solve the problem of passing athletes to the child component, the component must declare an input property. This is done using the directive `@Input` inside the component that exposes the property. It can be set in the view like any other HTML property, using one-way binding:

```
<app-athlete [athlete]="athlete"></app-athlete>
```

As implemented in Listing 3-10 and Listing 3-11, the list of athletes is a list of anonymous objects (like any standard JavaScript). It works, but it's not taking advantage of the strongly typed nature of TypeScript.

So, a "model" class can be created, either manually or again with the CLI tools, to hold the data (Listing 3-14).

LISTING 3-14: Athlete.ts (app/athlete.ts)

```
export class Athlete {
  name: string;
  country: string;
  time: string;
}
```

After this, the `AthleteComponent` looks like Listing 3-15.

LISTING 3-15: AthleteComponent (app/athlete.component.ts)

```
import { Component, Input } from '@angular/core';
import { Athlete } from './Athlete';

@Component({
  selector: 'app-athlete',
  template: `{{athlete.name}} ({{athlete.country}}): {{athlete.time}}`
})
export class AthleteComponent {
  @Input() athlete: Athlete;
  constructor() { }
}
```

Notice the usage of @Input to define the name and type of the property exposed outside of the component.

Also the AthleteListComponent has changed, as shown in Listing 3-16.

LISTING 3-16: AthleteListComponent (app/athlete-list.component.ts)

```
import { Component } from '@angular/core';
import { AthleteService } from './athlete.service';
import { Athlete } from "./athlete";

@Component({
  selector: 'app-athlete-list',
  template: `
  <ol>
    <li *ngFor="let athlete of athletes">
      <app-athlete [athlete]="athlete">
    </app-athlete></li>
  </ol>
  `,
})
export class AthleteListComponent {
  athletes: Array<Athlete>;
  constructor(private athleteService: AthleteService){
    this.athletes=athleteService.getAthletes();
  }
}
```

If there is an @Input directive, there must be also an @Output one. It is used to expose events that can be raised from within the component.

Let's use an @Output directive to show how to inform the root component that somone clicked on an athlete, so that it can display a more detailed view on his race.

For this to happen, the `AthleteListComponent` must bind to the click event on the athlete, and it must raise the custom event inside the handler for the click. Listing 3-17 highlights the new lines of code added for this purpose.

LISTING 3-17: AthleteListComponent (app/athlete-list.component.ts)

```
import { Component, Output, EventEmitter } from '@angular/core';
import { AthleteService } from './athlete.service';
import { Athlete } from "./athlete";

@Component({
  selector: 'app-athlete-list',
  template: `
  <ol>
    <li *ngFor="let athlete of athletes">
      <app-athlete (click)="select(athlete)" [athlete]="athlete">
    </app-athlete></li>
  </ol>
  `,
})
export class AthleteListComponent {
  athletes: Array<Athlete>;
  @Output() selected = new EventEmitter<Athlete>();

  constructor(private athleteService: AthleteService){
    this.athletes=athleteService.getAthletes();
  }

  select(selectedAthlete: Athlete){
    this.selected.emit(selectedAthlete);
  }
}
```

Now the parent component, the root `AppComponent`, listens to the selected event and handles it as any other event. Listing 3-18 shows the changes.

LISTING 3-18: AppComponent (app/app.component.ts)

```
import { Component } from '@angular/core';
import { Athlete } from "app/Athlete";

@Component({
  selector: 'app-root',
  template: `<h1>Kona Ironman Top 5 men</h1>
  <app-athlete-list (selected)=showDetails($event)>Loading athlete
list...</app-athlete-list>
  You selected: {{selectedAthlete}}`
})
```

```
export class AppComponent {
  selectedAthlete: string;

  constructor (){
    this.selectedAthlete="none";
  }

  showDetails(selectedAthlete: Athlete) {
    this.selectedAthlete=selectedAthlete.name;
  }
}
```

The parameter of the event, which contains the athlete being selected, is referenced by the `$event` variable.

The name of the athlete is then displayed at the bottom of the screen (Figure 3-4).

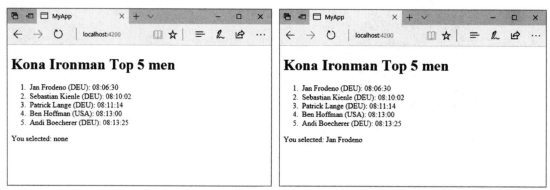

FIGURE 3-4: List of athletes and the selected athlete

TALKING TO THE BACK END

All the main concepts have been explained, and you have also seen how to better structure the application using multiple components. But the data is still coming from hardcoded values and not from a real REST API from a server. This last section before moving to the integration with ASP .NET Core and Visual Studio 2017 shows how to connect to a remote source of information using the `Http` module and the *Reactive Extensions* (RxJS).

By using nested components and services, the logic that is now getting the list of athletes is all in the `AthleteService` class. That is the only class that needs to be changed in order to retrieve data from a JSON end-point, which could be either a static .json file or a web service that returns data in JSON format. In this section we are using the .json file (Listing 3-19), but later in the chapter we'll use a web API done with ASP.NET Core MVC.

LISTING 3-19: Athletes.json file

```
{
  "data": [
    {"name":"Jan Frodeno", "country": "DEU", "time": "08:06:30"},
    {"name":"Sebastian Kienle", "country": "DEU", "time": "08:10:02"},
    {"name":"Patrick Lange", "country": "DEU", "time": "08:11:14"},
    {"name":"Ben Hoffman", "country": "USA", "time": "08:13:00"},
    {"name":"Andi Boecherer", "country": "DEU", "time": "08:13:25"}
  ]
}
```

In order to use the Http module, our app has to be instructed on where to find it. This is done by importing the HttpModule in the imports property inside the @NgModule annotation on the root AppModule. The one generated by the Angular CLI tools (Listing 3-2) is already configured, but if you created your app manually, you have to include it.

Using the Http Module

Inside the service class now we can use the Http module to retrieve the data available in the JSON file. Listing 3-20 shows the complete code for the athlete service.

LISTING 3-20: AthleteService using http (app/athlete.service.ts)

```
import { Injectable } from '@angular/core';
import { Athlete } from './Athlete';
import { Http, Response } from "@angular/http";
import 'rxjs/add/operator/map';

@Injectable()
export class AthleteService {
  constructor(private http: Http){}

  getAthletes(){
    return this.http.get('api/athletes.json')
      .map((r: Response)=><Athlete[]>r.json().data);
  }
}
```

The core of the functionality is the http.get method, which connects over HTTP to the specified URL and returns an RxJS Observable object. It then uses the map function of the Observable to modify the data before sending it back to the component. In this case it returns the data property of the JSON file and casts it to an array of Athlete.

For this to work first the Http module needs to be injected using the constructor, as it is done for any other modules or services. For the application to compile correctly, the objects Http and

Response as well as the map method must be imported. This last act of importing is necessary because the Reactive Extensions for JavaScript is a big library, so it is better to import only the parts of it that are actually used.

Consuming the RxJS Observable

Before running the sample, another change is needed. With the hardcoded values, the method in the service was directly returning the array of items. With the Http module, the method returns an RxJS Observable that cannot be directly used with *ngFor.

There are few options for consuming the observable, which are subscribing to the Observable, using the async pipe, or using promises.

Subscribing to the Observable

The first option for consuming the Observable is subscribing to it.

```
export class AthleteListComponent {
  athletes: Array<Athlete>;
  constructor(private athleteService: AthleteService) {  }

  getAthletes() {
    this.athleteService.getAthletes()
      .subscribe(
        athletes => this.athletes = athletes
      );
  }

  ngOnInit(){this.getAthletes();}
}
```

Instead of just setting the property athletes with the return value of the service's method, now the code is using the subscribe method and is registering a function that assigns to the component's property the array coming from the service. Also notice that the call to this method doesn't happen in the constructor any more, but inside a method called ngOnInit, which is called when the component gets initialized.

Using the async Pipe

Another option for consuming the Observable is using the async pipe. It is a short-hand version of the subscribe process done in the previous section. With this notation we can assign the Observable that comes from the service directly to the property of the component. Inside the *ngFor we use the async pipe to instruct Angular that that property it is iterating over is coming asynchronously. Listing 3-21 shows the code for the component modified to use the async pipe.

LISTING 3-21: Updated AthleteListComponent using async pipe

```
import { Component, Output, EventEmitter, OnInit } from '@angular/core';
import { AthleteService } from './athlete.service';
import { Athlete } from "./athlete";
import { Observable } from "rxjs/Observable";
```

```
@Component({
  selector: 'app-athlete-list',
  template: `
  <ol>
    <li *ngFor="let athlete of athletes | async">
      <app-athlete (click)="select(athlete)" [athlete]="athlete">
      </app-athlete></li>
  </ol>
  `,
})
export class AthleteListComponent implements OnInit {
  athletes: Observable<Athlete[]>;
  @Output() selected = new EventEmitter<Athlete>();
  constructor(private athleteService: AthleteService){   }

  getAthletes() {
    this.athletes = this.athleteService.getAthletes();
  }

  ngOnInit(){this.getAthletes();}

  select(selectedAthlete: Athlete){
    this.selected.emit(selectedAthlete);
  }
}
```

Notice that from being an array of Athlete now the athletes property is an Observable of an array of athletes.

> **NOTE** *The term "pipe" is used because it is indentified with the | character, and also because it is a function that processes the bound property before displaying it on the screen. If you know AngularJS 1, a pipe is just another name for filters.* async *is one of the pipes available, but there are others like* date *to render a* Date *object as a string, or* uppercase/lowercase *to convert a string all uppercase or lowercase, and other examples exist as well. You can also easily build custom pipes if you need them.*

Using Promises

If you are used to promises, as was done in AngularJS 1, you still can do so. But since Angular uses Observable by default, you have to convert it to a promise using the toPromise method of Observable and return it to the component.

```
getAthletes(){
  return this.http.get('api/athletes.json')
    .map((r: Response)=><Athlete[]>r.json().data)
    .toPromise();
}
```

Then the promise can be handled using the `then()` function as was done with AngularJS 1. Listing 3-22 shows this approach.

LISTING 3-22: Component handling promise

```
import { Component, Output, EventEmitter, OnInit } from '@angular/core';
import { AthleteService } from './athlete.service';
import { Athlete } from "./athlete";
import { Observable } from "rxjs/Observable";


@Component({
  selector: 'app-athlete-list',
  template: `
  <ol>
    <li *ngFor="let athlete of athletes">
      <app-athlete (click)="select(athlete)" [athlete]="athlete">
    </app-athlete></li>
  </ol>
  `,
})
export class AthleteListComponent implements OnInit {
  athletes: Athlete[];
  @Output() selected = new EventEmitter<Athlete>();
  constructor(private athleteService: AthleteService){  }

  getAthletes() {
    this.athleteService.getAthletes()
    .then(list => this.athletes=list);
  }

  ngOnInit(){this.getAthletes();}

  select(selectedAthlete: Athlete){
    this.selected.emit(selectedAthlete);
  }
}
```

Since the `async` pipe works with both `Observable` and promises, you could also use it instead of handling the promise in code.

At the end of the day, you have four options for consuming the `Observable`:

➤ Using `Observable` and subscribing to changes with code

➤ Using `Observable` and using the `async` pipe

➤ Using promises and handling it in code

➤ Using promises with the `async` pipe

REACTIVE EXTENSIONS FOR JAVASCRIPT (RXJS)

The Reactive Extensions is a set of libraries for asynchronous and event-based programming based on the `Observable` pattern. This project is developed by Microsoft and is available not only for JavaScript but also for many other languages like .NET, Java, Node, Swift, and many more.

Typically, asynchronous programming is implemented using callbacks, functions, or promises. Those are good for simple scenarios, but when the complexity increases, as with cancellation or synchronization and even error handling, working with them becomes error-prone. Using the `Observable` object together with all its methods makes all these scenarios easier to deal with.

RxJS is not developed by the Angular team, but it is used extensively throughout the framework.

You can learn more about RxJS at the website `http://reactivex.io/`.

There is much more to Angular than what this chapter covers. There are pipes to format the value of a property directly in the views, there are routes to allow easier navigation between the views and components of the application, and there is a module for simplifying the writing of forms and validating. There is so much that a book twice this size would not be enough to cover them all.

USING ANGULAR WITH ASP.NET MVC

Using Angular with ASP.NET Core and ASP.NET MVC Core is not any more complicated than what was necessary to connect to the static JSON file. Changing the URL to an ASP.NET MVC Core Web API is all that is needed on the client side. Building the server-side part of the service is also easy. You just create a controller that returns the list of items you need to show in the Angular component.

Listing 3-23 shows a very simple API that responds to the URL /api/athletes and returns a list of objects with names and times. In a real-world scenario, that data would probably come from a database or some other storage. Chapter 9 shows a complete sample that uses the database.

LISTING 3-23: Athlete controller

```
using System.Collections.Generic;
using Microsoft.AspNetCore.Mvc;
using API.Models;
using Newtonsoft.Json;

namespace API.Controllers
{
```

```
[Route("api/[controller]")]
public class AthletesController : Controller
{
    // GET: api/values
    [HttpGet]
    public AthletesViewModel Get()
    {
        return new AthletesViewModel(new[] {
            new Athlete("Jan Frodeno", "DEU", "08:06:30"),
            new Athlete("Sebastian Kienle", "DEU", "08:10:02"),
            new Athlete("Patrick Lange", "DEU", "08:11:14"),
            new Athlete("Ben Hoffman", "USA", "08:13:00"),
            new Athlete("Andi Boecherer", "DEU", "08:13:25")
        });
    }
}

public class AthletesViewModel
{
    public AthletesViewModel(IEnumerable<Athlete> items)
    {
        Items = items;
    }
    [JsonProperty(PropertyName = "data")]
    public IEnumerable<Athlete> Items { get; set; }
}

public class Athlete
{
    public Athlete(string name, string country, string time)
    {
        Name = name;
        Country = country;
        Time = time;
    }
    public string Name { get; set; }
    public string Country { get; set; }
    public string Time { get; set; }
}

}
```

Names of .NET properties are converted to JavaScript properties using camelCase by default (so Name will become the JavaScript property name), but if needed this name can be changed using the JsonProperty attribute specifying the PropertyName.

Combining Angular and ASP.NET Core Projects

The complicated part is integrating Angular and ASP.NET Core together during the development process.

There are three possible approaches:

➤ Do not integrate them. Have the Angular project built with the Angular CLI tool in its own folder, and keep an ASP.NET Core project with just the API services. The glue between the two is just the URLs.

➤ Put them both inside one project, maintaining the Angular part using the Angular CLI and building the artifacts inside the wwwroot of the ASP.NET Core project.

➤ Use a new feature of ASP.NET Core called JavaScriptServices, which makes it possible to build the entire project without using the Angular CLI.

Let's briefly explore the three options in more detail.

> ### HOW AN ANGULAR APPLICATION IS BUILT FOR THE BROWSER USING WEBPACK
>
> To understand why it is not possible to just drop a JavaScript library in an ASP .NET Core project and have everything working, you have to understand how an Angular project is built.
>
> As you might have noticed, Angular is a very modular framework. Each different piece of the application, both your own and from the framework, is in a separate file or module and imported as needed. Styles are spread among numerous files, potentially one per component. All these files have to be bundled together to avoid sending hundreds of files to the browser. In addition to this, Angular applications are built using TypeScript, which needs to be converted into standard ES5 JavaScript to be consumed by browsers.
>
> Discovering the dependencies and relationships between the various pieces, transpiling JavaScript to TypeScript, bundling JavaScript and CSS, and finally including the correct references in HTML files are all steps that are needed before anyone can run an Angular application. As you can imagine, it's a pretty daunting task.
>
> It could have been done with a generic front-end build tool like Gulp, but the Angular team decided to use a build tool focused only on module bundling, called WebPack, which takes care of everything. And the Angular CLI tools use it to run the Angular project during development and to build the artifacts needed when publishing the application.

Keeping Angular and ASP.NET Core as Two Separate projects

The first and easiest of the integration solutions is to not integrate. On one side we have a simple ASP.NET Core Web API application that returns the list of athletes (as in Listing 3-23) and on the other side we have the same Angular application used throughout the chapter. Just launch both at the same time, the first from Visual Studio and the second using the `ng serve` command of the Angular CLI tools.

The only difference is in the service class for Listing 3-20, where the URL used in the `http.get` method needs to be changed to `http.get('http://localhost:57663/api/athletes')` (with whichever port number Visual Studio starts the project with).

There is a problem, though. Here, one application running on a domain (the Angular app running on `localhost:4200`) is trying to access the API from another domain (`localhost:57663`). This violates the *same-origin policy* implemented by browsers to block scripts that access resources hosted on different origins (URLs with different domains, sub-domains, ports, or schemas).

The first solution is to configure a proxy in the Angular development server configuration (Listing 3-24). This way the scripts talk to the same origin, which then proxies the request to the real API.

LISTING 3-24: Proxy configuration (proxy.config.json)

```
{
    "/api/*": {
        "target": "http://localhost:57663",
        "secure": false
    }
}
```

Now, the URL used by the service must be on the same domain, so change it to `http.get('/api/athletes')`.

Finally, restart the angular development server specifying the configuration:

```
ng serve --proxy-config proxy.config.json
```

This is fine for development, but it is not enough as a permanent solution, which needs to configure the ASP.NET Core application to allow cross-origin resource sharing (CORS) requests. First, reference the `Microsoft.AspNetCore.Cors` package to your project. Then the policies need to be configured in the `Configure` method of the `Startup` class.

```
app.UseCors(builder => {
    builder.WithOrigins("http://localhost:4200");
});
```

To try it out, restart the Angular development server without the proxy configuration.

Combining Angular and ASP.NET Core into One Project Using the Angular CLI

The previous solution is the one that requires less setup and completely separates the two projects. It is probably the best solution if the front end is pure Angular and is decoupled from the back end. However, if the application is a mix of server-side rendering and Angular code, the two parts need to be in the same project.

The general concept behind this approach is to create both projects inside the same folder, one with Visual Studio and the other with the Anguar CLI tools. Then you configure the CLI tools to put the build artifacts in the `wwwroot` folder of the ASP.NET Core project.

First create a standard ASP.NET Core MVC application and add a Web API service (the one from Listing 3-23).

Then create an Angular project using the CLI tools and copy it over inside the same folder so that the `package.json` of the Angular project is on the same folder as the project's `.csproj` file. Figure 3-5 shows what the project tree should look like after copying the project.

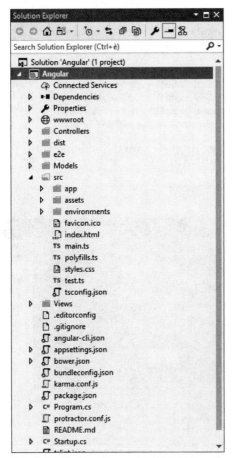

FIGURE 3-5: Angular and ASP.NET Core in one project

The next step is to modify the `angular-cli.json` file so that the build output goes into the `wwwroot` folder instead of the the default `dist` folder. Because the build process empties the content of the output folder, you also need to make sure the output goes in a subfolder to avoid deleting all the files that already exist within the folder.

```
...
    "apps": [
      {
        "root": "src",
        "outDir": "wwwroot/js",
```

```
  "assets": [
    "assets",
    "favicon.ico"
  ],
...
```

Then run the `ng build` command, and the Angular CLI will create a publishable version of the scripts inside the `wwwroot/js` folder.

The final step is to insert the `<app-root>` tag where the Angular application needs to appear (for example in the `Home/Index.cshtml` view) and to reference the files generated in the `_Layout.cshtml` file as shown below:

```
<script type="text/javascript" src="~/js/inline.bundle.js"></script>
<script type="text/javascript" src="~/js/styles.bundle.js"></script>
<script type="text/javascript" src="~/js/vendor.bundle.js"></script>
<script type="text/javascript" src="~/js/main.bundle.js"></script>
```

Figure 3-6 shows the homepage of the default ASP.NET Core template with the addition of the Angular application that displays the list coming from the Web API.

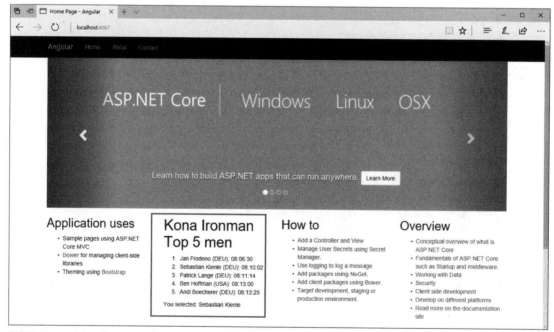

FIGURE 3-6: Mixed server-side and Angular rendering

To make development easier, the Angular CLI can be configured to run the build whenever a file changes, bringing back the fast feedback process you might be accustomed to from using the Angular development server: `ng build --watch`. The browser won't refresh automatically, but at least the scripts are recreated every time a file changes.

The setup of this solution for combining Angular and ASP.NET Core is a bit cumbersome, but it needs to be done only at the beginning of a project. If you want a faster and less manual start and an even deeper integration, there is a third option: using JavaScriptServices.

Using JavaScriptServices

This last option makes use of JavaScriptServices, a library released by Microsoft in ASP.NET Core v2. This library aims at simplifying the development of single-page applications with ASP.NET Core. Besides providing an easier setup of the project, it adds features like server-side rendering of Angular applications and integrates the WebPack build process, decoupling from the Angular CLI. All this is possible thanks to a lower-level library that allows execution of any Node.js application inside ASP.NET Core. It also provides support not only for Angular but also for React.

A project using JavaScriptServices can be created directly within Visual Studio 2017 by selecting the Angular project template (Figure 3-7) or by using the `dotnet new` command using the `angular` template.

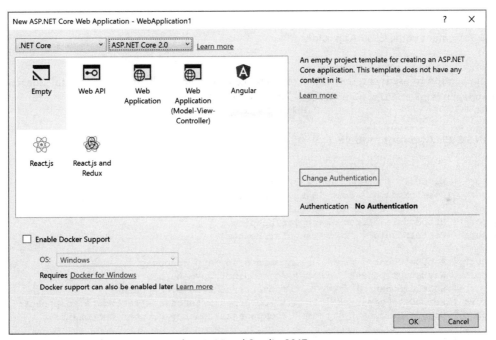

FIGURE 3-7: Angular project template in Visual Studio 2017

The resulting project is more of a sample than a template, but it provides a good starting point for single-page applications with ASP.NET Core.

Adding the sample app we used so far requires a bit of tweaking.

Let's start by copying all the components, including the root app component, into the `ClientApp/ app/components/athletes` folder. You need to change the name of the root app component to `athletes-app.component.ts` since this app already has a root app component. Figure 3-8 shows what is inside the ClientApp folder.

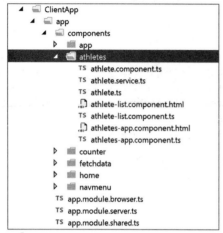

FIGURE 3-8: Content of the ClientApp folder

For the application to use them, they must be referenced from the application root module located at `ClientApp/app/app.module.shared.ts` (Listing 3-25).

LISTING 3-25: App root module

```
import { NgModule } from '@angular/core';
import { CommonModule } from '@angular/common';
import { FormsModule } from '@angular/forms';
import { HttpModule } from '@angular/http';
import { RouterModule } from '@angular/router';

import { AppComponent } from './components/app/app.component';
import { NavMenuComponent } from './components/navmenu/navmenu.component';
import { HomeComponent } from './components/home/home.component';
import { FetchDataComponent } from './components/fetchdata/fetchdata.component';
import { CounterComponent } from './components/counter/counter.component';

import { AthletesAppComponent } from './components/athletes/athletes-
app.component';
import { AthleteService } from './components/athletes/athlete.service';
import { AthleteListComponent } from './components/athletes/athlete-list.
component';
import { AthleteComponent } from './components/athletes/athlete.component';
```

```
@NgModule({
    declarations: [
        AppComponent,
        NavMenuComponent,
        CounterComponent,
        FetchDataComponent,
        AthletesAppComponent,
        AthleteListComponent,
        AthleteComponent,
        HomeComponent
    ],
    providers: [AthleteService],
    imports: [
        CommonModule,
        HttpModule,
        FormsModule,
        RouterModule.forRoot([
            { path: '', redirectTo: 'home', pathMatch: 'full' },
            { path: 'home', component: HomeComponent },
            { path: 'counter', component: CounterComponent },
            { path: 'fetch-data', component: FetchDataComponent },
            { path: 'athletes', component: AthletesAppComponent },
            { path: '**', redirectTo: 'home' }
        ])
    ]
})
export class AppModuleShared {
}
```

Apart from the import statements, the `declarations`, and `providers` arrays configured with the new components and services, there is something new: the configuration of the route. Routes are used in Angular to map URLs to specific components and to make navigating between components easier. Thanks to these routes, users can also bookmark or navigate directly to a part of the application as if it were a server-side rendered page.

Deciding Which Integration Method to Use

We've seen three possible ways of integrating an Angular project inside a ASP.NET Core application. Keeping Angular and ASP.NET Core as two separate projects is the best approach if you have a clear separation between the front end and the API, and it is also the one that allows you to develop clearly with the Angular tools. Combining Angular and ASP.NET Core into one project using the Angular CLI is a good solution for managing the whole application from inside one Visual Studio project and still uses the Angular tools for development, but this approach require a bit more manual work. Using JavaScriptServices is probably the best way if you need to combine traditional ASP.NET development together with SPA. It also provides most of the features needed by complex applications like server-side pre-rendering and hot swap of components for easier development. But this is a very dynamic and opinionated world and new solutions come out every day.

VISUAL STUDIO 2017 SUPPORT FOR ANGULAR

Until now you have written a lot of code. What if I told you that you can save a good number of keystrokes by using the native integration of Angular in Visual Studio? Visual Studio 2017 has three features that help with writing Angular applications:

➤ Code snippets to help writing Angular elements

➤ IntelliSense in TypeScript files

➤ IntelliSense in HTML files

Next you will have a look at each of these in more detail.

Code Snippets

Visual Studio comes with native support for TypeScript, so to create any new TypeScript file, including any Angular-related file, you can use Add New Item and select the TypeScript file, as shown in Figure 3-9.

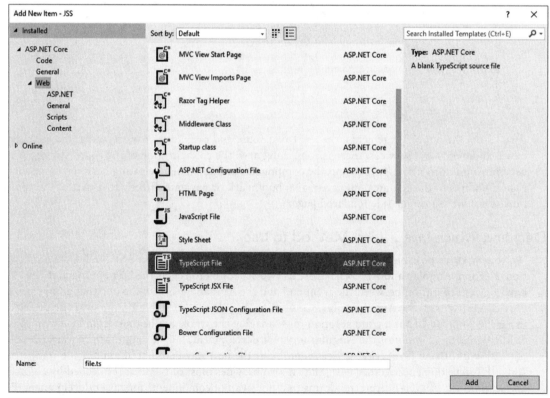

FIGURE 3-9: Add New Item dialog

Once you have created an empty TypeScript file, you can use the Angular snippets to create the skeleton for components, modules, services, and other Angular elements.

For example, the `ng2component` snippet expands to the following code:

```
import { Component } from 'angular/core';

@Component({
    selector: 'my-component',
    template: 'Hello my name is {{name}}.'
})
export class ExampleComponent {
    constructor() {
        this.name = 'Sam';
    }
}
```

Snippets also expand to other recurring blocks of code, such as connecting to HTTP (`ng2httpget`)

```
return this.http.get('url')
    .map((response: Response) => response.json());
```

or subscribing to `Observable` (`ng2subscribe`).

```
this.service.function
    .subscribe(arg => this.property = arg);
```

> **WARNING** *Angular2 snippet packs are not part of the default Visual Studio installation, but need to be download separately from the Visual Studio Extension Gallery:* `https://marketplace.visualstudio.com/items?itemName=MadsKristensen.Angular2SnippetPack`

IntelliSense in TypeScript Files

Visual Studio 2017 also provides complete (and relevant) IntelliSense for Angular by retrieving the documentation directly from TypeScript's typings (the documentation for TypeScript files) for Angular.

Figure 3-10 shows the autocompletion list that appears when typing inside the `@Component` annotation. Notice that the list only contains the methods that are exposed by the `module` class and that a full explanation of the function is provided.

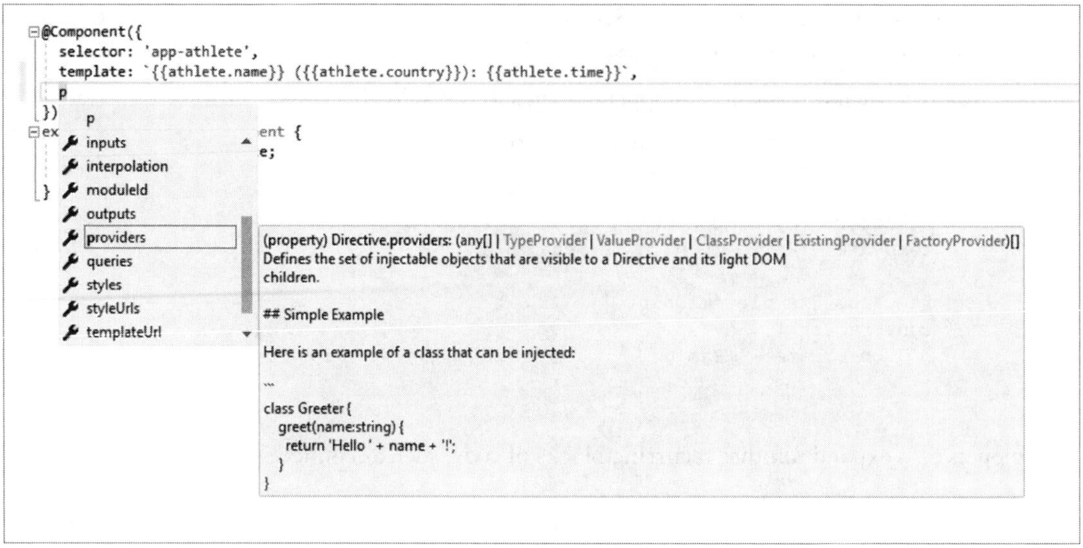

```
@Component({
    selector: 'app-athlete',
    template: `{{athlete.name}} ({{athlete.country}}): {{athlete.time}}`,
    p
})
ex    p
                              ent {
      inputs                  e;
      interpolation
}     moduleId
      outputs
      providers        (property) Directive.providers: (any[] | TypeProvider | ValueProvider | ClassProvider | ExistingProvider | FactoryProvider)[]
      queries          Defines the set of injectable objects that are visible to a Directive and its light DOM
      styles           children.
      styleUrls
      templateUrl      ## Simple Example

                       Here is an example of a class that can be injected:

                       ```

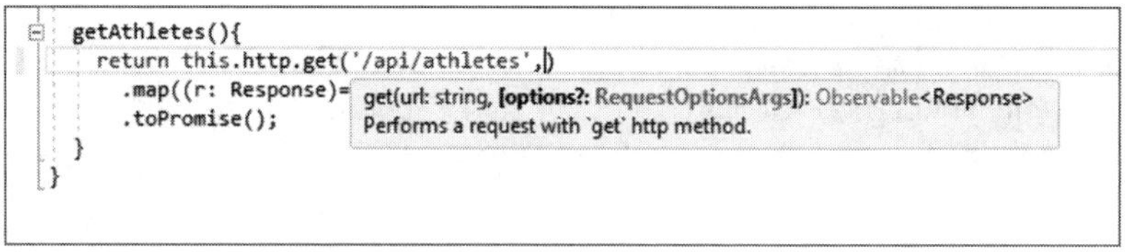

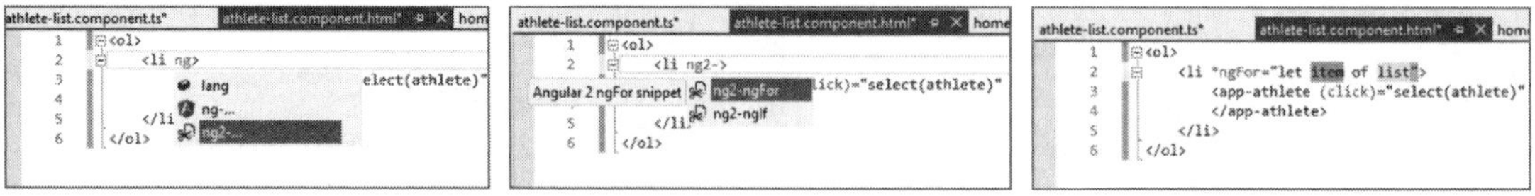

                       class Greeter {
                         greet(name:string) {
                           return 'Hello ' + name + '!';
                         }
                       }
```

**FIGURE 3-10:** IntelliSense autocompletion

When you are about to enter the parameters, the usual Parameter Info tooltip appears, as shown in Figure 3-11.

```
getAthletes(){
    return this.http.get('/api/athletes',)
    .map((r: Response)=    get(url: string, [options?: RequestOptionsArgs]): Observable<Response>
    .toPromise();          Performs a request with `get` http method.
}
}
```

FIGURE 3-11: Parameter info

IntelliSense in HTML Files

The power of Angular lies in its declarative approach, achieved with directives applied to HTML elements. Visual Studio 2017 with the snippet pack installed also helps in this context. Together with the standard HTML attributes, Visual Studio's IntelliSense also provides autocompletion for all the Angular structural directives. First it shows the ng2- indicator, then it expands to the list of Angular directives, as shown in Figure 3-12, and then it expands to the full format of the directive.

FIGURE 3-12: Angular autocompletion in HTML
```

SUMMARY

Angular can be used independently from any specific server-side technology, but the features introduced with the latest versions of Visual Studio and ASP.NET Core make it a perfect match for doing front-end development on the Microsoft.NET platform. Angular is a very powerful JavaScript framework with a lot of concepts. This chapter was just an introduction, but I hope you got the main points so you can start your journey into more advanced topics and experimenting on your own.

Bootstrap in a Nutshell

WHAT'S IN THIS CHAPTER?

➤ Introduction to Bootstrap

➤ Building responsive sites with Bootstrap

➤ Customizing Bootstrap with Less

➤ Features of Visual Studio 2017 that make developing with Bootstrap easier

Now that you have seen how to add client-side behavior to a web application, this chapter shows you how to make it look beautiful, by introducing Bootstrap.

Until a few years ago, putting the style on a website was a necessary evil for developers. CSS is not exactly a programming language, and it was not designed with maintainability in mind. Styling a website was a nightmare for web designers, who were using it every day and had to repeat their work with every new project. This led to the creation of hundreds of micro-libraries with the purpose of reducing repetition (or copy-paste operations) in the basic and standard CSS definitions.

Luckily, one company, Twitter, decided to publish their internal "blueprint" as an open-source project known as Bootstrap. This quickly became the most popular CSS "library" available, because of its default styles and components, its modularity, and the ease with which it can be customized via the CSS pre-processing language Less (and recently also with Sass). Bootstrap is responsive by default, which means that sites and web apps built with it adapt automatically to the screen size of the device, be it a TV screen, desktop, laptop, tablet, or smartphone. This framework has good support in Visual Studio 2017, which makes working with it faster and more enjoyable.

This chapter starts by introducing Bootstrap, discusses some of its features, and later expands on how to use it with ASP.NET Core and Visual Studio 2017.

INTRODUCTION TO BOOTSTRAP

Bootstrap is a very simple framework to work with. You just install it (via Bower, by downloading it, or by simply referencing it from the CDN), add the styles to your page, and everything "magically" gets a more professional and over-all polished style.

Installing Bootstrap

Three files (with a fourth optional file) have to be referenced for all the features of Bootstrap to work:

➤ The Bootstrap CSS file is `<link href="bootstrap/css/bootstrap.min.css" rel="stylesheet">`.

➤ The optional Bootstrap theme `<link href="bootstrap/css/bootstrap-theme.min.css" rel="stylesheet">` adds some nice colors to the page.

➤ The Bootstrap JavaScript library is `<script src="bootstrap/js/bootstrap.min.js"></script>`.

JQuery is also necessary since Bootstrap is based on it.

If you need to support older versions of IE (before IE9), the shim libraries html5shiv and Respond.js must be added. Listing 4-1 shows the basic template as suggested in the official documentation.

LISTING 4-1: Basic Template

```
<!DOCTYPE html>
<html lang="en">
  <head>
    <meta charset="utf-8">
    <meta http-equiv="X-UA-Compatible" content="IE=edge">
    <meta name="viewport" content="width=device-width, initial-scale=1">
    <!-- The above 3 meta tags *must* come first in the head; any other head
content must come *after* these tags -->
    <title>Basic template</title>

    <!-- Bootstrap -->
    <link href="css/bootstrap.min.css" rel="stylesheet">
    <link href="css/bootstrap-theme.min.css" rel="stylesheet">
```

```
    <!-- HTML5 shim and Respond.js for IE8 support of HTML5 elements and media
queries -->
    <!-- WARNING: Respond.js doesn't work if you view the page via file:// -->
    <!--[if lt IE 9]>
      <script src="https://oss.maxcdn.com/html5shiv/3.7.2/html5shiv.min.js"></
script>
      <script src="https://oss.maxcdn.com/respond/1.4.2/respond.min.js"></script>
    <![endif]-->
  </head>
  <body>

    <h1>Hello, world!</h1>

    <!-- jQuery (necessary for Bootstrap's JavaScript plugins) -->
    <script src="https://ajax.googleapis.com/ajax/libs/jquery/1.12.4/jquery.min.
js"></script>
    <!-- Include all compiled plugins (below), or include individual files as
needed -->
    <script src="js/bootstrap.min.js"></script>
  </body>
</html>
```

Figure 4-1 shows how the only text there, a simple "Hello, World!" statement, looks compared to an un-styled page. Notice the different font and margins.

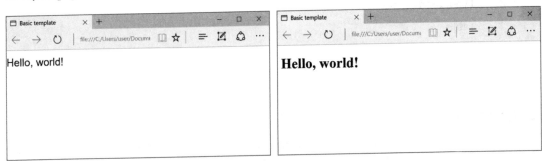

FIGURE 4-1: Styled and un-styled version of the same page

Figure 4-1 shows an example of the core CSS styles of Bootstrap for typography, which is covered more in detail in the next pages.

> **NOTE** *This chapter uses Bootstrap version 3.3. Bootstrap version 4 has long been in development and at the time of this writing is still in its beta version. When it is released, it is expected that the biggest changes will be a switch from Less to Sass, the rewriting of all JavaScript plugins, and the removal of nonresponsive layouts.*

The Main Features

Bootstrap is basically made of three different types of features:

➤ **Core CSS classes:** These style classes enhance the style of elements, either automatically or by applying a simple CSS class.

➤ **Components:** These implement more complex UI elements, such as navigation bars, drop-down menus, input groups, progress bars, and so on.

➤ **JavaScript plugins:** These bring the various components to life.

The following sections will examine these features in more detail.

BOOTSTRAP STYLES

The first core feature that Bootstrap offers is a set of CSS classes that enhance the look of the site and make it responsive.

These styles can be broadly grouped into these categories:

➤ Grid System

➤ Typography

➤ Tables

➤ Forms

➤ Buttons

Grid System

A basic feature of any CSS framework, the grid system allows you to create a page layout based on a series of rows and columns. On top of the basic behavior, Bootstrap provides a 12-column fluid grid layout that adapts to the size of the screen.

A few instructions need to be kept in mind when making a layout with the Bootstrap grid system:

➤ The whole grid must be inside an HTML element marked with `.container`.

➤ This container includes rows, defined as `<div class="row">...</div>`.

➤ Rows include columns. The width of each column is defined by specifying the number of grid cells it spans using the class `.col-sm-*`, replacing * with the actual number. For example, 4 `.col-sm-3` (4 × 3 is 12) would be used to make four equally sized columns.

Listing 4-2 shows these basic rules in action. There are four rows, with different columns per row (12 × 1, 8 + 4, 4 × 3, and 6 × 2). The class applied is `.col-sm-*`, which defines the behavior from "small devices" (a screen size bigger than 768px) and up. Figure 4-2 shows how the grid appears on a normal width, and when the window of the browser goes below 768px, you can see that all columns are stacked one below the other.

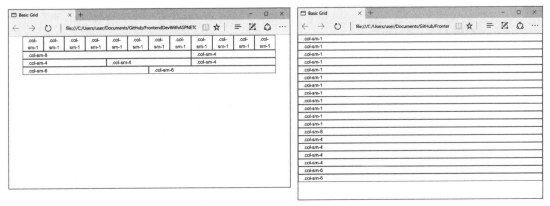

FIGURE 4-2: Grid shown in desktop and smartphone mode

LISTING 4-2: Basic Grid

```
<!DOCTYPE html>
<html lang="en">
...
<body>
  <div class="container">
    <div class="row">
      <div class="col-sm-1">.col-sm-1</div>
      <div class="col-sm-1">.col-sm-1</div>
      <div class="col-sm-1">.col-sm-1</div>
      <div class="col-sm-1">.col-sm-1</div>
      <div class="col-sm-1">.col-sm-1</div>
      <div class="col-sm-1">.col-sm-1</div>
      <div class="col-sm-1">.col-sm-1</div>
      <div class="col-sm-1">.col-sm-1</div>
      <div class="col-sm-1">.col-sm-1</div>
      <div class="col-sm-1">.col-sm-1</div>
      <div class="col-sm-1">.col-sm-1</div>
    </div>
    <div class="row">
     <div class="col-sm-8">.col-sm-8</div>
      <div class="col-sm-4">.col-sm-4</div>
    </div>
    <div class="row">
      <div class="col-sm-4">.col-sm-4</div>
      <div class="col-sm-4">.col-sm-4</div>
      <div class="col-sm-4">.col-sm-4</div>
```

```
      </div>
      <div class="row">
        <div class="col-sm-6">.col-sm-6</div>
        <div class="col-sm-6">.col-sm-6</div>
      </div>
    </div>
    ...
    </body>
  </html>
```

To understand this better, you will next explore how the responsive grid works.

Bootstrap defines four classes of devices, and for each of them there is a different CSS class prefix:

➤ **Extra small devices**, like smartphones, with a screen size smaller than 768px (.col-xs-)

➤ **Small devices**, like tablets, with a screen size bigger than 768px but smaller than 992px (.col-sm-)

➤ **Medium devices**, like normal laptops, with a screen size bigger than 992px but smaller than 1200px (.col-md-)

➤ **Large devices**, like desktops, with a screen size bigger than 1200px (.col-lg-)

In Listing 4-2 the size of columns was specified with class .col-sm-*, which means that everything smaller than 768px would get the default vertical stacked layout, as shown in Figure 4-2. To get the cells stacked for both smartphones and tablets but to be horizontal on desktops, the class .col-md-* should be used.

But more complicated layouts can be achieved by combining different classes. For example, if you do not want the smartphone version to stack horizontally but you want two columns per row, you can define this behavior by using col-xs-6 col-sm-1.

On the other hand, if you want the same layout in all device sizes, you just need to apply the class for the smallest size, and all bigger sizes will inherit it. For example, if you always want two columns per row, no matter the size, just apply col-xs-6. Listing 4-3 shows an example of these approaches.

LISTING 4-3: A More Complex Layout

```
<!DOCTYPE html>
<html lang="en">
...
<body>
  <div class="row">
    <div class="col-xs-6 col-sm-1">.col-sm-1</div>
    <div class="col-xs-6 col-sm-1">.col-sm-1</div>
    <div class="col-xs-6 col-sm-1">.col-sm-1</div>
    <div class="col-xs-6 col-sm-1">.col-sm-1</div>
    <div class="col-xs-6 col-sm-1">.col-sm-1</div>
    <div class="col-xs-6 col-sm-1">.col-sm-1</div>
    <div class="col-xs-6 col-sm-1">.col-sm-1</div>
```

```
    <div class="col-xs-6 col-sm-1">.col-sm-1</div>
    <div class="col-xs-6 col-sm-1">.col-sm-1</div>
    <div class="col-xs-6 col-sm-1">.col-sm-1</div>
    <div class="col-xs-6 col-sm-1">.col-sm-1</div>
    <div class="col-xs-6 col-sm-1">.col-sm-1</div>
  </div>
  <div class="row">
    <div class="col-xs-6 col-sm-8">.col-sm-8</div>
    <div class="col-xs-6 col-sm-4">.col-sm-4</div>
  </div>
  <div class="row">
    <div class="col-xs-6 col-sm-4">.col-sm-4</div>
    <div class="col-xs-6 col-sm-4">.col-sm-4</div>
    <div class="col-xs-6 col-sm-4">.col-sm-4</div>
  </div>
  <div class="row">
    <div class="col-xs-6">.col-sm-6</div>
    <div class="col-xs-6">.col-sm-6</div>
  </div>
  ...
  </body>
</html>
```

The grid system supports other interesting features. For example, you can specify an offset if there is the need to add a margin to a row, you can nest columns inside rows, and you can change the order in which columns are displayed.

This last feature is very important if the order in which columns appear in the horizontal layout is different from the order in the vertically stacked layout. The right sidebar is an example of this. Columns are stacked in the same order in which they appear in code, so normally a right sidebar would go below the content on the bottom of the page, which is not what you want. Bootstrap provides the classes .col-*-push-* and .col-*-pull-* to change this behavior. When applied to a column, they respectively push it to the right or pull it to the left.

Listing 4-4 shows the scenario of a right sidebar that goes on top of the content in the smartphone view. Notice that the columns are arranged in the desired order for the vertically stacked view, and the classes change their behavior for tablets and larger device sizes.

LISTING 4-4: Column Reordering

```
<!DOCTYPE html>
<html lang="en">
...
<body>
  <div class="row">
    <div class="col-sm-4 col-sm-push-8">Sidebar</div>
    <div class="col-sm-8 col-sm-pull-4">Content</div>
  </div>
  ...
  </body>
</html>
```

Other useful classes, still related to responsive design even if not specifically to the grid system, are the ones that hide elements based on screen size. They are:

➤ `.visible-xs-*` shows an element only in a specific device size (a smartphone in this case). In this case `*` is not the number of columns but how the visibility has to be applied (`block`, `inline`, `inline-block`).

➤ `.hidden-xs` hides an element for the specific device size.

Another possibility is to hide an element when a page is printed:

➤ `.visible-print-*` shows the element only when printing.

➤ `.hidden-print` hides the element during printing.

Typography

As shown at the beginning of the chapter in Figure 4-1, just by adding the Bootstrap library, the `H1` started looking more modern. This enhancement works not just for headers but also for all the other standard HTML elements. There is no need to use any special syntax, just the standard HTML tags.

For example, the `blockquote` element is rendered as in Figure 4-3. The code used to achieve it is shown in Listing 4-5.

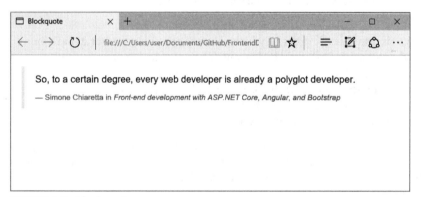

FIGURE 4-3: Blockquote

LISTING 4-5: BLOCKQUOTE

```
<!DOCTYPE html>
<html lang="en">
...
<body>

  <blockquote>
    <p>So, to a certain degree, every web developer is already a polyglot
developer.</p>
```

```
    <footer>Simone Chiaretta in <cite title="Front-end development with ASP.NET
Core, Angular, and Bootstrap">Front-end development with ASP.NET Core, Angular, and
Bootstrap</cite></footer>
  </blockquote>
  ...
  </body>
</html>
```

Code listings also get a style boost with the Bootstrap library. Figure 4-4 shows what happens when the `<code>` and `<pre>` elements are used.

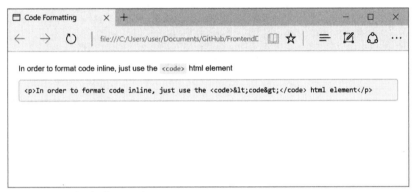

FIGURE 4-4: Code formatting

Tables

Unlike the other HTML elements, which get the Bootstrap styles without any class required, tables need a class to be specified. This is because applying styles to all tables will cause problems when they are used in many UI components such as calendars or date pickers.

All that is needed to apply the Bootstrap styles is adding the `.table` class to the `<table>` element. This will render a standard table with horizontal dividers between rows. There are also a few additional classes for different styles of tables:

➤ `.table-striped` adds a gray background to alternate rows.

➤ `.table-bordered` adds a border to the table itself and all cells.

➤ `.table-hover` adds a roll-over to rows.

➤ `.table-condensed` reduces the padding between rows, making the visualization a bit more compact.

In addition to these table-related classes, there are also row- and cell-specific classes to indicate whether the row represents information (`.info`), a warning (`.warning`), a danger (`.danger`), or the success of an operation (`.success`).

Finally, by wrapping a table in `<div class="table-responsive">`, a horizontal scrollbar will appear with screen sizes smaller than 768px.

Forms

Another area where Bootstrap brings a lot of enhancement is forms and form fields. Similar to tables, forms require a class to be specified. Every field of the form must have a `.form-control` class and must be enclosed, together with its label and optional help, into an element with the class `.form-group`. These classes put fields at 100% width, apply optimal spacing, and show labels and help text in an appropriate style, as is shown in Figure 4-5. (Listing 4-6 is the code used to render that login form.)

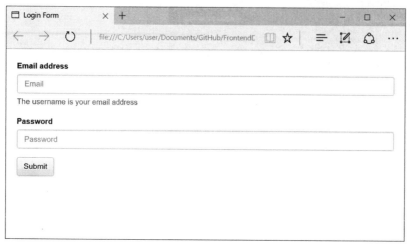

FIGURE 4-5: Login form

LISTING 4-6: Code for Login Form

```
<!DOCTYPE html>
<html lang="en">
...
<body>
  <form>
    <div class="form-group">
      <label for="email">Email address</label>
      <input type="email" class="form-control" id="email" placeholder="Email">
      <p class="help-block">The username is your email address</p>
    </div>
    <div class="form-group">
      <label for="password">Password</label>
      <input type="password" class="form-control" id="password"
             placeholder="Password">
    </div>
    <button type="submit" class="btn btn-default">Submit</button>
  </form>
  ...
  </body>
</html>
```

Two classes exist to change the layout of forms: `.form-inline` puts all fields on the same line, and `.form-horizontal` puts the label and field on the same line and each form group on a different row. When you use a second class, the form layout uses the grid layout described at the beginning of the chapter, so the number of columns used by the label and input box can be specified using the same class names.

Fields can also be styled according to their state or validation result. When you apply the `disabled` boolean attribute to disable an input element, this element will be also grayed out. To achieve the same visual effect without actually disabling the input element, apply the `readonly` attribute.

To show the validation result for a field, apply the validation-related classes to the form-group element. These classes are `.has-success` to indicate the validation is okay, `.has-error` to indicate a validation error, and `.has-warning` for something in between.

```
<div class="form-group has-success">
  <label for="email">Email address</label>
  <input type="email" class="form-control" id="email" placeholder="Email">
  <p class="help-block">The username is your email address</p>
</div>
```

Buttons

Bootstrap also provides classes to style buttons, just by applying `.btn` to the `<button>` element.

You can use classes in combination with `.btn` to change the semantics of buttons. You can use `.btn-primary` to identify the main button on the form, `.btn-success` to identify a positive action, or `.btn-danger` for actions leading to dangerous outcomes (such as unrecoverable delete operations).

There also exist modifiers for making buttons bigger or smaller. You can use `.btn-lg`, `.btn-sm`, `.btn-xs`, or `.btn-block` to make the button take over all the width of the parent element.

To see all the classes available in Bootstrap, see the official documentation on the Bootstrap website.

COMPONENTS

The second level of features provided by Bootstrap is Components. They are made of HTML snippets that are enhanced by Bootstrap's own JavaScript plugins. There are 21 components available in Bootstrap, from small features like glyphs, badges, and alerts to bigger UI controls like navigation bars, dropdowns, pagination, and input fields. It's impossible to cover them all in this short introductory chapter, so the next pages just cover a few of them. I suggest you to read the official documentation to see how they work.

Glyphicons

Bootstrap includes more than 250 Halfling Glyphicons for free. Glyphs are lightweight icons implemented via web fonts and CSS classes. To use them in your page, you have to add a `<span>` element with the relevant glyph class. The only important rule to remember is that CSS classes for glyphs have to be used on their own element without any other class applied and without nested elements.

Listing 4-7 shows the code needed to create the confirm button of Figure 4-6, which basically is a glyph inside a button together with a caption.

LISTING 4-7: Confirm Button

```
<!DOCTYPE html>
<html lang="en">
...
<body>

  <button type="button" class="btn btn-success btn-lg">
    <span class="glyphicon glyphicon-ok-circle" ></span> Confirm
  </button>
  ...
  </body>
</html>
```

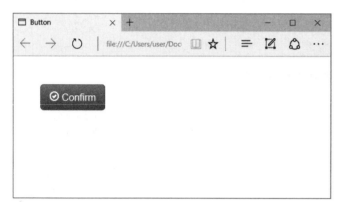

FIGURE 4-6: Confirm Button

Dropdown

One of the most important UI components is the drop-down menu. In Bootstrap a dropdown has a slightly different connotation, though. It is not meant to be used to select a value, like in the HTML select element, but more like a menu with items.

A dropdown is made of two parts. The first is the trigger, which, when clicked, will open the menu. The second is the `<ul>` with the items of the menu. These two elements have to be put inside an element with the `.dropdown` class. Listing 4-8 shows an example of a dropdown menu.

LISTING 4-8: Dropdown Menu

```
<!DOCTYPE html>
<html lang="en">
...
<body>
```

```
<div class="dropdown">
  <button class="btn btn-default dropdown-toggle" type="button"
          data-toggle="dropdown">
    User Profile
    <span class="caret"></span>
  </button>
  <ul class="dropdown-menu" aria-labelledby="dropdownMenu1">
    <li class="dropdown-header">Settings</li>
    <li><a href="#">Update password</a></li>
    <li><a href="#">Update profile</a></li>
    <li class="disabled"><a href="#">Payment information</a></li>
    <li role="separator" class="divider"></li>
    <li><a href="#">Logout</a></li>
  </ul>
</div>
...
</body>
</html>
```

Listing 4-8 also shows other optional elements for the dropdown:

➤ A header, specified with the `.dropdown-header` class

➤ A disabled link, applying the class `.disabled`

➤ A divider to separate links, using the `.divider` class

Figure 4-7 shows the menu with all the optional elements.

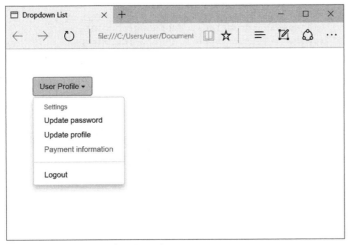

FIGURE 4-7: User Profile dropdown menu

Input Groups

The most important concern of every developer should be to make it easier for the users of web apps to enter data. The input group is a component that helps with that by extending the standard input field and adding text, symbols, or buttons before and after the field itself.

An input group is defined by a container element marked with the class `.input-group`. This class includes a `<span>` element with the class `.input-group-addon` if the add-on is text or `.input-group-btn` if it's a button, and the actual input field, with the class `.form-control`.

Only one add-on per side is allowed.

Listing 4-9 shows all the various options. Notice that the button can also be used as a trigger for a dropdown menu (shown in Figure 4-8).

LISTING 4-9: Various Samples of Input Groups

```
<!DOCTYPE html>
<html lang="en">
...
<body>
  <div class="input-group">
    <span class="input-group-addon">http://twitter.com/</span>
    <input type="text" class="form-control" placeholder="Twitter Handle">
  </div>

  <div class="input-group">
    <input type="text" class="form-control" placeholder="Email">
    <span class="input-group-addon">@example.com</span>
  </div>

  <div class="input-group">
    <input type="text" class="form-control" placeholder="Search for...">
    <span class="input-group-btn">
      <button type="button" class="btn btn-default dropdown-toggle"
              data-toggle="dropdown">Search <span class="caret"></span>
      </button>
      <ul class="dropdown-menu dropdown-menu-right">
        <li><a href="#">Races</a></li>
        <li><a href="#">Athletes</a></li>
        <li><a href="#">News</a></li>
      </ul>
    </span>
  </div>
  ...
  </body>
</html>
```

Navigation

Well-designed navigation can mark the difference between a successful UI and an unusable site. Bootstrap provides components for various type of navigation UIs. They all share the same approach as they are all wrapped inside a `<nav>` element, and the elements of the navigation are all items of an HTML list.

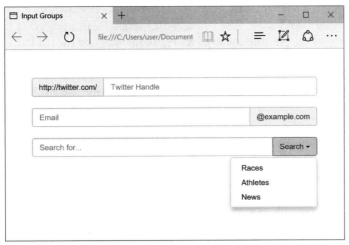

FIGURE 4-8: Various samples of input groups

Navigation Bar

Probably the most well known Bootstrap component, easily recognizable from Twitter's UI a few years ago, is the navigation bar. This component acts as a responsive container for all the other elements and components that can be used in an application's main navigation bar.

The container for navbar is marked with the `.navbar` class. It includes the bar header, which is a `<div>` element with the class `.navbar-header` that can be either an image or simply the name of the app. All elements of the bar are simply `<li>` items inside a `<ul class="nav navbar-nav">` list element, and each of them can contain a normal link or a nested list if a submenu (achieved with a dropdown menu) is needed. Figure 4-9 shows a complete bar that also includes a form element.

FIGURE 4-9: Example of navbar

One interesting feature is the fact that the navbar can be configured to collapse into a vertical mobile menu when the screen is smaller than 768px. (See Figure 4-10.) To enable this feature, a button for opening and closing the bar must be put into the header area of the bar, and the list that contains the items must be put inside a collapsible element.

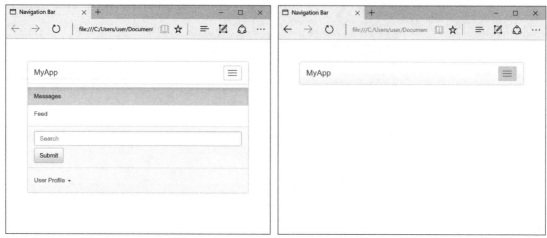

FIGURE 4-10: Responsive navbar, both open and collapsed

Listing 4-10 shows all the basic features of the navbar, including how to mark an element as active.

LISTING 4-10: Responsive navbar

```
<!DOCTYPE html>
<html lang="en">
...
<body>
  <nav class="navbar navbar-default">
    <div class="container-fluid">
      <div class="navbar-header">
        <button type="button" class="navbar-toggle collapsed" data-
toggle="collapse" data-target="#example-navbar-collapse-1" aria-expanded="false">
          <span class="icon-bar"></span>
          <span class="icon-bar"></span>
          <span class="icon-bar"></span>
        </button>
        <a class="navbar-brand" href="#">MyApp</a>
      </div>

      <div class="collapse navbar-collapse" id="example-navbar-collapse-1">
        <ul class="nav navbar-nav">
          <li class="active"><a href="#">Messages</a></li>
          <li><a href="#">Feed</a></li>
        </ul>
```

```
            <form class="navbar-form navbar-left" role="search">
              <div class="form-group">
                <input type="text" class="form-control" placeholder="Search">
              </div>
              <button type="submit" class="btn btn-default">Submit</button>
            </form>
            <ul class="nav navbar-nav navbar-right">
              <li class="dropdown">
                <a class="dropdown-toggle" type="button" data-toggle="dropdown">
                  User Profile
                  <span class="caret"></span>
                </a>
                <ul class="dropdown-menu" aria-labelledby="dropdownMenu1">
                  <li class="dropdown-header">Settings</li>
                  <li><a href="#">Update password</a></li>
                  <li><a href="#">Update profile</a></li>
                  <li class="disabled"><a href="#">Payment information</a></li>
                  <li role="separator" class="divider"></li>
                  <li><a href="#">Logout</a></li>
                </ul>
              </li>
            </ul>
          </div>
        </div>
      </nav>
      ...
    </body>
  </html>
```

The navbar has many other options, which can be found by reading the official Bootstrap documentation on their website.

Pagination

The pagination component is used to move through the pages of a listing. In this case the list element needs to have the .pagination class. All the pages of the control are normal list items that can be disabled by applying the .disabled class or marked as active with the .active class.

Listing 4-11 shows the code for the pagination control, and Figure 4-11 shows how it appears.

LISTING 4-11: Pagination Control

```
<!DOCTYPE html>
<html lang="en">
...
<body>
  <nav>
    <ul class="pagination">
      <li class="disabled"><a href="#"><span>&laquo;</span></a></li>
      <li class="active"><a href="#">1</a></li>
      <li><a href="#">2</a></li>
      <li><a href="#">3</a></li>
```

```
            <li><a href="#">4</a></li>
            <li><a href="#">5</a></li>
            <li><a href="#"><span>&raquo;</span></a></li>
         </ul>
      </nav>
      ...
      </body>
   </html>
```

FIGURE 4-11: Pagination control

Breadcrumbs

Breadcrumbs help users to find their way in hierarchical content structures as shown in Figure 4-12. Compared to the navbar this element is pretty easy, as it doesn't require anything more than an ordered list with the class `.breadcrumb`, as shown in Listing 4-12.

FIGURE 4-12: Breadcrumb

LISTING 4-12: Breadcrumb

```
<!DOCTYPE html>
<html lang="en">
...
```

```
<body>
  <ol class="breadcrumb">
    <li><a href="#">Home</a></li>
    <li><a href="#">Profile</a></li>
    <li class="active">Connections</li>
  </ol>
  ...
  </body>
</html>
```

Tabs and Pills

Another type of navigation is in-page navigation. In-page navigation is usually implemented with tabs or pills. Listing 4-13 shows how tabs are implemented.

LISTING 4-13: Tabbed Navigation

```
<!DOCTYPE html>
<html lang="en">
...
<body>
  <ul class="nav nav-tabs">
    <li role="presentation" class="active"><a href="#home">Home</a></li>
    <li role="presentation"><a href="#profile">Profile</a></li>
    <li role="presentation"><a href="#messages">Messages</a></li>
  </ul>
  ...
  </body>
</html>
```

To create pills navigation, just replace the class with `.nav-pills`. Figure 4-13 shows the two different in-page navigation options.

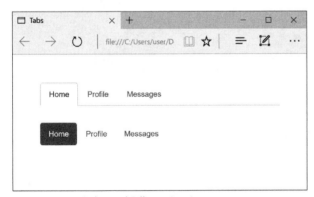

FIGURE 4-13: Tabs and Pills navigation

As shown later in this chapter, these two types of navigation can be enhanced using the Bootstrap JavaScript library to automatically switch panes when clicking on the items.

Other Components

You can also use Bootstrap to create other components, including labels, badges, and alerts. Listing 4-14 shows some code that you can use to render these other basic Bootstrap components, which are shown in Figure 4-14.

LISTING 4-14: Labels, Badges, and Alerts

```
<!DOCTYPE html>
<html lang="en">
...
<body>

    <!-- Label -->
    <p>Your password is about to expire <span class="label label-warning">Warning</span></p>
    <!-- Badage -->
    <p>Messages <span class="badge">4</span></p>
    <!-- Alert -->
    <div class="alert alert-danger" role="alert">Your order couldn't be processed
due to an error in our system.</div>

    ...
    </body>
</html>
```

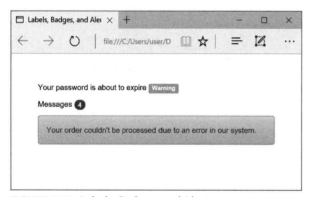

FIGURE 4-14: Labels, Badges, and Alerts

JAVASCRIPT

The final level of enhancement brought by Bootstrap is its JavaScript plugins library. Some of the plugins are automatically used to bring some of the components, like the dropdown menu or tabbed navigation, to life. Others are pure JavaScript APIs that can be used autonomously.

This chapter does not cover the JavaScript plugins library in detail and mainly focuses on some simple usages of the API, because the usage of JavaScript plugins library in Bootstrap is quite advanced and is beyond the scope of this book.

Tabbed Content

Tabbed navigation was explained earlier in this chapter. With the help of the Toggable Tabs plugin, the navigation can open and close the various panes. This can be achieved in two different ways: via JavaScript or just by the usage of markup and data attributes.

Activating Tab Navigation with JavaScript

After setting up the tab navigation as in Listing 4-13, the panes must be created. They are just simple `<div>` elements that specify `role="tabpanel"`.

```
<div class="tab-content">
  <div role="tabpanel" class="tab-pane active" id="home">Home</div>
  <div role="tabpanel" class="tab-pane" id="profile">Profile</div>
  <div role="tabpanel" class="tab-pane" id="messages">Messages</div>
</div>
```

Notice that the IDs of the panes match the anchors in the links used in the navigation. This is very important because the JavaScript function that is used to open a pane, `.tab('show')`, relies on the `href` in the links and the `id` in the panes to be the same. This method has to be called as the click event of the link, like `$('#myTabs a[href="#profile"]').tab('show')`, to enable the tab feature on the profile link.

A better approach would be to enable the tab feature on all links using a simple JQuery selector. Listing 4-15 shows the complete code for tabs activated via jQuery.

LISTING 4-15: Tabbed Navigation with JavaScript

```
<!DOCTYPE html>
<html lang="en">
...
  <body>

    <ul id="myTabs" class="nav nav-tabs">
      <li role="presentation" class="active"><a href="#home">Home</a></li>
      <li role="presentation"><a href="#profile">Profile</a></li>
      <li role="presentation"><a href="#messages">Messages</a></li>
    </ul>

    <div class="tab-content">
      <div role="tabpanel" class="tab-pane active" id="home">Homediv>
      <div role="tabpanel" class="tab-pane" id="profile">Profilediv>
      <div role="tabpanel" class="tab-pane" id="messages">Messages</div>
    </div>
```

```
    <script src="https://ajax.googleapis.com/ajax/libs/jquery/1.12.4/jquery.min.
js"></script>
    <script src="js/bootstrap.min.js"></script>

    <script type="text/javascript">
    $('#myTabs a').click(function (e) {
      e.preventDefault()
      $(this).tab('show')
    });
    </script>

  </body>
</html>
```

Activating Tab Navigation with Data Attributes

Activating via data attributes in the markup is even easier. All that is needed is to add `data-toggle="tab"` in the navigation as shown in Listing 4-16.

LISTING 4-16: Using Data Attributes for Tab Navigation

```
<!DOCTYPE html>
<html lang="en">
...
<body>
  <ul id="myTabs" class="nav nav-tabs">
    <li role="presentation" class="active"><a href="#home"
        data-toggle="tab">Home</a></li>
    <li role="presentation"><a href="#profile"
        data-toggle="tab">Profile</a></li>
    <li role="presentation"><a href="#messages"
        data-toggle="tab">Messages</a></li>
  </ul>

  <div class="tab-content">
    <div role="tabpanel" class="tab-pane active" id="home">Home</div>
    <div role="tabpanel" class="tab-pane" id="profile">Profile</div>
    <div role="tabpanel" class="tab-pane" id="messages">Messages</div>
  </div>
  ...
</body>
</html>
```

Modal Dialog

Another commonly used UI control is the modal dialog. The functionality of the Bootstrap plugin is pretty basic: It displays and closes the modal dialog. On the other hand, the HTML code needed for the modal dialog itself is a bit verbose, but once you understand it, it is pretty logical.

It starts with an external `<div>` element with the class `.modal`, which represents the overlay that goes over the whole page. Inside there is another `<div>` element marked with the class `.modal-dialog`. This is the actual modal dialog, which contains three separate areas:

➤ The modal header, defined by `<div class="modal-header">`, contains the title of the dialog and the close button.

➤ The actual content of the dialog is contained inside `<div class=modal-body">`.

➤ The footer, inside `<div class=modal-footer">`, is where the action buttons of the dialog are supposed to be.

Listing 4-17 shows the complete code that is used to render the dialog of Figure 4-15.

LISTING 4-17: Modal Dialog

```
<!DOCTYPE html>
<html lang="en">
...
<body>
  <!-- Button trigger modal -->
  <button type="button" class="btn btn-primary btn-lg"
          data-toggle="modal" data-target="#myModal">
    Launch logout modal
  </button>

  <!-- Modal -->
  <div class="modal fade" id="myModal" tabindex="-1" role="dialog">
    <div class="modal-dialog" role="document">
      <div class="modal-content">
        <div class="modal-header">
          <button type="button" class="close"
                  data-dismiss="modal">&times;</button>
          <h4 class="modal-title" id="myModalLabel">Logout</h4>
        </div>
        <div class="modal-body">
          You are about to log out from the system. Do you want to proceed?
        </div>
        <div class="modal-footer">
          <button type="button" class="btn btn-default"
                  data-dismiss="modal">Cancel</button>
          <button type="button" class="btn btn-primary">Logout</button>
        </div>
      </div>
    </div>
  </div>
  ...
</body>
</html>
```

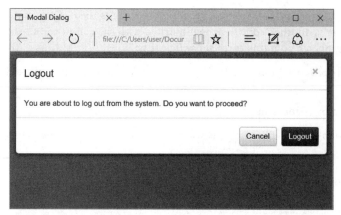

FIGURE 4-15: Modal dialog

Opening the module is very easy. As with most of the other Bootstrap plugins, it can be done with markup or with code. In order to do it with markup, as shown in Listing 4-17, just set `data-toggle="modal"` on the element that should open the dialog and `data-target="#myModal"` to indicate which modal to open.

```
<button type="button" class="btn btn-primary btn-lg" data-toggle="modal" data-
target="#myModal">Launch logout modal</button>
```

The method `$('myModal').modal('show')` can be used to open the modal in JavaScript.

Tooltips and Popovers

Other core plugins that do not require much work to implement are tooltips and popovers. (See Figure 4-16.) They basically are the same thing, bubbles of text appearing next to an element, with a couple of small but significant differences. Tooltips appear when you hover over the element, while popovers appear when click on it. Popovers also have a title, which tooltips lack.

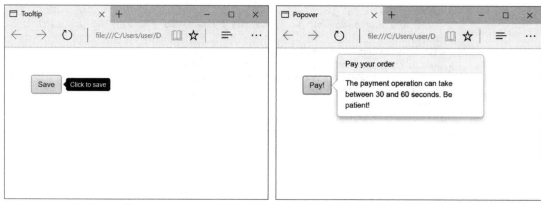

FIGURE 4-16: Tooltip and popover

Both tooltips and popovers can be configured either with JavaScript or via markup similarly to the other plugins.

To create them via markup, just set `data-toggle="tooltip"` or `data-toggle="popover"` on the element. You can also optionally set the position of the tooltip with `data-placement="left"`. The text of the tooltip and title of the popover are then specified with the `title` attribute, and the content of the popover is specified via the `data-content` attribute. For performance reasons, unlike the other plugins that were automatically enabled, tooltips and popovers have to be manually opted-in via the JavaScript methods `$().tooltip()` and `$().popover()`. Code for both components is shown in Listings 4-18 and 4-19.

LISTING 4-18: Tooltip

```html
<!DOCTYPE html>
<html lang="en">
...
<body>
  <button id="saveBtn" type="button" class="btn btn-default"
          data-toggle="tooltip"
          data-placement="right"
          title="Click to save">Save</button>
  ...
  <script type="text/javascript">
    $('#saveBtn').tooltip();
  </script>
  ...
</body>
</html>
```

LISTING 4-19: Popover

```html
<!DOCTYPE html>
<html lang="en">
...
<body>
  <button id="payBtn" type="button" class="btn btn-default"
          data-toggle="popover"
          data-placement="right"
          title="Pay your order"
          data-content="The payment operation can take between 30 and 60 seconds.
Be patient!">Pay!</button>
  ...
  <script type="text/javascript">
    $('#payBtn').popover();
  </script>
  ...
</body>
</html>
```

CUSTOMIZING BOOTSTRAP WITH LESS

Bootstrap is built with Less, one of the CSS pre-processing languages. A benefit is that it can be easily customized for a better fit of the look and feel of your application without the need to override everything in all your CSS files. This can be done in two different ways: via the Bootstrap website or by downloading the source code and manually updating the Less or Sass files.

Customizing via the Website

The Bootstrap official website provides a customization page that allows developers to change the default styles of the framework. (See Figure 4-17.) In addition to this, it also offers the possibility to select which styles, components, and plugins to include in the compiled file. Use this last option if you want to reduce the size of the files that will be downloaded from your website.

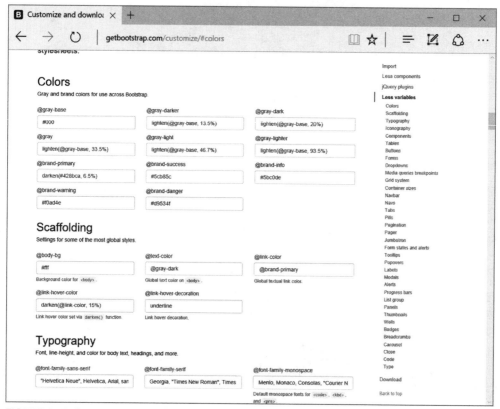

FIGURE 4-17: Bootstrap customizer

The customization page is accessible at the URL `http://getbootstrap.com/customize/`.

From there you can scroll down to find the variables you need or you can select the area of the framework you want to customize from the menu on the right. If, for example, you want the green of the "success" style for buttons, bars, and labels to be a different tone of green, you can change the @brand-success variable.

When all the customization is done, scroll down to the bottom of the page and click on the Compile and Download button. This will generate a zip file with your specific version of Bootstrap. It will also save your specific configuration as gist on GitHub and inside a config.json file inside the zip file just downloaded. You can see a snippet of this file in Listing 4-20. Notice that at the end it includes the URL to open the customization tool directly with this specific configuration.

LISTING 4-20: Config.json File

```
{
  "vars": {
    "@gray-base": "#000",
    ...
    "@brand-primary": "darken(#428bca, 6.5%)",
    "@brand-success": "#00FF00",
    "@brand-info": "#5bc0de",
    "@brand-warning": "#f0ad4e",
    "@brand-danger": "#d9534f",
    ...
  },
  "css": [
    "print.less",
    "type.less",
    "code.less",
    ...
  ],
  "js": [
    "alert.js",
    "button.js",
    ...
  ],
  "customizerUrl": "http://getbootstrap.com/customize/?id=b21b62d56781c2e2ea87"
}
```

This tool is very useful if you need to do a quick adjustment to the styles and you do not use Less (or Sass) already in your development workflow. But if a more iterative approach is needed and you are using already Less, it's probably better to modify the variables directly.

Customizing with LESS

In order to directly edit the Less variables, you need to download the source code of Bootstrap. The folder with the actual code of the CSS styles is called less. It contains one Less file per CSS area and component, and also one file called variables.less. This is the file that needs to be modified to change the styles of any component in Bootstrap. Listing 4-21 shows the beginning of the file, with the variable @brand-success that was changed with the online customization tool.

LISTING 4-21: Beginning of variables.less File

```
/
// Variables
// --------------------------------------------------


//== Colors
//
//## Gray and brand colors for use across Bootstrap.

@gray-base:             #000;
@gray-darker:           lighten(@gray-base, 13.5%); // #222
@gray-dark:             lighten(@gray-base, 20%);   // #333
@gray:                  lighten(@gray-base, 33.5%); // #555
@gray-light:            lighten(@gray-base, 46.7%); // #777
@gray-lighter:          lighten(@gray-base, 93.5%); // #eee

@brand-primary:         darken(#428bca, 6.5%); // #337ab7
@brand-success:         #5cb85c;
@brand-info:            #5bc0de;
@brand-warning:         #f0ad4e;
@brand-danger:          #d9534f;
...
```

Once all the changes have been made, Grunt will take care of compiling the Less code into the final CSS files. Chapter 6 explains more in detail how to use Grunt to run these build tasks, but if it is already set up, just type `grunt dist` and the updated CSS files will be generated.

BOOTSTRAP SUPPORT IN VISUAL STUDIO 2017 AND ASP.NET CORE

As you might have noticed, Bootstrap uses a lot of CSS classes and snippets of HTML code for all its styles and components. Without good autocomplete functionality and a good snippet library, developers would have to rely on memory and documentation.

Visual Studio helps by providing a CSS autocomplete feature that shows all the classes available in Bootstrap and identifies them with a **B** icon, as shown in Figure 4-18.

Visual Studio 2017 also includes a good snippet library in which developers can save their most used snippets. Snippets in Visual Studio are very powerful because they clearly mark which parts are fixed and which parts (typically just names or IDs) can be changed.

Visual Studio doesn't come with a list of Bootstrap snippets, but it can understand if a project is using Bootstrap and provides possible third-party extensions that can help with it, as shown in Figure 4-19. Visual Studio suggests installing the following two extensions:

➤   Bootstrap Snippet Pack

➤   Glyphfriend

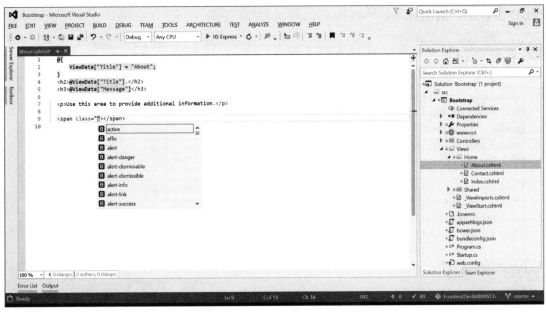

FIGURE 4-18: Bootstrap autocomplete

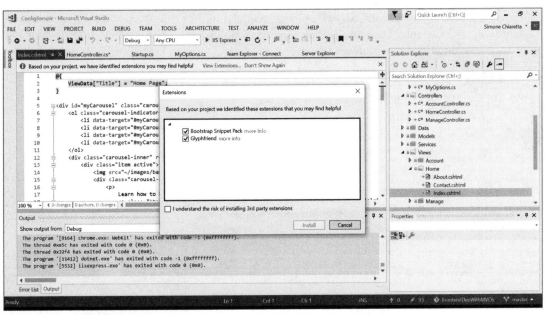

FIGURE 4-19: Suggested third-party extensions

Bootstrap Snippet Pack

As the name implies, this is a collection of 30+ snippets that can be added to an HTML page by simply dragging them from the Visual Studio toolbox (see Figure 4-20).

Most Bootstrap components are made of long pieces of HTML, most of which has to be copied as it is, and only few strings need to be updated. Development becomes very easy as the strings that can be modified are clearly marked and you can cycle through them with the Tab key.

For example, in the snippet for the modal dialog (Listing 4-17), the only strings needing customization are the ID, the title, the content, and the text of the two buttons. As you can see in Figure 4-21, these strings are highlighted for easy identification.

Glyphfriend

This extension helps with choosing from the glyphicons available in Bootstrap by showing their preview in the autocomplete dropdown (see Figure 4-22).

This extension is not limited to Bootstrap. It supports all the other Font Awesome icons, as well as Ionic, Foundation, IcoMoon, and GitHub's Octicons. It even supports Emoji when using Visual Studio as a markdown editor.

FIGURE 4-20: Bootstrap Snippet Pack Toolbox

```
About.cshtml + X
  1   @{
  2        ViewData["Title"] = "About";
  3   }
  4   <h2>@ViewData["Title"].</h2>
  5   <h3>@ViewData["Message"]</h3>
  6
  7   <p>Use this area to provide additional information.</p>
  8
  9   <div class="modal fade" id="myModal" tabindex="-1" role="dialog" aria-labelledby="myModal-label">
 10       <div class="modal-dialog" role="document">
 11           <div class="modal-content">
 12               <div class="modal-header">
 13                   <button type="button" class="close" data-dismiss="modal" aria-label="Close"><span aria-hidden="true">&times;</span></button>
 14                   <h4 class="modal-title" id="myModal-label">Modal title</h4>
 15               </div>
 16               <div class="modal-body">
 17                   <p>Lorem ipsum dolor sit amet, consectetur adipiscing elit.</p>
 18               </div>
 19               <div class="modal-footer">
 20                   <button type="button" class="btn btn-default" data-dismiss="modal">Close</button>
 21                   <button type="button" class="btn btn-primary">Save</button>
 22               </div>
 23           </div>
 24       </div>
 25   </div>
```

FIGURE 4-21: Modal dialog snippet

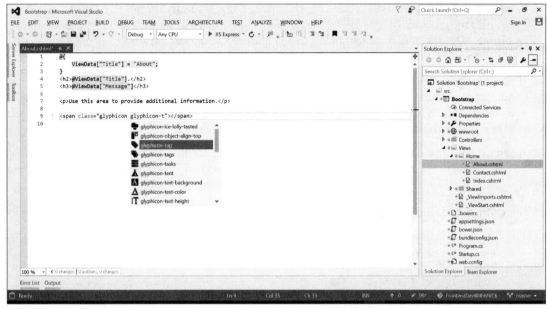

FIGURE 4-22: Glyphicons in the autocomplete dropdown

Tag Helpers for ASP.NET Core

Another possible approach to make it easier to write Bootstrap components is ASP.NET Core tag helpers. Tag helpers are custom tags that can render arbitrary HTML markup at runtime.

Unfortunately, there is no library that provides tag helpers for all the Bootstrap components, but there is a community-driven tag helper project that includes helpers for Alert, ProgressBar, and Modal Dialog components. This library can be downloaded from NuGet under the name TagHelperSamples.Bootstrap. Regarding the Modal Dialog, using the tag helper provided by this library, the verbose HTML snippet becomes the few lines shown in Listing 4-22.

LISTING 4-22: Modal Dialog with the Tag Helper (Views\Home\Index.cshtml)

```
<button type="button" class="btn btn-primary" bs-toggle-modal="simpleModal">
    Launch modal
</button>
<modal id="simpleModal" title="Modal Title">
    <modal-body>
        <h4>Something happened</h4>
        <p>Something happened</p>
    </modal-body>
</modal>
```

A `bs-toggle-modal` attribute is added to the dialog trigger, specifying the name of the modal to open. And then, obviously, the modal dialog has to be defined, using the `<modal>` tag. As shown in Listing 4-22, the actual content of the dialog goes inside the `<modal-dialog>` tag. Optionally, a `<modal-footer>` can be used to specify additional buttons for the dialog.

If you need helpers for other Bootstrap components, you can always write them yourself. As seen in Chapter 1, writing a tag helper is not particularly difficult, especially if you are doing it only for your specific needs and not with the intent of covering all the possible scenarios needed when releasing the code for the community.

As an example of how easy it is to build a simple tag helper for Bootstrap, Listing 4-23 shows a simplified version of the Alert tag helper that is part of the aforementioned Bootstrap tag helper library.

LISTING 4-23: Simplified Alert Tag Helper (TagHelpers\AlertSimpleTagHelper.cs)

```
using System.Threading.Tasks;
using Microsoft.AspNet.Razor.TagHelpers;

namespace AlertTagHelper.TagHelpers
{
    [HtmlTargetElement("alert")]
    public class AlertSimpleTagHelper : TagHelper
    {
        [HtmlAttributeName("type")]
        public string AlertType { get; set; }
        public override void Process(TagHelperContext context, TagHelperOutput
output)
        {
            output.TagName = "div";
            var cssClass = "alert alert-"+AlertType;
            output.Attributes.Add("class", cssClass);
            output.Attributes.Add("role", "alert");
        }
    }
}
```

This helper is used with the tag `<alert type="danger">Something Went Wrong!</alert>`, which is much more concise than writing the snippet needed for the Bootstrap component of Listing 4-14.

SUMMARY

Bootstrap CSS makes it extremely easy, even for non-designers, to build a compelling UI by making use of all the best practices both in UX and in responsive design. To make Bootstrap fit visually better with your application, several themes are available via the community, and for very specific cases, all the aspects of Bootstrap can be easily customized with Less. And even though sometimes it is a little verbose, Visual Studio provides some facilities to make working with it easier, and if you prefer abstracting the client-side snippets behind some server-side code, the tag helpers of ASP.NET Core allows you to define your own server-side tags.

5

Managing Dependencies with NuGet and Bower

WHAT'S IN THIS CHAPTER?

> ➤ Introduction to package managers

> ➤ Usage instructions for NuGet, Bower, NPM

> ➤ How to redistribute your components

> ➤ Visual Studio 2017 support for package managers

The previous chapters showed that modern software development, both front-end and server-side, is based on small and very focused components that can be composed as needed.

Unfortunately, while it is good to avoid the monolithic frameworks of the past, this new approach introduces a problem: how do you manage all these components? Components usually depend on other components, which depend on yet other components, which depend... well, you got the idea. To make things more difficult, there might be a component, let's call it **A**, that depends on component **B**, but also another component, **C**, that also depends on **B**, but a different version of it. And on top of this, all components must be kept up-to-date. Finally, in some cases, to correctly install a component, additional operations might be needed, like compiling some native library or changing some configuration files.

Fortunately, all these tasks are automated by specific tools that are called *package managers*. In the context of front-end development with ASP.NET Core MVC, there are three package managers you need to know:

> ➤ NuGet, for managing .NET libraries

> ➤ Bower, for managing client-side (JavaScript and CSS) libraries

> ➤ NPM, for managing the installation of tools used during the development

The rest of this chapter will show how to use these three package managers and also how to publish components as packages. But before looking at the specifics of each of them, you need to look at some concepts that apply to all package managers.

WROX.COM CODE DOWNLOADS FOR THIS CHAPTER

The wrox.com code downloads for this chapter are found at www.wrox.com Search for the book's ISBN (978-1-119-18131-6), and you will find the code in the chapter 5 download and individually named according to the names throughout the chapter.

GENERAL CONCEPTS

All package managers, apart from the obvious differences given by the different technologies or languages they target, are practically identical. Here are their common concepts:

➤ They all rely on a public registry that contains all published packages. The registry might also store the actual package or just provide the URL where the package can be downloaded.

➤ Packages are downloaded and stored in a local folder (usually within the current user folder) that acts as a local cache. This way when a project needs a package that has been already downloaded, it's directly copied from the cache instead of being downloaded again (providing that it is the latest version). This saves bandwidth and time (especially if packages are restored every time a project is built). It also allows some kind of offline development experience that would be otherwise impossible.

➤ Projects declare which third-party libraries they depend on. This is usually done by specifying in a JSON file the names of the packages and their versions.

➤ Package managers take care of downloading not only the projects' dependencies but also the libraries they depend on, descending the entire tree of packages.

With these basic general concepts in mind, it is time to look at the .NET package manager, called NuGet.

NUGET

NuGet is the package manager for .NET libraries. It has been available inside Visual Studio since 2010. With Visual Studio 2017 and ASP.NET Core, things changed a bit. Whereas before it was used to manage everything, now with the introduction of Bower, its scope has been limited to .NET libraries only.

> **NOTE** *Technically, you can still make client-side packages, but the package explorer will understand and will send the user to look for the same package on Bower, as seen in Figure 5-1.*

FIGURE 5-1: How the NuGet Package Manager shows client-side only packages

It might have lost the support for client-side packages, but it gained an important new feature as with the introduction of .NET Core, NuGet became the delivery method also for all system libraries.

> **SHORT HISTORY OF NUGET**
>
> I clearly remember how NuGet was born, because I was there at the ALT.NET Seattle Conference in 2008. A panel lead by Scott Hanselman discussed how to encourage .NET developers to use open-source by making it easier to discover, download, and install libraries.
>
> People were talking about reusing the ruby-gem infrastructure to deliver libraries, but eventually it was agreed on to build something similar that was closer to the .NET toolset. A few open-source projects started on that day. One of them, initially called NuPack, became what is known as NuGet.

Getting Packages via NuGet

NuGet packages can be installed in many ways. The choice of which installation to use depends on the context in which the package manager will be used and on personal preferences.

Using the Package Manager GUI

The first option for getting packages is to use the Package Manager GUI. It is accessible within Visual Studio either from the main menu ⇨ Tools ⇨ NuGet Package Manager or by right-clicking on the Dependencies node of the solution's tree in the Solution Explorer window. Both options are shown in Figure 5-2.

From the GUI (shown in Figure 5-3), you can search for packages and install them into your current project, optionally choosing which version to install.

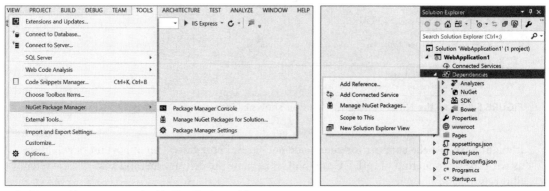

FIGURE 5-2: How to open the NuGet Package Manager

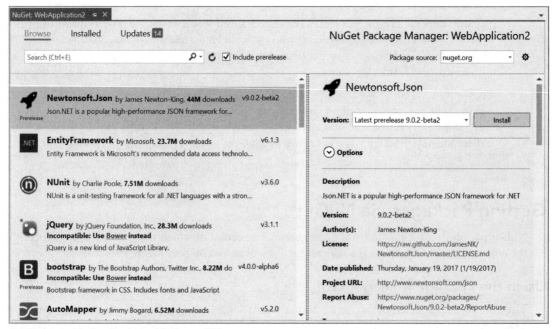

FIGURE 5-3: NuGet Package Manager GUI

Using the Package Manager Console

If you are more into command-line tools, the second option for getting packages, still within Visual Studio, is to use the Package Manager Console, usually already available among the bottom windows in Visual Studio. If the window is not there, it can be opened via the TOOLS ⇨ NuGet Package Manager menu.

There you can use some commands to look for and install packages into the project.

➤ Use `Find-Package -Id Json` to look for packages. The output of this command is shown in Figure 5-4.

➤ Use `Install-Package Newtonsoft.Json` to install a new package.

➤ Use `Get-Package` to list all installed packages.

➤ Use `Uninstall-Package Newtonsoft.Json` to uninstall an installed package.

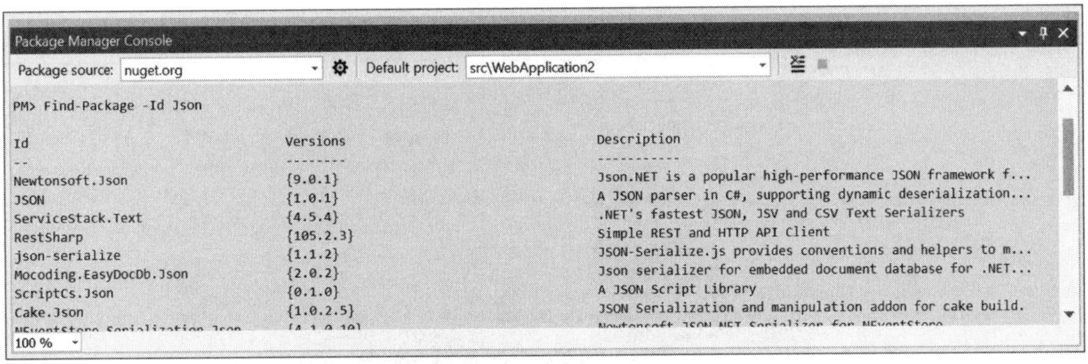

FIGURE 5-4: NuGet Package Manager Console

Manually Editing the .csproj Project File

The last available option is to edit directly the `.csproj` project file.

The new `.csproj` project file format that has been introduced for .NET Core projects contains many different sections, but the one you are currently interested in is the `<ItemGroup>` section that contains `<PackageReference>` elements, which is used to specify which packages and which versions the project depends on. Listing 5-1 shows the `.csproj` project file of a sample ASP.NET Core project from version 2.0. As mentioned in Chapter 1, it only contains the reference to the `Microsoft.AspNetCore.All` meta-package.

LISTING 5-1: Sample ASP.NET Core project configuration file

```
<Project Sdk="Microsoft.NET.Sdk.Web">

  <PropertyGroup>
    <TargetFramework>netcoreapp2.0</TargetFramework>
  </PropertyGroup>

  <ItemGroup>
    <PackageReference Include="Microsoft.AspNetCore.All" Version="2.0.0" />
  </ItemGroup>
```

```
  <ItemGroup>
    <DotNetCliToolReference Include="Microsoft.VisualStudio.Web.CodeGeneration.
Tools" Version="2.0.0" />
  </ItemGroup>

</Project>
```

If you don't know the name of packages or their version, Visual Studio 2017 shows an autocomplete menu, providing a search feature also in this context. Autocomplete is available both for the package name and for the version number, as shown in Figure 5-5.

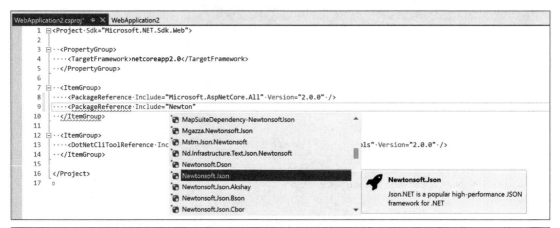

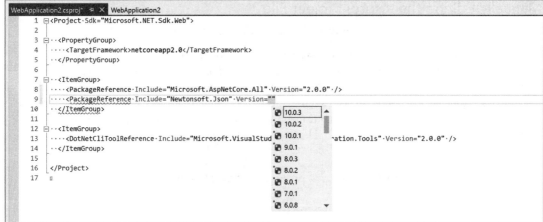

FIGURE 5-5: IntelliSense in action inside the .csproj project file.

Also, if you don't know exactly which version number or you want to be open to future patches, you can specify the version using the floating version range notation, for example 8.0.*.

PACKAGE REFERENCES' AUTOCOMPLETE

The autocomplete of package references might not be in Visual Studio 2017 at the time of publishing, but this feature is available in the Visual Studio extension Project File Tools, which can be downloaded from `https://marketplace .visualstudio.com/items?itemName=ms-madsk.ProjectFileTools`.

What Happens Once You Install a Package

A big difference from the previous version of NuGet is that the installation of a package only means adding a new entry in the `.csproj` project file. Also, when the Package Manager GUI or Console is used, nothing is downloaded. They also just write the package ID and version inside the file.

As soon as the `.csproj` file changes, Visual Studio launches the .NET Core CLI specifying the `restore` command (Figure 5-6). It is this cross-platform tool that connects to the nuget.org server, downloads the packages, and saves them inside the user folder (`C:\Users\user\.nuget\ packages\`). Unlike previous versions, packages are not also saved inside a folder in the current project, but are directly referenced from the user folder.

FIGURE 5-6: Restore notification

Publishing Your Own Packages

Eventually you might find yourself needing to publish a NuGet package, either because you want to make something you developed available to the .NET community or because you want to share your library in a way that is easy for co-workers in your organization to reuse.

In order to create a package, you need the dotnet command line tool, which is installed as part of the .NET Core SDK.

Adding Metadata for the Package

For building a NuGet package you need to specify some metadata: author details, package name and version, various URLs for the project, and a list of the dependencies needed by the package. The metadata is added directly in the `.csproj` file, as you can see in Listing 5-2.

LISTING 5-2: webapplication.csproj metadata

```
<Project Sdk="Microsoft.NET.Sdk">

  <PropertyGroup>
    <TargetFramework>netcoreapp2.0</TargetFramework>
    <PackageId>Wrox.Book</PackageId>
    <PackageVersion>1.0.0</PackageVersion>
```

```
    <Authors>Simone Chiaretta</Authors>
    <Description>Show the title of the book</Description>
    <PackageReleaseNotes>First release</PackageReleaseNotes>
    <Copyright>Copyright 2017 (c) Wrox</Copyright>
    <PackageTags>book title wrox</PackageTags>
    <PackageProjectUrl>http://example.com/Wrox.Book/</PackageProjectUrl>
    <PackageIconUrl>http://example.com/Wrox.Book/32x32icon.png</PackageIconUrl>
    <PackageLicenseUrl>http://example.com/Wrox.Book/mylicense.html</
PackageLicenseUrl>
  </PropertyGroup>

</Project>
```

Creating the Package

With all the metadata set, you just need to go to the root folder of your project (where the `.csproj`
file is) and type `dotnet pack -c Release` This command will gather all the dependencies and the
metadata from the `.csproj` file, copy them to the NuSpec file (the NuGet definition file), build
the project for all supported frameworks, and package everything into a NuGet package file, saved
in the `bin/Release` (or `bin/Debug`).

If you then open the package just created using the NuGet Package Explorer, you can see all the
properties and files that are included in the package (Figure 5-7).

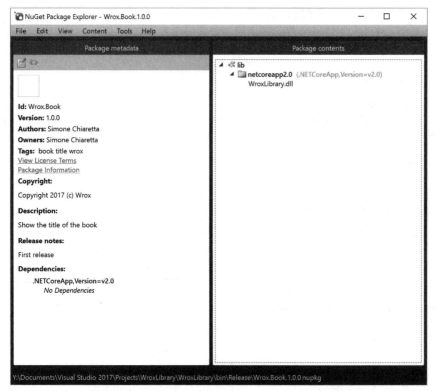

FIGURE 5-7: NuGet Package Explorer

Publishing to the Nuget.org Gallery

If you want to publish your package to an internal repository, you can just copy the file to the folder (or follow your own procedures), but if you want the package to be available for anyone in the .NET community, you have to publish on the official repository, the NuGet.org gallery. In order to do so, you need to do two things:

➤ Download the NuGet command line utility (which you can also download from the Package Manager Console with `Install-Package NuGet.CommandLine`).

➤ Create an account on the NuGet.org gallery (`http://nuget.org/`).

Once you have done both of these things, you need to register the API key that will be used to link your package with your account:

```
nuget setApiKey Your-API-Key
```

and then publish the package:

```
nuget push YourPackage.nupkg
```

NPM (NODE.JS PACKAGE MANAGER)

NPM is the Node.js Package Manager. In the context of front-end development with ASP.NET Core, NPM is used mainly to install development tools and utilities.

Installing NPM

If you are using Visual Studio 2017, you might already have NPM installed on your machine. (There was an option to install Node.js tools in VS2017 setup.) To check whether it is installed, type `npm -v` at the command prompt. If it shows a version number (such as 4.1.1), you have NPM and you can skip to the next section. Otherwise, keep on reading.

The best approach is to install NPM via the Node.js installer. Node.js recently changed their version number and release policy, and now they provide two channels:

➤ The LTS (*long-term support*) version is supported in production environments, gets a major release every year, and has an additional year and half of maintenance.

➤ The stable version is the latest stable version, without support for production, but it is released more frequently (a major release every six months).

For the purpose of this book, the latest LTS is sufficient.

Once Node.js is installed, make sure you have the latest version of NPM by upgrading it with `npm install npm -g`.

NPM Usage

You can install NPM packages in two ways. Either you use the command-line tool directly or, if within Visual Studio, you can edit the `package.json` file and the installation will happen automatically, just like it does for NuGet packages.

Using the NPM Command Line

The NPM command line is the main access to all the features of NPM. The most important commands are:

➤ npm `install` restores the packages specified in the `package.json` file.

➤ npm `install` <package-name> installs the package specified in the command.

➤ npm `init` helps you create an initial `package.json` file with some default values.

➤ npm `update` updates your dependencies to the latest versions.

The `install` command has a few switches that you should know. The first is -g, which is used to install the package as *global* package. This is mostly for command-line tools built with Node.js, like NPM itself or Bower.

Two other switches, `--save` (also -S) and `--save-dev` (also -D), will save the installed package in the `package.json` file so that you don't have to update it manually. The first saves the package as an application dependency, while the latter saves it as a development dependency. In the context of ASP.NET Core projects, NPM is used only for tools, not for the actual application itself, so only the `--save-dev` switch will be used.

Listing 5.3 shows an example of `package.json` that comes with the default ASP.NET Core application when you add NPM (for example when enabling Gulp support). As you can see, only the `devDependencies` section contains packages. In this instance they are the task runner `gulp` and some of its tasks.

LISTING 5-3: Package.json

```json
{
  "name": "app",
  "version": "1.0.0",
  "private": true,
  "devDependencies": {
    "del": "^2.2.2",
    "gulp": "^3.9.1",
    "gulp-concat": "^2.6.1",
    "gulp-cssmin": "^0.1.7",
    "gulp-htmlmin": "^3.0.0",
    "gulp-uglify": "^2.0.0",
    "merge-stream": "^1.0.1"
  }
}
```

Using NPM within Visual Studio

There is no Package Manager GUI like there was for NuGet, but Visual Studio still has pretty good support for NPM.

You can edit the `package.json` file directly within Visual Studio, and, as with NuGet, you have autocomplete for both package names and version numbers. As you can see in Figure 5-8, there is also a more detailed tooltip that appears when you hover with the mouse on the package name. You can also perform some basic operations via the bulb menu.

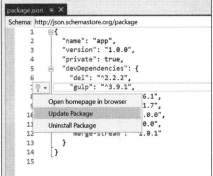

FIGURE 5-8: IntelliSense extensions for package.json

As soon as the file is saved, Visual Studio launches the `npm install` command explained in the previous section, and packages are installed. Another nice touch is the dependencies tree in Solution Explorer, which shows the packages together with their dependencies (see Figure 5-9).

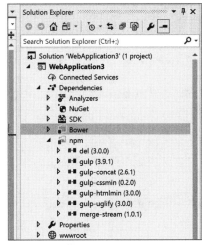

Where Packages Are Installed

Unlike NuGet, where packages are installed in the current user's folder and referenced via their name in the `.csproj` project file, NPM packages are installed directly in a sub-folder of the project, called `node_modules`. A copy of the files is also saved in a local cache under the user's folder where global packages also are installed.

FIGURE 5-9: Packages tree

BOWER

With NuGet you can add server-side dependencies, NPM is for tools, and Bower is for adding client-side libraries. But apart from this obvious difference, it works more or less the same way as the other two package managers.

THE FATE OF BOWER

Visual Studio templates come with client side references with Bower, so this chapter explains how to use it. But the maintainers of the project have posted a note on their GitHub repository that suggests to use Yarn (which is a third-party npm client) and WebPack (which was mentioned in Chapter 3 and is covered more in detail in Chapter 6) for new projects.

Installing Bower

The first step is to install Bower (if you haven't installed it already with Visual Studio or if you are using it within Visual Studio Code or any other IDE). This is done via NPM by using `npm install bower -g`.

In order to use Bower, git must be installed as well. This is one significant difference between Bower and the other systems. While still having a central repository at `http://bower.io/search/` for listing packages names, it is not used to store the packages, which are retrieved directly from GitHub or any other git endpoint. So, for that reason, it needs git to get the actual packages.

Getting Packages with Bower

Bower packages can be installed in a few different ways, similar to NuGet and NPM. You can get them with the command-line tool, which is its native interface and has the most complete feature set. If you are using Bower within Visual Studio, you can install packages with the Package Manager or by directly editing the dependencies configuration file, which is called `bower.json`.

Using the Bower Command Line

The command-line tool for Bower is the standard and most flexible way to interact with Bower. It allows you not only to install, update, and remove packages, but also to register packages on the central repository. You can also perform any kind of package management operation using just a local cache without going on the network, which is a feature that saved me a few times when on a plane.

The commands are basically the same as with NPM:

➤ `bower install` installs all the packages defined in the `bower.json` file.

➤ `bower install <package>` installs the specified package. In this case a package can be a registered package, an URL, or a git (or svn) endpoint.

➤ `bower update` updates the installed packages.

➤ `bower uninstall <package>` uninstalls the specified package.

➤ `bower init` creates a new `bower.json` file.

Also with Bower, as with NPM, you can save yourself some time and automatically add a package to the `bower.json` file by specifying the `--save` flag.

Using the Bower Package Manager GUI in Visual Studio

If you are using Visual Studio, you can search for packages and install them directly by using the package manager. This is exactly the same as with NuGet, just listing Bower packages (see Figure 5-10). This window can be opened by right-clicking on the project root in the Solution Explorer and selecting the "Manage Bower packages" menu item.

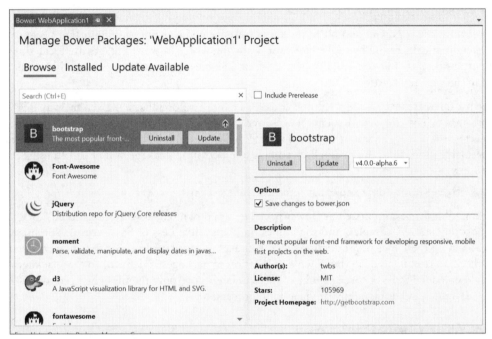

FIGURE 5-10: Bower package manager

Editing the bower.json File

As with the other package managers, manually editing and saving the definition file will trigger the automatic installation. In this case Visual Studio will launch the `bower install` command.

Also with Bower, IntelliSense will help autocomplete package names and versions.

The `bower.json` format is similar to NPM's `package.json`, as you can see in the default ASP.NET Core project configuration file shown in Listing 5-4.

LISTING 5-4: Bower.json

```
{
  "name": "asp.net",
  "private": true,
  "dependencies": {
    "bootstrap": "3.3.6",
```

```
    "jquery": "2.2.0",
    "jquery-validation": "1.14.0",
    "jquery-validation-unobtrusive": "3.2.6"
  }
}
```

Where Packages Are Installed

Knowing exactly where NuGet and NPM packages were located was not that important because they were automatically found by tools. However, knowing where Bower packages are located is more important because they are usually JavaScript or CSS files that have to be manually included or linked in the web application.

Normally, packages are installed in a sub-folder called bower_components, but given the way ASP .NET Core apps behave, the default location of Bower packages installed from within an ASP.NET Core project is wwwroot/lib. Since the root of an ASP.NET Core app is the wwwroot folder, all packages are available inside the libs folder. For example, the bootstrap package will be linked using the reference:

```
<link href="lib/bootstrap/dist/css/bootstrap.css" rel="stylesheet" />.
```

This might not be the best approach as Bower packages are downloaded with the git repository, including documentation, samples, and sometimes build files (like Less or Sass scripts). You might not want to put all these files in production when you deploy your site. In this case you might want to delete the .bowerrc file (where the download location of packages is defined) so that packages are again downloaded to bower_components. You can later move only the files you need to the wwwroot/lib folder, either manually or via a build process.

Creating Your Own Packages

When it comes to sharing your JavaScript or CSS libraries, there is not much that needs to be done. Actually nothing has to be done (as long as there is already a bower.json file) if you just want to share your library within your company or even with the world without registering in the repository.

If you want to register the package for the public repository, something more is needed:

➤ Some other metadata is recommended. You can use description, moduleType to specify how the library interacts with the application, main to list the entry points of the library (the ones that have to be included in the HTML file), and ignore to list the folders and files from the git repository that do not have to be copied when installing the package.

➤ The package must be stored in a git repository and must be publicly accessible.

➤ Versions have to be tagged with git tags, named complying to the semver (Semantic Versioning) schema (for example, v1.0.0-beta).

Once these preconditions are met, the package can be registered on the official repository by calling the following command:

```
bower register <package-name> <git-endpoint>
```

SUMMARY

Going away from the monolithic framework approach to the small, focused libraries approach required solving the problem of finding, installing, and managing dependencies. Package managers solved this pretty effectively.

In this chapter you learned about three types of packages used in ASP.NET Core applications: NuGet for .NET libraries, NPM for development tools, and Bower for client-side dependencies.

Apart from NuGet, the other two are not "native" to the Microsoft ecosystem. They are integrated into Visual Studio, which makes it easy for developers who are not used to command-line tools to use them as well.

Finally, you also learned how easy it is to share your libraries with either the developers' community or just within your organization.

6

Building Your Application with Gulp and webpack

WHAT'S IN THIS CHAPTER?

➤ The role of build automation systems

➤ Introduction to webpack

➤ A more in depth overview of Gulp

➤ How Visual Studio 2017 integrates with Gulp and build systems

Build systems have been around in the world of server-side software development for many years, starting from make files used for compiling C/C++ code or simple batch files used in the '80s and '90s and evolving into task-based systems with the arrival of Java's Ant in early 2000. And from Ant, NAnt and later MSBuild came to life and brought task-based build automation systems to .NET.

Until recently, front-end development did not require as many build steps as server-side developments, but with the increasing complexity of JavaScript-based applications, front-end-specific build systems started to appear.

This chapter covers Gulp and webpack, two of many build automation systems for front-end development. It also covers the features of Visual Studio 2017 that make working with them easier and more integrated into the IDE.

Before seeing these tools in practice, you will have a look at the typical operations that are performed in the context of front-end builds.

WHAT FRONT-END BUILD SYSTEMS ARE FOR

In the context of server-side compiled languages, build systems are used to compile code into binaries, to run tests, to compute metrics, and to perform transformations of configuration files from development to a production setup. Other typical operations include moving files around and creating release files.

Front-end build systems are also used for more or less the same reasons as server-side build systems because even front-end development requires "compiling" code files into "binaries" (for example Less or Sass to CSS or TypeScript to JavaScript) or running JavaScript test suites or metrics (JSLint for example). However, front-end development also requires some tasks that are specific to JavaScript and CSS development and that are used during the development phase and not just during the final release. One such task is automatically including references to Bower files. Another example is minification and concatenation of JavaScript and CSS files to reduce the size and number of files downloaded by the client.

The rest of the chapter explains how to perform some of the most common tasks. It will show how to:

➤ Automatically include references to Bower packages

➤ Compile Sass files to CSS

➤ Compile TypeScript to JavaScript

➤ Combine and minify JavaScript and CSS files

➤ Run JSLint to detect JavaScript problems

➤ Perform tasks and automatically reload the browser when changes are detected in a file

The tool used to show how to perform these tasks is Gulp, since it is the tool the .NET community is mostly leaning toward. Later in the chapter there is also a quick introduction to webpack, which was already briefly mentioned in Chapter 3 since it is used by the Angular Command Line tool and is gaining a lot of traction in the front-end development community.

A DEEPER LOOK AT GULP

The first JavaScript task runner was Grunt, but despite its relatively large user base, its adoption is constantly dropping in favor of Gulp, which has been developed to overcome the problems of Grunt. The approach is very different. It is code-based instead of being configuration-based. Steps of the build process are connected together using Node.js streams, where the output of one step streams into the input of the following. That is why it is called "the streaming build system."

Getting Started with Gulp

Gulp must be installed via NPM. First install the command-line tool:

```
npm install --global gulp-cli
```

Then, within the project's folder, also install the `gulp` package itself, again from NPM:

```
npm install gulp --save-dev
```

The Gulpfile.js File

As already mentioned, build automation with Gulp is done with code instead of by configuring a series of tasks. For this reason `gulpfile.js` looks like a standard Node.js code file.

A `gulpfile.js` file starts with the initialization of the `gulp` library itself and of all the plugins and modules that will be used in the build script. This is done by using the Node.js `require()` function.

```
var gulp = require("gulp"),
    del = require("del"),
    concat = require("gulp-concat"),
    cssmin = require("gulp-cssmin"),
    uglify = require("gulp-uglify");
```

Once all the external libraries are loaded, the build process can be developed using Gulp's APIs. There are just four top-level methods in the Gulp APIs. Two are used to define entry points for tasks, and two are for representing input files and the output folder.

gulp.task()

The `task` method defines a gulp task. Its parameters are:

➤   name, which is the name of the task

➤   deps, an optional array of the other tasks on which the task being defined depends on (and that have to be completed before the task can run)

➤   fn, the function to be executed

An example of a call to this method is:

```
gulp.task("dist", ["build"], function(){
  //do something after the build task has run
});
```

The task named `default` will be executed if you launch the gulp process without specifying any task.

```
gulp.task("default",["dist","build"])
```

An important point to mention is that all tasks are executed for maximum concurrency, which means that all tasks are launched at the same time in parallel. If you want tasks to be executed in a specific order, in addition to specifying the dependencies with the parameter `deps`, the task's function must have a "hint" that tells the system when it is done with its job. This can be achieved by accepting a callback function, by returning a stream object, or by returning a promise.

gulp.watch()

The `watch` method is used to run a task or a function when the specified files change. Its parameters are:

➤ `glob`: Either a string or an array of strings representing the files to watch, using the typical wildcards normally used in command-line tools (such as `scripts/*.js`)

➤ `opts`: Options used to configure the watch process, for example `interval` to specify how frequently to check for changes or `debounceDelay` to delay the execution if there are many changes in rapid succession

➤ `tasks`: The array of tasks to be executed

➤ `cb`: The callback function to be executed

The two parameters `tasks` and `cb` cannot be specified together. Hence, there are two variation of the `watch` method. There is one that specifies tasks to run:

```
gulp.watch("js/*.js",["jshint"])
```

And there is a version that executes a function:

```
gulp.watch('js/*.js', function(event) {
  console.log('File ' + event.path + ' was ' + event.type);
});
```

gulp.src()

This method usually is the starting point of each task. It returns a stream of files (hence the name of "streaming build system") that can be piped into the various plugins that make up the task. If you want the task to be a dependency for another task, this is the stream that has to be returned by the task's function.

```
return gulp.src("js/*.js")
  .concat(...)
  .pipe(uglify())
  .pipe(gulp.dest("lib"));
```

gulp.dest()

This method is used as a function inside a `pipe` method. It takes the stream and will write the files to the specified folder.

```
.pipe(gulp.dest("lib"));
```

A Typical Gulp Build File

Now you will see how to put all this information into practice by implementing a typical build file. There are several steps in doing this, but the core aspects include the following:

1. JavaScript files are checked for possible errors.

2. JavaScript and CSS files are concatenated into a single file.

3. The concatenated JavaScript file is then minified.

As an example take the file structure shown in Figure 6-1.

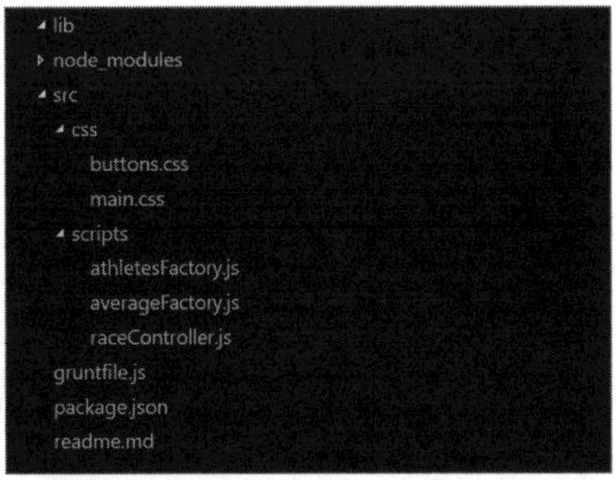

FIGURE 6-1: Project's file structure

First, the plugins need to be installed, as always with `npm install ... --save-dev`:

➤ `gulp-concat` is used to concatenate multiple files into one.

➤ `gulp-uglify` is used to minify the JavaScript files.

➤ `gulp-cssmin` is used to minify the CSS files.

➤ `del` is a standard deep deletion npm package.

In the build process, first you are going to delete the old artifacts and then do all the rest.

```
gulp.task("clean", function() {
  return del("lib/*");
});
```

The next step is the concatenation and minification of scripts and CSS files.

Scripts are treated using the following task:

```
gulp.task("minjs", ["clean"], function(){
  return gulp.src("src/scripts/*.js")
    .pipe(concat("all.min.js"))
    .pipe(uglify())
    .pipe(gulp.dest("lib"));
});
```

The JavaScript files are read in memory and concatenated into an `all.min.js` file (still in memory). This file is what was minified and finally saved to the `lib` folder.

You do the same for the minification of the CSS files by just replacing `uglify` with `cssmin` (gulp has a separate plugin for this).

```
gulp.task("mincss", ["clean"], function(){
  return gulp.src("src/css/*.css")
    .pipe(concat("styles.css"))
    .pipe(cssmin())
    .pipe(gulp.dest("lib"));
});
```

The `gulpfile.js` file, complete with all the `require` statements and the definition of the default task, is shown in Listing 6-1.

LISTING 6-1: Gulpfile.js

```
var gulp  = require('gulp'),
    del = require('del'),
    concat = require('gulp-concat'),
    cssmin = require('gulp-cssmin'),
    uglify = require('gulp-uglify');

gulp.task("clean", function() {
  return del("lib/*");
});

gulp.task("minjs", ["clean"], function(){
  return gulp.src("src/scripts/*.js")
    .pipe(concat("all.min.js"))
    .pipe(uglify())
    .pipe(gulp.dest("lib"));
});

gulp.task("mincss", ["clean"], function(){
  return gulp.src("src/css/*.css")
    .pipe(concat("styles.css"))
    .pipe(cssmin())
    .pipe(gulp.dest("lib"));
});

gulp.task("default", ["mincss","minjs"]);
```

More Gulp Recipes

There is much more that can be done with Gulp than just minifying and combining files. Gulp plugins' repository counts more than 2800 plugins. On top of that, Gulp is just a standard Node.js file, so any npm package can be used.

The following sections discuss some recipes for other common tasks.

Naming Output Files from a Package Name

The content of the `package.json` file can be read and its values reused with Gulp. Because it is a JSON object, it can be read and loaded in memory with the `require` method:

```
var pkg = require('./package.json')
```

Then the concatenated script file can be named after it:

```
pkg.name+"-"+pkg.version+".min.js"
```

The JavaScript minification task now looks like this:

```
var pkg = require('./package.json');

gulp.task("minjs", ["clean","lint"], function(){
  return gulp.src("src/scripts/*.js")
    .pipe(concat(pkg.name+"-"+pkg.version+".min.js"))
    .pipe(uglify())
    .pipe(gulp.dest("lib"));
});
```

Generating Source maps

Minification reduces the size of scripts, but it makes it impossible to debug code. One solution to this is to create source maps that can be used by JavaScript debugging tools to map the minified source to the original code.

In order to generate source maps with Gulp, you need to install the `gulp-sourcemaps` plugin. The simplest way of using the plugin is to call the `init()` method before any processing starts, read the original files, and finally call the `write()` method to write the maps on disk.

```
return gulp.src("src/scripts/*.js")
  .pipe(sourcemaps.init())
    .pipe(concat(pkg.name+"-"+pkg.version+".min.js"))
    .pipe(uglify())
  .pipe(sourcemaps.write())
  .pipe(gulp.dest("lib"));
```

By calling the `write()` method without parameters, the source map is saved embedded into the destination file, but by passing a path relative to the destination, like `sourcemaps.write('.')`, a separate file will be saved with the same filename as the destination, plus the `.map` extension.

> **NOTE** *The plugins used between* init *and* write *must support* gulp-sourcemaps, *like the ones used in the samples in this book:* uglify, concat, *and* cssmin.

Checking JavaScript Using JSHint

Running JSHint can also be done with Gulp by using the `gulp-jshint` plugin. It is easy to use. First you execute the `jshint()` method, and then pipe the result into the `jshint.reporter('REPORTER-NAME')` method to print the result of the analysis on the console.

There are many reporters in the wild and all the JSHint reporters should also work within this plugin. The most popular, used in the context of `gulp-jshint`, is the default that comes with the plugin, `default`, and optional `jshint-stylish`. Figure 6-2 shows how the output of the two reporters compare. Default is on top and the stylish on the bottom.

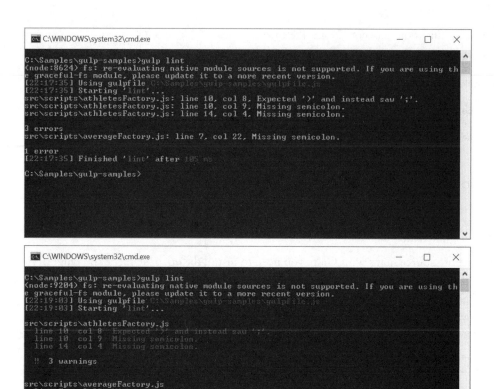

FIGURE 6-2: Default and stylish reporters compared

In addition, if you do not want the task to go on even if there are warnings or errors, the `fail` reporter can be used to stop the execution of the build process. The following snippet shows a task that runs JSHint, prints the report, and fails if some errors happen.

```
gulp.task("lint", function() {
  return gulp.src("src/scripts/*.js")
    .pipe(jshint())
    .pipe(jshint.reporter('jshint-stylish'))
    .pipe(jshint.reporter('fail'));
});
```

This stops the execution of all the tasks that depend on the `lint` task, as shown in Figure 6-3.

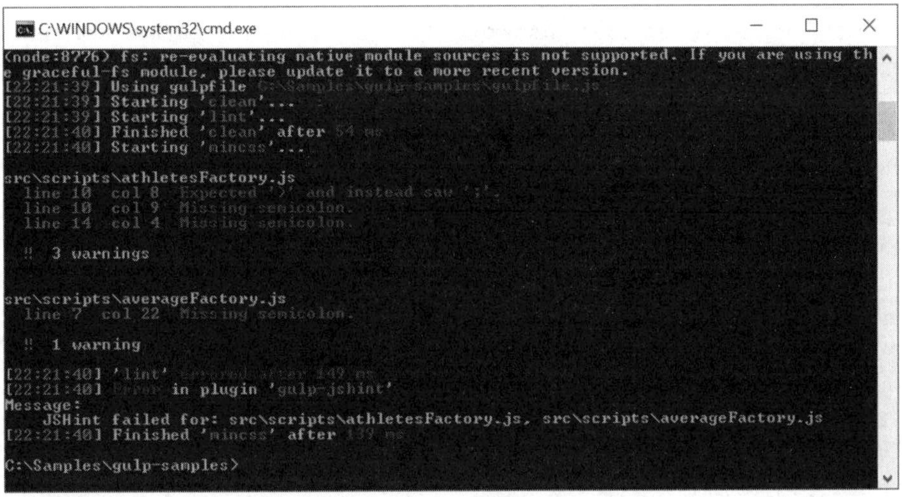

FIGURE 6-3: Execution stopped after JSHint failed

Executing Tasks When Files Change

Gulp has a `watch` method that triggers the execution of tasks when files change. For example, if you want to run JSHint every time a JavaScript file changes, you can create a new task and within that task call the `watch` method.

```
gulp.task('watch', function() {
  gulp.watch('src/scripts/*.js', ['lint']);
});
```

Then launch Gulp specifying the `watch` task: `gulp watch`. As soon as a JavaScript file is saved in the `scripts` folder, the JSHint check will start.

Managing Bower Dependencies

Bower installs all the dependencies in a subfolder of the project, named `bower_components`. As seen in Chapter 5, the easy way to include these dependencies in an HTML file is to directly reference the components inside the Bower's folder. This might be okay in development, but it is not a good approach for deploying the application because a Bower package is basically its git repository, so it includes a lot of files you do not want in the production environment.

A better approach is to copy to a different folder only the files needed to run the application. This can be done manually, or it can be automated with Gulp.

To make this easier, there is a Gulp plugin called `main-bower-files` that goes through all the dependencies defined in `bower.json` and for each of them takes the main files defined by the developer of the package. These files are the ones needed to use the library. Its usage is straightforward: Just call the plugin to define the source files for the task and then pipe them to the destination folder. Listing 6-2 copies the components to the folder `dist/libs`.

LISTING 6-2: Managing Bower components with Gulp

```
var gulp = require('gulp');
var mainBowerFiles = require('main-bower-files');

gulp.task("default", function(){
  return gulp.src(mainBowerFiles())
    .pipe(gulp.dest("dist/lib"));
});
```

> **WARNING** *Not all Bower packages define the main files correctly. Bootstrap, for example, includes a .less file as main but not the CSS file or the fonts. In such cases you can override the file returned by* mainBowerFiles, *either in your bower.json file or directly in the* gulp *task.*
>
> ```
> gulp.task("default", function(){
>   return gulp.src(mainBowerFiles({
>           overrides: {
>               bootstrap: {
>                   main: [
>                       './dist/js/bootstrap.js',
>                       './dist/css/*.min.css',
>                       './dist/fonts/*.*'
>                   ]
>               }
>           }
>   }))
>     .pipe(gulp.dest("dist/lib"));
> });
> ```

Replacing References Directly in the HTML Files

Earlier in the chapter you saw how to concatenate and minify JavaScript and CSS files. Wouldn't it be nice if you could also update the reference inside the HTML files? This is possible thanks to a very powerful plugin called gulp-inject.

It takes a list of references and inserts them into HTML files in an area delimited by special comments. While adding the new references, it deletes whatever was between these comments. This way, the development version of the HTML file references the individual JavaScript and CSS files, while the production version generated with the Gulp task references the combined and minified version.

Now you will take a look at how this is done. First, the HTML file must contain the scripts surrounded by the comments.

```
<!-- inject:js -->
  <script src="/scripts/athletesFactory.js"></script>
  <script src="/scripts/averageFactory.js"></script>
  <script src="/scripts/raceController.js"></script>
<!-- endinject -->
```

Then the minification happens inside the `gulp` task as shown in Listing 6-3.

LISTING 6-3: Replacing script references via Gulp

```
var gulp  = require('gulp'),
    concat = require('gulp-concat'),
    inject = require('gulp-inject'),
    cssmin = require('gulp-cssmin'),
    uglify = require('gulp-uglify');

var pkg = require('./package.json');
var fileName = pkg.name+"-"+pkg.version+".min.js";

gulp.task("minjs", function(){
  return gulp.src("./src/scripts/*.js")
    .pipe(concat(fileName))
    .pipe(uglify())
    .pipe(gulp.dest("./dist/lib"));
});

gulp.task("mincss", function(){
  return gulp.src("./src/css/*.css")
    .pipe(concat("styles.css"))
    .pipe(cssmin())
    .pipe(gulp.dest("./dist/lib"));
});

gulp.task("inject",["minjs","mincss"], function(){
  return gulp.src("./src/index.html")
    .pipe(inject(gulp.src(["./dist/lib/*.js","./dist/lib/*.css"]),
        {ignorePath: 'dist'}))
    .pipe(gulp.dest("./dist"));
});

gulp.task("default", ["inject"]);
```

In Listing 6-3 you can see how the `gulp-inject` plugin works. It receives the HTML file stream as input via piping, and it outputs the version modified with the references to the files specified as parameters.

After the task has run, the references in the HTML file will change to the minified script and styles that were copied to the `dist` folder.

```
<!-- inject:css -->
<link rel="stylesheet" href="/lib/styles.css">
<!-- endinject -->

<!-- inject:js -->
<script src="/lib/gulp-inject-sample-0.0.1.min.js"></script>
<!-- endinject -->
```

INTRODUCTION TO WEBPACK

Webpack is *module bundler* that loads all the dependencies of a JavaScript application and bundles them to optimize the loading time in the browser. Although it is not strictly speaking a task runner, webpack can be used to accomplish most of the tasks performed by Gulp, like minification, bundling, and linting. Let's see how this works.

webpack's Main Concepts

Webpack has a bit steeper learning curve compared to Gulp, so before seeing some examples, let's have a look at the main concepts: *entry, output, loaders,* and *plugins.* It all starts with the entry point of the application, which is where webpack starts to follow the dependencies tree from. The end of the process is the output, which is where webpack will save the bundle once it has completed its job. Between the entry and the output, all the processing happens, which is done by loaders and plugins.

Webpack is a JavaScript module bundler, which means that it discovers JavaScript modules and their dependencies and bundles them. However, webpack can also treat .css files, sass files, TypeScript files, and even images and .html files. Loaders are used to "convert" any kind of file in a module treatable by webpack. Plugins do not work on the individual source files but are used to perform general operations on the final output of the bundling.

The configuration of webpack is stored in a `webpack.config.js` file.

Let's now see how to use webpack to perform the same operations done with Gulp in Listing 6-1.

Using webpack

The first step is obviously installing webpack. This is done with NPM. It could be installed globally like the other tools, but it is a better practice to install it on a per-project basis to avoid version conflicts between different projects on the same machine.

Once you have a new folder and have an empty `package.json` file in the folder, you can run `npm install webpack --save-dev` to install webpack and add it as a development reference for the project.

Bundling JavaScript

Next is creating the `webpack.config.js` file with the minimum configuration, which specifies the entry file and the output file for the bundle. The configuration file in Listing 6-4 instructs webpack to start discovering dependencies from the file `./src/index.js` and store the bundled version in a file `bundle.js`. For the automatic discovery to work, it is not enough to have just a bunch of files in the same folder. They have to reference each other using the ECMAScript 5 export/import of modules. Listing 6-5 shows how the two files used in this example are linked together.

LISTING 6-4: Simple webpack configuration file (webpack.config.js)

```javascript
var path = require('path');

module.exports = {
  entry: './src/index.js',
  output: {
    filename: 'bundle.js',
    path: path.resolve(__dirname, 'dist')
  }
}
```

LISTING 6-5: JavaScript files used in the sample

INDEX.JS

```javascript
import {greet} from './greeting.js';

function component() {
  var element = document.createElement('div');

  element.innerHTML = greet("readers");
  element.classList.add('hello');

  return element;
}
document.body.appendChild(component());
```

GREET.JS

```javascript
export function greet(who) {
  return "Hello " + who;
}
```

Notice the use of import to import the dependency and export to export the function for other files to use. Now just running webpack without any additional configuration will bundle the two files together into one file.

To run webpack, since it's just installed locally in the project, there are two options. The first is to use its relative path ./node_modules/.bin/webpack. This is where all the executables are stored when installed via npm. The other option is to use an *npm script*. To do so, just add a script element to the package.json file and later just type npm run build to execute webpack. The following snippet shows what needs to be added.

```json
"scripts": {
  "build": "webpack"
},
```

Bundling Stylesheets

In order to add stylesheets to the bundle, you must trick webpack into thinking the .css file is another module and installing and configuring the right module loader. The first part is done by importing the .css file as if it was another javascript module:

```
import './style.css';
```

Then the style and CSS loaders must be installed via npm and configured inside the `webpack.config.js` file.

This is the command to install the two modules:

```
npm install style-loader css-loader --save-dev
```

Listing 6-6 shows the configuration file after the CSS loader has been added.

LISTING 6-6: webpack.config.js with css loader

```
var path = require('path');


module.exports = {
  entry: './src/index.js',
  output: {
    filename: 'bundle.js',
    path: path.resolve(__dirname, 'dist')
  },
  module: {
    rules: [
      {
        test: /\.css$/,
        use: [
          'style-loader',
          'css-loader'
        ]
      }
    ]
  }
}
```

Listing 6-6 shows how loaders are added within a `module` property. Each different module loader needs a `test` to specify when the loader must be used and a list of loaders to use. The test could be a RegEx with the extension of the files or a more complex function.

Once webpack is run, the style will be bundled together with the JavaScript files and injected into the header section of the HTML file at runtime. If you want the style to be referenced in the HTML file from its own file, you need to use the **ExtractTextWebpackPlugin**. Listing 6-7 shows what the configuration file looks like with this plugin.

LISTING 6-7: webpack.config.js using the extract-text-webpack-plugin

```javascript
var path = require('path');
const ExtractTextPlugin = require("extract-text-webpack-plugin");

module.exports = {
  entry: './src/index.js',
  output: {
    filename: 'bundle.js',
    path: path.resolve(__dirname, 'dist')
  },
  module: {
    rules: [
      {
        test: /\.css$/,
        use: ExtractTextPlugin.extract({
         fallback: "style-loader",
         use: "css-loader"
        })
      }
    ]
  },
  plugins: [
    new ExtractTextPlugin("styles.css")
  ]
};
```

With this change, now the CSS files get bundled into just one file instead of being injected into the header section of the HTML file.

Minifying and Adding Sourcemaps

After having bundled the files, you still need to minify them. This is done using another plugin, called **UglifyJsPlugin**. To use this plugin, it's enough to add it to the list of plugins (after having imported it into the configuration file).

```javascript
new webpack.optimize.UglifyJsPlugin()
```

In order to have sourcemaps for both JavaScript and .css files, another parameter, called devtool, must be specified in the configuration. This can have many different values based on the type of sourcemap needed (inline or in a separate file) and its accuracy. Listing 6-8 shows the configuration file after minification with sourcemaps has been added.

LISTING 6-8: webpack.config.js with minification and sourcemaps

```javascript
var path = require('path');
const webpack = require('webpack');
const ExtractTextPlugin = require("extract-text-webpack-plugin");
```

```
module.exports = {
  entry: './src/index.js',
  output: {
    filename: 'bundle.js',
    path: path.resolve(__dirname, 'dist')
  },
  devtool: "source-map",
   module: {
    rules: [
      {
        test: /\.css$/,
        use: ExtractTextPlugin.extract({
         fallback: "style-loader",
         use: "css-loader"
        })
      }
    ]
  },
  plugins: [
    new ExtractTextPlugin("styles.css"),
    new webpack.optimize.UglifyJsPlugin({sourceMap:true})
  ]
};
```

More Things webpack Can Do

Although webpack is a module bundler, thanks to the different loader it is not limited to bundling JavaScript files. It can treat styles (also sass and less), script files that require some transpiling (like TypeScript, CoffeScript, or ECMAScript2015), images, fonts, and many types of files. Additionally, it can run JSHint while loading JavaScript file. Via plugins it can also automatically add script and style tags into the HTML file (using the HtmlWebpackPlugin), minify the bundle as seen earlier, compress files, and do much more.

However, it is a module bundler, so it doesn't have the flexibility of a general purpose task runner like Gulp, and it requires that applications are written in a modular way, which is not always done, especially when not using the latest JavaScript frameworks.

But if you use Angular via the CLI, you get webpack compilation and bundling automatically without doing anything.

VISUAL STUDIO 2017 AND BUILD SYSTEMS

Now that you know about Gulp, it is important to understand how it is integrated into Visual Studio 2017.

The Bundler and Minifier Extension

Microsoft realized that developers use task runners mostly for minifying and bundling files, so the ASP .NET Core project template doesn't include a `gulpfile.js` file. Instead it includes the `bundleconfig` `.json` file, which contains the configuration for new feature of Visual Studio 2017: the Bundler and

Minifier. The Bundler and Minifier simplifies the process of managing CSS and JavaScript files by providing menu items for creating bundles during development in Visual Studio.

Minification of a file can simply be configured by right-clicking on the file in the Project Explorer and selecting Bundler & Minifier ➪ Minify File, and bundles can be created by selecting multiple files and selecting Bundler & Minifier ➪ Bundle and Minify File (see Figure 6-4).

FIGURE 6-4: The Bundler and Minifier menu items

These commands from the menu just update the `bundleconfig.json` file. Listing 6-9 shows an example of bundling configuration.

LISTING 6-9: An example of bundleconfig.json file

```
[
  {
    "outputFileName": "wwwroot/css/site.min.css",
    "inputFiles": [
      "wwwroot/css/site.css"
    ]
  },
  {
    "outputFileName": "wwwroot/js/site.min.js",
    "inputFiles": [
      "wwwroot/js/site.js"
    ],
    "minify": {
      "enabled": true
    }
  },
  {
    "outputFileName": "wwwroot/js/bundle.js",
    "inputFiles": [
      "wwwroot/js/site2.js",
      "wwwroot/js/site.js"
    ],
    "sourceMap": true
  }
]
```

The file contains a list of bundles, each one defined by the output file name, a list of input files, and optional additional configuration settings, like enabling source maps.

This new feature doesn't preclude the usage of Gulp. If the front-end build process becomes more than just bundling files, a gulpfile that uses the `bundleconfig.json` file can be created from the menu (Figure 6-5), and it can then be expanded to include other tasks. This way the configuration of the bundles can still be done via menu items, making it easier to manage, even when using Gulp.

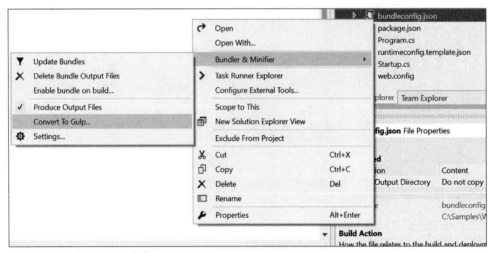

FIGURE 6-5: Convert to Gulp

Listing 6-10 shows the `gulpfile.js` file created by the Bundler & Minifier extension.

LISTING 6-10: Gulpfile.js generated by the Bundler & Minifier extension

```
"use strict";

var gulp = require("gulp"),
    concat = require("gulp-concat"),
    cssmin = require("gulp-cssmin"),
    htmlmin = require("gulp-htmlmin"),
    uglify = require("gulp-uglify"),
    merge = require("merge-stream"),
    del = require("del"),
    bundleconfig = require("./bundleconfig.json");

var regex = {
    css: /\.css$/,
    html: /\.(html|htm)$/,
    js: /\.js$/
};

gulp.task("min", ["min:js", "min:css", "min:html"]);

gulp.task("min:js", function () {
```

```javascript
    var tasks = getBundles(regex.js).map(function (bundle) {
        return gulp.src(bundle.inputFiles, { base: "." })
            .pipe(concat(bundle.outputFileName))
            .pipe(uglify())
            .pipe(gulp.dest("."));
    });
    return merge(tasks);
});

gulp.task("min:css", function () {
    var tasks = getBundles(regex.css).map(function (bundle) {
        return gulp.src(bundle.inputFiles, { base: "." })
            .pipe(concat(bundle.outputFileName))
            .pipe(cssmin())
            .pipe(gulp.dest("."));
    });
    return merge(tasks);
});

gulp.task("min:html", function () {
    var tasks = getBundles(regex.html).map(function (bundle) {
        return gulp.src(bundle.inputFiles, { base: "." })
            .pipe(concat(bundle.outputFileName))
            .pipe(htmlmin({ collapseWhitespace: true, minifyCSS: true, minifyJS:
true }))
            .pipe(gulp.dest("."));
    });
    return merge(tasks);
});

gulp.task("clean", function () {
    var files = bundleconfig.map(function (bundle) {
        return bundle.outputFileName;
    });

    return del(files);
});

gulp.task("watch", function () {
    getBundles(regex.js).forEach(function (bundle) {
        gulp.watch(bundle.inputFiles, ["min:js"]);
    });

    getBundles(regex.css).forEach(function (bundle) {
        gulp.watch(bundle.inputFiles, ["min:css"]);
    });

    getBundles(regex.html).forEach(function (bundle) {
        gulp.watch(bundle.inputFiles, ["min:html"]);
    });
});

function getBundles(regexPattern) {
    return bundleconfig.filter(function (bundle) {
        return regexPattern.test(bundle.outputFileName);
    });
}
```

The Task Runner Explorer

Tasks, both from the bundler and minifier and for Gulp, can also be run manually via the Task Runner Explorer. This window can be opened by right-clicking on the `gulpfile.js` file from the Project Explorer (see Figure 6-6) or from the View ⇨ Other Windows ⇨ Task Runner Explorer menu item.

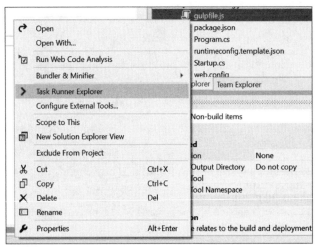

FIGURE 6-6: Opening the Task Runner Explorer

The Task Runner Explorer shows all the tasks available inside the `gulpfile.js` file and all the file bundles specified in the `bundleconfig.json` file. It also allows you to specify which tasks to run when some operation runs in Visual Studio. A task can be configured to run:

➤ When the project is opened

➤ When the Clean operation is invoked

➤ Before the build of the project starts

➤ After the build of the project completes

Figure 6-7 depicts the Task Runner Explorer showing the tasks in the tree on the left, the bindings of tasks and VS operations on the right, and the dropdown menu to configure those bindings.

IntelliSense for Gulp

Finally, since gulp files are just JavaScript files, the standard JavaScript IntelliSense triggers auto-complete and shows information about gulp and gulp's plugin methods, as shown on Figure 6-8.

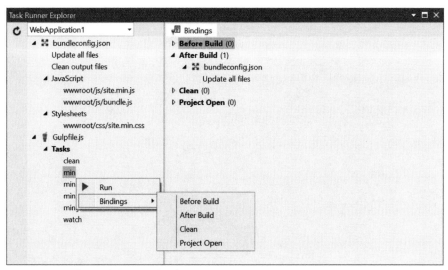

FIGURE 6-7: The Task Runner Explorer in action

```
gulp.task("min:html", function () {
    var tasks = getBundles(regex.html).map(function (bundle) {
        return gulp.src(bundle.inputFiles, { base: "." })
            .pipe(concat(bundle.outputFileName))
            .pipe(htmlmin ▲ 1 of 2 ▼ concat(filename: string, [options?: IOptions]): NodeJS.ReadWriteStream
            .pipe(gulp.de
    });
    return merge(tasks);
});
```

FIGURE 6-8: IntelliSense for Gulp

SUMMARY

Even though build automation tools have existed for more than 40 years, they were just recently brought to the world of front-end development. Eventually, .NET web development, while still using MSBuild, also started adopting these front-end build systems like Gulp.

Grunt was the first tool to appear, but recently Gulp, thanks to its more code-based approach, is getting more traction, and Microsoft has chosen it as the default build tool supported inside Visual Studio and ASP.NET Core projects.

In this chapter you learned how to prepare your front-end artifacts for release. The next chapter explains how to leverage those tasks to deploy projects to your servers, either on premise or on the cloud, and on demand or in continuous deployment fashion.

7

Deploying ASP.NET Core

WHAT'S IN THIS CHAPTER?

- ➤ The new hosting model of ASP.NET Core
- ➤ How to deploy on-premise
- ➤ How to use Azure
- ➤ Continuous deployment with git and Azure
- ➤ How to deploy to Docker Containers

After having learned how to build front-end applications with ASP.NET Core MVC, Angular, Bootstrap, and Gulp, it is finally time to show the application to other people. In order to do this, you need to deploy applications.

WROX.COM CODE DOWNLOADS FOR THIS CHAPTER

The wrox.com code downloads for this chapter are found at www.wrox.com Search for the book's ISBN (978-1-119-18131-6), and you will find the code in the chapter 7 download and individually named according to the names throughout the chapter.

THE NEW HOSTING MODEL OF ASP.NET CORE

Before exploring the deployment of ASP.NET Core applications, it is important to understand how they are hosted inside servers.

In classic ASP.NET, applications are DLLs that are hosted inside the IIS Application Pool (also known as Worker Process, w3wp.exe). They are instantiated from IIS's runtime manager. When requests come in, they are sent to the HttpRuntime of the right site, which lives inside an AppPool. In short, they are basically modules controlled by IIS itself.

In ASP.NET Core, it is totally different. Console applications run their own web server using Kestrel. Each application already hosts itself and can directly respond to requests over HTTP, so you might be wondering why you need IIS in first place. The reason is that Kestrel is a web server that has been optimized for performance, but it lacks all the management features that IIS has. So it is okay to run applications directly on Kestrel for development, but you need IIS for exposing them to the outside world.

In this case IIS basically acts as a reverse proxy, receiving the requests and forwarding them to the ASP.NET Core application self-hosted on a Kestrel web server. Then it waits for the execution pipeline to complete its processing and sends back the HTTP output to the originator of the request.

This is accomplished by `AspNetCoreModule`, which calls the `dotnet run` command to fire up the application the first time it is requested. The `AspNetCoreModule` makes sure the application stays loaded should it crash, and the module keeps the mapping of the HTTP port on which the application is running. This module is configured via the `web.config` file in the root of the application. Listing 7-1 shows a sample of the configuration.

LISTING 7-1: web.config that configures the AspNetCoreModule

```xml
<configuration>
  <system.webServer>
    <handlers>
      <add name="aspNetCore" path="*" verb="*"
        modules="AspNetCoreModule"
        resourceType="Unspecified"/>
    </handlers>
    <aspNetCore
        processPath="dotnet"
        arguments=".\PublishingSample.dll"
        stdoutLogEnabled="false"
        stdoutLogFile=".\logs\stdout"/>
  </system.webServer>
</configuration>
```

The important configuration attributes are `processPath`, which contains the path to the executable that will listen to HTTP requests, and `arguments`, with the arguments to pass to the process. In standard ASP.NET Core applications, `processPath` is `dotnet` and `arguments` is the path to the DLL with the actual application.

INSTALLING ON INTERNET INFORMATION SERVICES ON PREMISE

Now that you understand the background theory, it's important to see how to install the application on IIS.

Making Sure All Is Well

Normally, applications are installed on a server, but if you do not have access to one, you can follow the steps of this book on your local development machine. Before starting, make sure IIS is installed. If you know it is already installed, you can skip this part and go straight to the "Installing AspNetCoreModule" section.

The first step is to check whether IIS is installed. Type **http://localhost** in a browser: If you get the welcome page of Figure 7-1, all is good. Otherwise, if you get a server not found error, it means the local website is not running, either because IIS is not installed or it is stopped.

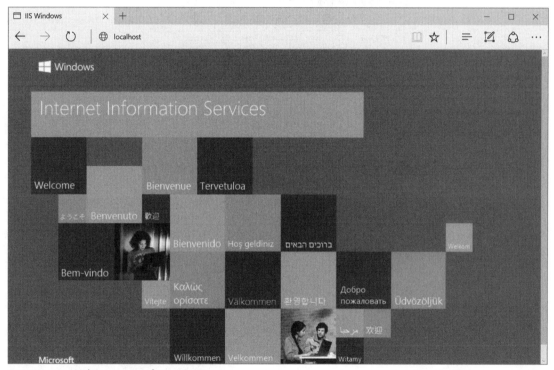

FIGURE 7-1: Welcome page from IIS 10

Now try to turn it on. For that, open IIS Manager. Select All Apps ⇨ Windows Administrative tools), open the Default Web Site, and press the Start button under Manage website, as shown in the Actions bar on the right side of Figure 7-2.

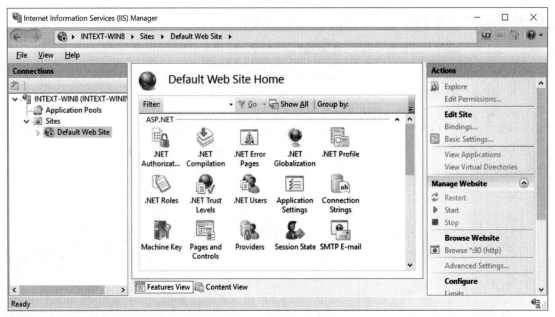

FIGURE 7-2: IIS Manager

If you do not have the IIS Manager, it means that Internet Information Services has not been installed on your machine. In order to install it, open the Windows Features window (accessible from Control Panel ⇨ Programs ⇨ Turn Windows features on or off) and check both World Wide Web Services and IIS Management Console, as in Figure 7-3, and then click OK.

FIGURE 7-3: Windows Features

Installing AspNetCoreModule

The glue between IIS and ASP.NET Core is provided by `AspNetCoreModule`. This module is installed as part of the .NET Core Windows Server Hosting bundle that also installs the .NET Core Runtime and .NET Core Library, providing a very convenient way to enable .NET Core hosting on web servers. `AspNetCoreModule` is also installed as part of the .NET Core SDK, so if you are running the SDK on your development machine, you should already have the module.

Either way, you should now be able to see the `AspNetCoreModule` in the list of modules in the IIS Manager (Figure 7-4).

Modules

Use this feature to configure the native and managed code modules that process requests made to the Web server.

Group by: No Grouping

Name	Code	Module Type	Entry Type
AnonymousAuthenticationM...	%windir%\System32\inetsrv\...	Native	Local
AnonymousIdentification	System.Web.Security.Anony...	Managed	Local
AspNetCoreModule	%SystemRoot%\system32\in...	Native	Local
ConfigurationValidationModule	%windir%\System32\inetsrv\...	Native	Local
CustomErrorModule	%windir%\System32\inetsrv\...	Native	Local
DefaultAuthentication	System.Web.Security.Default...	Managed	Local
DefaultDocumentModule	%windir%\System32\inetsrv\...	Native	Local
DirectoryListingModule	%windir%\System32\inetsrv\...	Native	Local
FileAuthorization	System.Web.Security.FileAuth...	Managed	Local
FormsAuthentication	System.Web.Security.FormsA...	Managed	Local
HttpCacheModule	%windir%\System32\inetsrv\...	Native	Local
HttpLoggingModule	%windir%\System32\inetsrv\l...	Native	Local
HttpRedirectionModule	%windir%\System32\inetsrv\r...	Native	Local
IsapiFilterModule	%windir%\System32\inetsrv\f...	Native	Local
IsapiModule	%windir%\System32\inetsrv\i...	Native	Local
OutputCache	System.Web.Caching.Output...	Managed	Local
Profile	System.Web.Profile.ProfileMo...	Managed	Local
ProtocolSupportModule	%windir%\System32\inetsrv\...	Native	Local
RequestFilteringModule	%windir%\System32\inetsrv\...	Native	Local

FIGURE 7-4: IIS Modules with AspNetCoreModule highlighted

Publishing Applications via the Command Line

With the setup of the infrastructure finalized (which luckily has to be done only once), it is time to publish the application.

The simple way of deploying is by using the `dotnet publish` command. By default this command publishes the application into the `./bin/[configuration]/[framework]/publish` folder, using the framework that has been specified as TargetFramework and building it in Debug mode.

This publishing operation builds the application in the same way as the `dotnet build` command, but it also copies all the dependencies and references into a self-contained folder that can easily be copied to the destination IIS folder (Figure 7-5). In addition to these, the `publish` command also runs all the MSBuild targets specified in the project file and can, for example, run the bundling and minification of scripts and styles.

It also creates a `web.config` file (or to update the file if it already existed) in the root folder so that it contains the right values similar to what is shown in Listing 7-1.

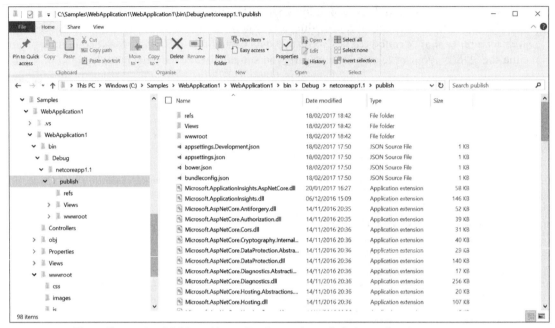

FIGURE 7-5: The self-contained folder with application code and all dependencies

The default folder is hidden inside the structure. You probably want to publish in Release mode. The `publish` command is usually issued by specifying all the options:

```
dotnet publish
        --framework netcoreapp1.1
        --output "c:\temp\PublishSample"
        --configuration Release
```

Creating the Website

The last step obviously is the creation of the web site (or web application) inside IIS. The procedure is very simple and is done just as with any other IIS website, with just one small peculiarity. Since IIS will only act as a proxy without executing any .NET code, an application pool must be configured to not instantiate a .NET runtime. This is done by selecting the No Managed Code option (Figure 7-6).

FIGURE 7-6: Creating AppPool with No Managed Code

Once this is done, a website (or a virtual application) can be created by specifying this newly created AspNetCore application pool and the folder where the application has been published (Figure 7-7).

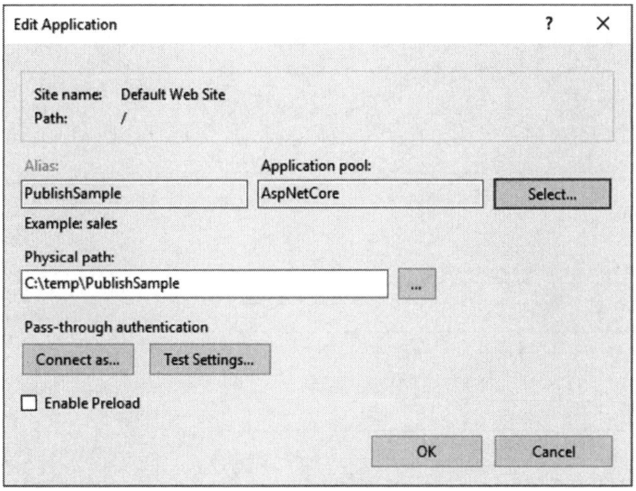

FIGURE 7-7: Creating a new virtual application in IIS

Now browse to `http://localhost/PublishSample` and enjoy the ASP.NET Core application served via IIS.

Publishing the Applications via Visual Studio

Publishing with `dotnet publish` doesn't deploy the application remotely, and it also doesn't support incremental updates. Therefore, a better option when developing within Visual Studio is to use the Publish dialog, accessible both from the Solution Explorer contextual menu and from the new overview screen introduced with Visual Studio 2017.

Typically, when deploying to a remote server, your system admin will have provided a publish profile. When you import it, Visual Studio will create a PowerShell script based on the information coming from the Publish dialog. This will call a PowerShell module, which will perform the actual WebDeploy operation.

If you do not have a publishing profile provided by the system admin, you can also create a custom publish profile, by configuring the connection parameters to your server. For testing on a remote IIS that has been configured as shown in this chapter (and on which Web Deploy has been correctly configured), Figure 7-8 contains the parameters to specify.

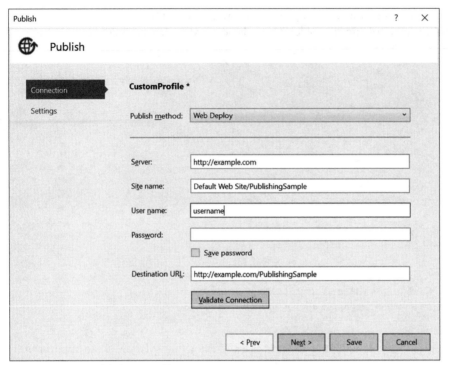

FIGURE 7-8: IIS publishing profile

DEPLOYING ON AZURE

Instead of deploying on-premise, another option is to deploy applications on the cloud. This mitigates a lot of the server configuration nightmare seen in the previous section and provides a more integrated experience into Visual Studio when using Azure. Other cloud hosting solutions are generally provisioning virtual machines, so deploying there is similar to doing it on a remote IIS that you manage yourself.

On Azure, two approaches are possible. The first involves using the Publish dialog and Web Deploy, while the second, used more in continuous deployment scenarios, uses git and builds the application directly on Azure using Kudu.

Deploying to Azure from Visual Studio with Web Deploy

Deploying on Azure from Visual Studio is not much different from the procedure for IIS on-premises, especially if all resources are already created on Azure. In this case just download the publishing profile from the Azure portal (Figure 7-9) and then import it from the Publish dialog.

The differences appear when new resources are needed. In this case there is no need to go in the Azure portal because everything can be done directly from the Publish Dialog by selecting

Microsoft Azure App Service as the publishing target (see Figure 7-10). In this screen, you can also choose to connect to an existing App Service (see Figure 7-11) by selecting Select Existing and clicking the Publish button or to create a new one by selecting Create New.

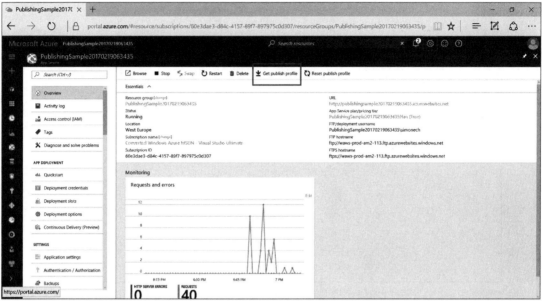

FIGURE 7-9: Getting a publishing profile from the Azure portal

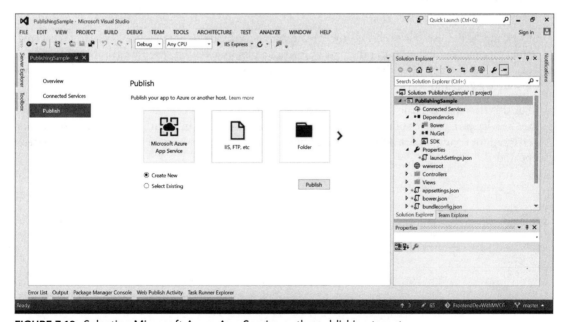

FIGURE 7-10: Selecting Microsoft Azure App Service as the publishing target

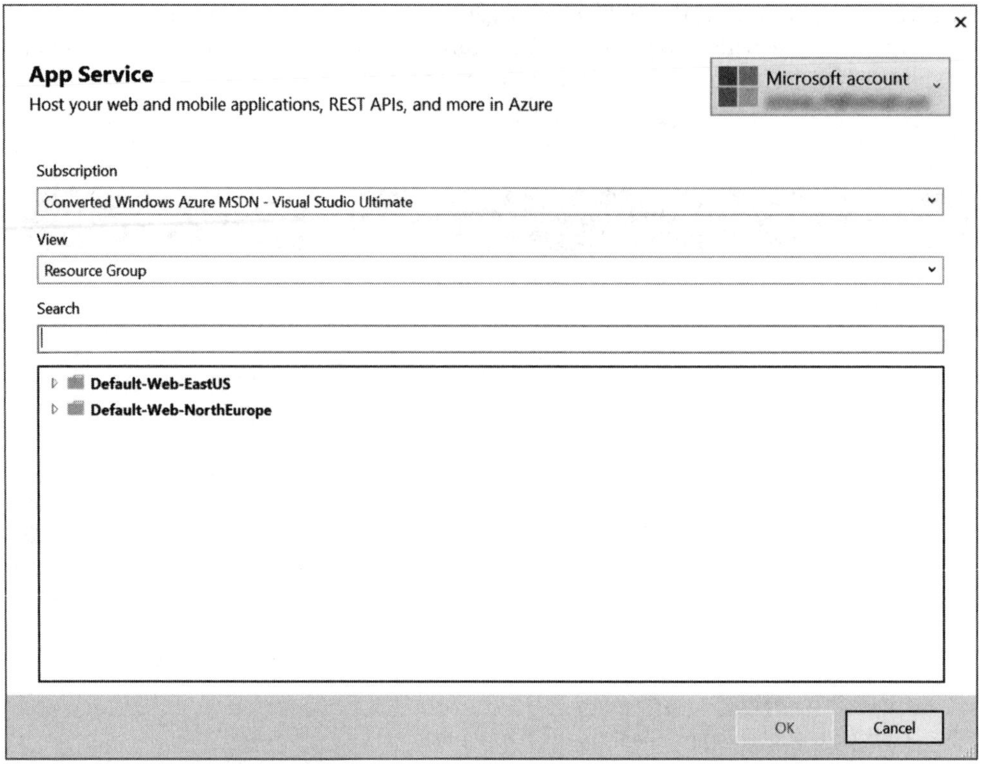

FIGURE 7-11: The App Service dialog

Clicking the Publish button brings the Create App Service dialog (see Figure 7-12). In this screen you can choose whether to put the new app service into an existing resource group and service plan or, as it is a best practice when creating a completely new and isolated application, create a new resource group and service plan.

For this example, call the resource group as the app name, and keep the auto-generated name for the service plan (make sure you select free as the size, as shown in Figure 7-13 so that you do not get charged for trying it out). At this point additional services (other app services or SQL databases) can be added.

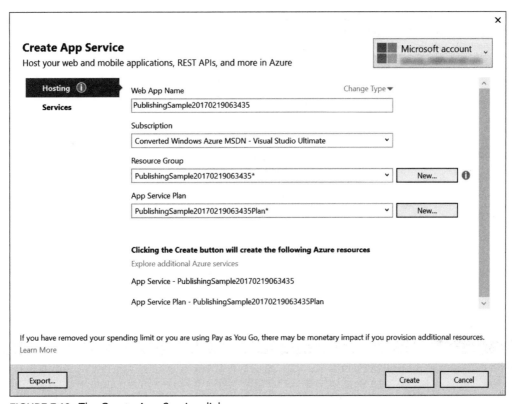

FIGURE 7-12: The Create App Service dialog

FIGURE 7-13: Configure App Service Plan dialog

Now click on Create and everything will be created on Azure and the publishing profile will be created inside Visual Studio. See Figure 7-14.

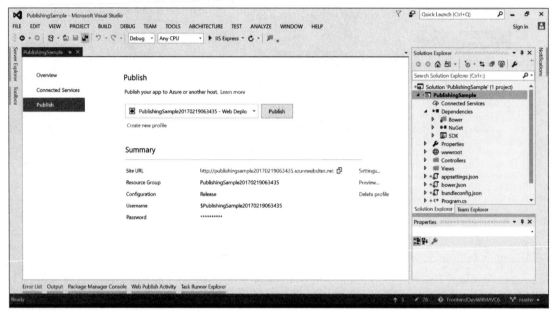

FIGURE 7-14: Publish on Azure Profile

From here on, the process is the same as seen before when using Web Deploy. You can choose Configuration (Release or Debug), Framework, database options, and you can preview what is going to be deployed on the server.

The actual publishing via Web Deploy consists on Visual Studio running `dotnet publish` to create the file bundle on a temporary folder, followed by Web Deploy moving the files to the server.

The beauty of Web Deploy compared to the other deployment method is the incremental publish. If files are changed later (for example the `About.cshtml` file), Web Deploy compares the new file with what has already been published and just sends the new files. From the Publish screen you can access the preview window (Figure 7-15) that shows what will happen when the actual deploy happens.

> **NOTE** *The preview also shows the files that are created during the publish process, like the updated* `web.config`, *the DLLs, the minified style-sheets, and the various dependency configuration files.*

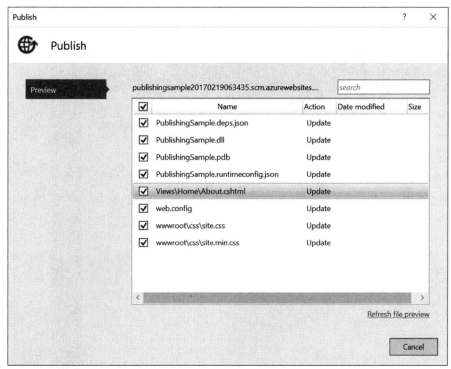

FIGURE 7-15: Web Deploy Preview

Continuous Deployment to Azure with Git

The other approach to deploy on Azure is via git and the continuous deployment features of Azure. The main difference of this approach is that instead of building in Visual Studio (or on a build machine) and later deploying to Azure, only the code is pushed to Azure while all the building and publishing happens directly on Azure via Kudu.

Configuring the Azure Web App

In order to have continuous deployment happening, the web app has to be configured on the Azure portal. This can be done by selecting the web app to be configured, finding the Deployment Source menu item inside Settings, and choosing the source. Here you find many different sources (Figure 7-16), both source control services like Visual Studio Team Services, git (both from GitHub and local) and Bitbucket, and file sharing services like OneDrive or Dropbox.

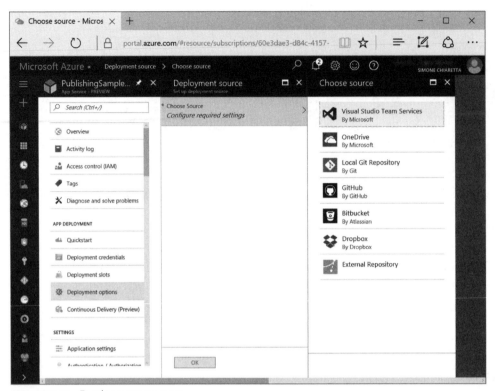

FIGURE 7-16: Deployment sources

For the sake of this book, it is easier to select Local Git Repository so that the code can be pushed directly from your machine without creating additional services, but any other source can be configured if necessary. Configuration steps for the other options might be different though.

Now in the overview pane of the web app, you can see the git clone URL (Figure 7-17), which is the one that needs to be configured as remote to the local git repository that contains the code to be deployed.

Configuring the Local Repository

Now some code has to be pushed to the Azure repository. There are various way of doing this. One is cloning the empty repository and creating an application inside it. Another is by creating the application in Visual Studio and checking the Add to Source Control flag in the project creation dialog. In this case the git repository on Azure must be specified as remote for the local repository. This can be achieved in many ways, but staying within Visual Studio, the remote can be configured from the Repository Settings in Team Explorer (Figure 7-18).

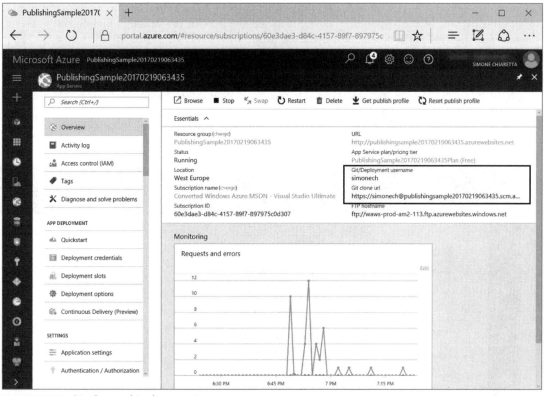

FIGURE 7-17: Git clone url in the overview pane

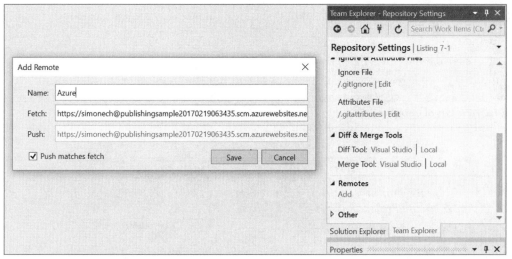

FIGURE 7-18: Add remote in Visual Studio

Now the code can be pushed to the remote, either directly from Visual Studio or from the command line. As part of the push operation, Azure launches the publish command, which restores all NuGet packages and builds the application using the project file. Every time a commit is pushed to the repository, the publish process starts, effectively implementing a continuous deployment scenario.

On Azure portal you can see the list of deployments and the log of each one of them. These are accessible from the same menu item used before to configure the Deployment Source (Figure 7-19).

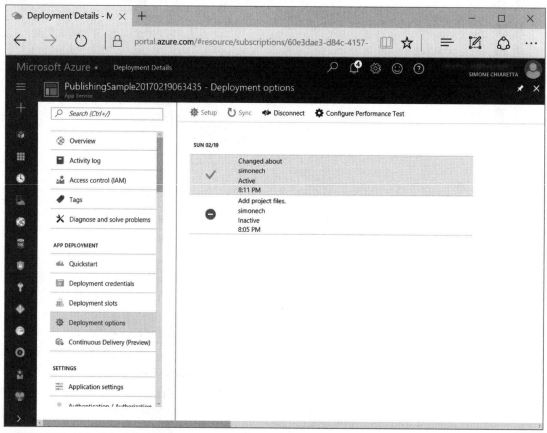

FIGURE 7-19: List of deployments

> **NOTE** *If you created the remote within Visual Studio, the remote is not tracked by the local repository, so the first time you want to push, you have to do it from the Command Prompt and type:*
>
> ```
> git push -u azure master
> ```
>
> *The* -u *option instructs git to start tracking the remote branch.*

In addition to these features, Azure also supports the concept of a deployment slot. It is like a "sub-web app" that works like a normal web app and can be used as a staging environment on which deployment can be tested before swapping the slot to the production application.

DEPLOYING TO DOCKER CONTAINERS

Visual Studio 2017 also supports publishing ASP.NET Core applications to Docker containers using the official aspnetcore Linux image for Docker provided by Microsoft. Visual Studio 2017 even supports debugging ASP.NET Core applications from within a Docker container, but that is not a feature installed by default, so a few steps are needed.

Installing the Docker Support

First, you have to install the Docker tools for Visual Studio 2017. This is done by opening the Visual Studio Installer application, modifying your current installation of Visual Studio, selecting the .NET Core Cross-Platform Development toolset, and on the right sidebar selecting the Container Development Tools optional component (Figure 7-20).

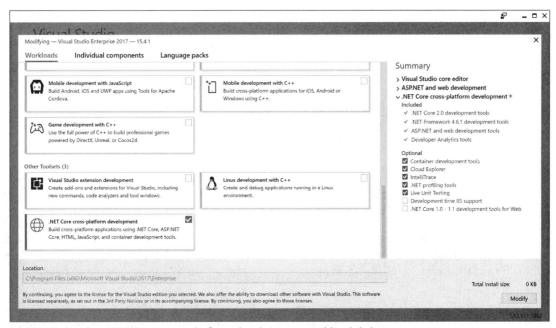

FIGURE 7-20: The .NET Core cross-platform development workload dialog

With the tools installed, you can create a new ASP.NET Core application and select Enable Docker Support directly from the new application dialog. This dialog, shown in Figure 7-21, also points to the link for installing Docker for Windows, which is a pre-requisite for running Docker.

This adds a few files to the project, the most important of which is the `Dockerfile` file. This file contains the instructions used by the Docker to build the container. Listing 7-2 shows the one used by Visual Studio 2017.

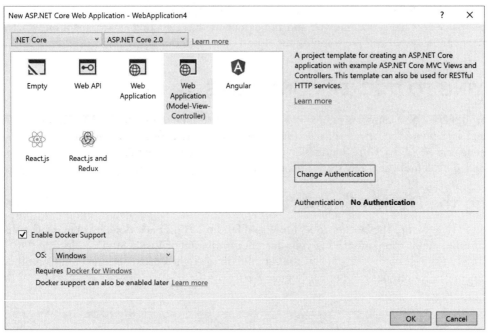

FIGURE 7-21: The Enable Docker Support option in the New Application dialog

LISTING 7-2: Dockerfile

```
FROM microsoft/aspnetcore:2.0
ARG source
WORKDIR /app
EXPOSE 80
COPY ${source:-obj/Docker/publish} .
ENTRYPOINT ["dotnet", "DockerSample.dll"]
```

This file instructs Docker to create a new container starting from the `microsoft/aspnetcore` official image, version 2.0, create a folder called `app` inside the newly create container, and copy there the files in the folder specified as argument `source` or by default all the content of the folder `obj/Docker/publish`.

It also makes the container listen to port 80 and defines, with the `ENTRYPOINT` command, the executable that will be run when the container is started. In this example, the `dotnet DockerSample .dll` command will be run to start the ASP.NET Core application.

If you now debug the application, it won't run in IIS Express as usual, but it will run inside the Docker container created using the `Dockerfile` of Listing 7-2. This is also clearly visible by the label on the debug button in the toolbar (Figure 7-22).

FIGURE 7-22: Debugging with Docker toolbar button

As additional proof that the application is running inside the container, you can replace the `About` action in the application template with the following code that shows the operating system on which the code is running.

```
public IActionResult About()
{
    ViewData["Message"] = System.Runtime.InteropServices.RuntimeInformation.
OSDescription;
    return View();
}
```

When running inside Docker, it shows "Linux Moby" (Figure 7-23), which is the distribution used by Microsoft for the official aspnetcore docker image.

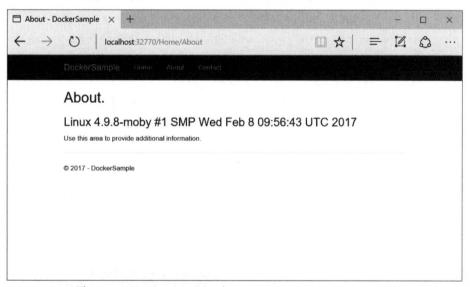

FIGURE 7-23: The operating system in Docker

If you want to add Docker to an application you have already created, you can do so from the Add menu in the Solution Explorer (Figure 7-24).

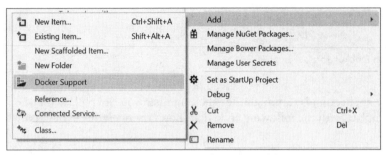

FIGURE 7-24: Selecting Docker Support from the Add menu

Publishing a Docker Image

From within Visual Studio 2017, you can also publish a Docker image directly to Azure by using the usual Publish dialog, selecting Container Registry, and following the same steps shown previously in the chapter. But what if you just want an image to run on your own Docker server? At the moment, you have to rely on the command line, both for dotnet and for Docker.

After opening the command prompt on the project's folder, first publish the application using the `dotnet publish` command:

```
dotnet publish -o obj/Docker/publish
```

Here you specify the `obj/Docker/publish` path because it is the default used in the `Dockerfile`.

Then you run the `docker build` command to create the image for the container:

```
docker build -t dockersample .
```

The `-t` parameter specifies the name of the image and `.` is the path to the `Dockerfile`.

If you now run the `docker images` command to list all the images in your system (Figure 7-25), you will see the newly created `dockersample`, together with the `microsoft/aspnetcore`, which has been downloaded from the docker repository in order to built it.

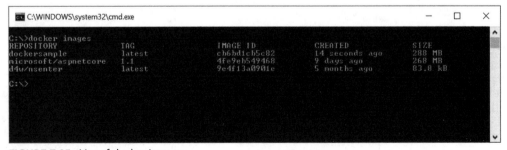

FIGURE 7-25: List of docker images

Now you can run the image directly using the `docker run` command:

```
docker run -t -p 8080:80 dockersample
```

The parameter -p tells the docker daemon to redirect the port 80 of the container to the port 8080 in the host. Now you can visit the application by going to the URL `http://localhost:8080`.

If you want to move the image to another server, you can save it to disk with the `docker save` command, copy it to your server, and load it with the `docker load` command.

SUMMARY

Hosting with ASP.NET Core is different from hosting with classic ASP.NET. Such a model might seem like a step backward, but in the next chapter you will see that this allows hosting ASP.NET Core applications on web servers that are different from IIS, even on different operating systems. To provide for the additional steps needed to deploy ASP.NET Core apps, taking care of all the build systems used to prepare applications for production and the capability to publish to other operating systems as well, Microsoft developed a range of better deployment tools. From simple manual deployment on a local server to continuous deployment via staging environments, the tooling provided within Visual Studio simplifies operations. But what about deploying to other operating systems? The next chapter covers how to develop ASP.NET Core applications without the help of Visual Studio, even when running on MacOS.

8

Developing Outside of Windows

WHAT'S IN THIS CHAPTER?

➤ How to set up ASP.NET Core on a Mac

➤ Visual Studio Core

➤ Hosting ASP.NET Core on Mac

➤ Using command-line tools

The first seven chapters of the book covered all the aspects of front-end development with ASP.NET Core, from the basic setup of a project within Visual Studio to the deployment of the final solution on Azure. But one of the main features for .NET Core, cross-platform support, has not been shown yet.

This chapter is all about cross-platform functionality. In fact, the procedures and all the samples used are described using a Mac, but everything can also be applied on a Linux machine or even a Windows machine that doesn't have Visual Studio installed.

You'll start your journey by installing ASP.NET Core on a Mac.

INSTALLING .NET CORE ON MACOS

Installing .NET Core on Windows was easy, because it comes with Visual Studio. But on a Mac, a Linux machine, or even on a Windows machine that doesn't have Visual Studio, the .NET Core framework and SDK have to be installed manually.

You can install the official SDK for macOS, downloading it from the dotnet core web site: https:// www.microsoft.com/net/core.

Now to make sure everything is installed properly, you can follow the same procedure shown in Chapter 1. Basically, from the terminal, move inside a newly created folder and type dotnet new console. This creates a very basic console application (the same shown in Listing 1-1). Then type dotnet restore to download all the packages needed (including the main CoreCLR), and finally run the console application by typing dotnet run.

The result should be similar to the one shown in Figure 8-1.

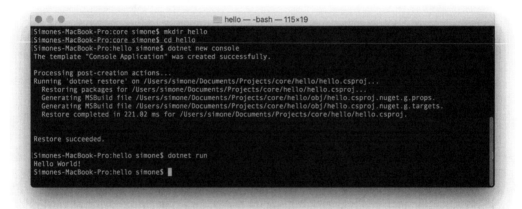

FIGURE 8-1: Creating the first console app on macOS

> **NOTE** *On Linux, the installation procedure depends on which distribution you are running, but it's pretty similar to the one for macOS. Download the prerequisites by using the package management tool that comes with the distribution, download the binaries, and unpack them. Detailed instructions on how to install for each distribution can be found on the Microsoft .NET Core site: https://www.microsoft.com/net/core. The supported distributions are Red Hat Enterprise 7, Ubuntu 14 and 16, Mint 17 and 18, Debian 8, Fedora 23 and 24, CentOS 7.1, Oracle Linux 7.1, and OpenSUSE 13.2 and 42.1, and new ones are added constantly.*

BUILDING THE FIRST ASP.NET CORE APP ON MACOS

Applications can be created either by using the dotnet command-line interface as you've done so far already or by using a more advanced tool like Yeoman.

Using dotnet Command-Line Interface

The easiest way of building an ASP.NET Core app is to use the `dotnet new` command, by specifying a new application type with the argument `mvc`. This creates a website similar to the one created by the default ASP.NET Core project in Visual Studio.

The `restore` command is run automatically, so just use the `run` command, and you'll have a default website up and running.

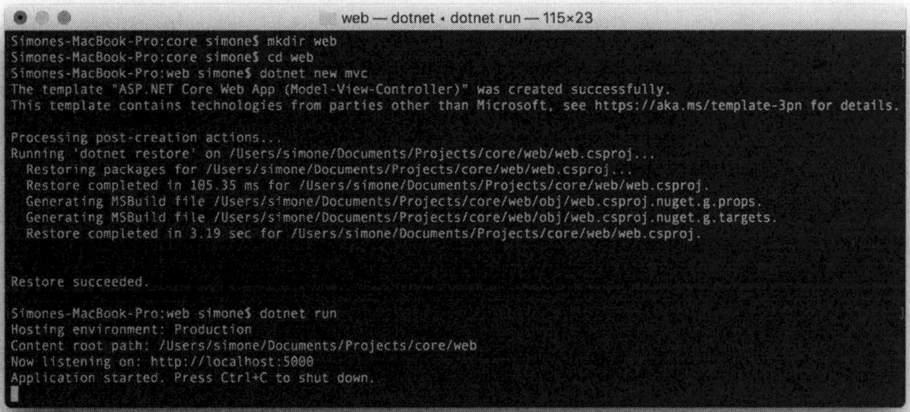

FIGURE 8-2: Creating a sample web app on macOS

Figure 8-2 shows what you see in the command line, and Figure 8-3 shows the resulting website, with MVC.

There are project templates available also for other types of projects, like class libraries (`classlib`), tests (`mstest` or `xunit`), and other types of web projects (`web` for an empty web project and `webapi`). New projects can be added over time. This can be done with updates to the tools or by downloading templates from the community. To see the list of templates available on your system, you can type the command `dotnet new --show-all` (Figure 8-4).

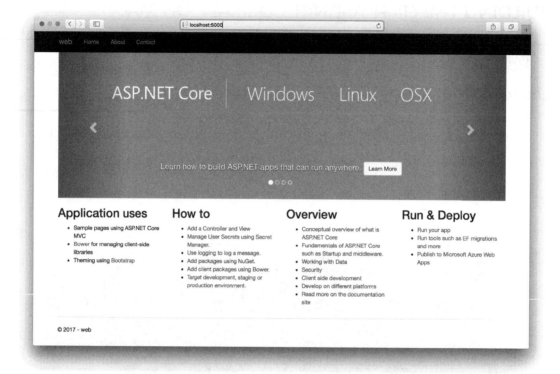

FIGURE 8-3: Sample website running on macOS

The creation of a project can be also controlled using template options. For example, for class libraries, the version of the framework can be specified with the `-f` or `--framework` option (`net-coreapp2.0` or `netstandard2.0`). The template for the MVC project can be created either with or without membership (and a ton of other options) and using either the cross-platform SQLite (the default) or the Windows-only LocalDB. To see the template-specific option, you can type the command `dotnet new <template name> --help`. Figure 8-5 shows the options of the MVC template.

So you can now create an MVC project with membership by typing the command:

```
dotnet new mvc -au Individual
```

The project created with the last command is also an example of a full-stack cross-platform project as it also includes the membership provider, which persists user data to a database using Entity Framework Core. Unlike the same kind of project created by Visual Studio, this one uses SQLite instead of SQL Server, so it can run on both Windows and Mac machines.

FIGURE 8-4: List of project templates

Before you can successfully run this project, including the part that saves a new login to the database, Entity Framework migrations must be run. This can be done by using the Entity Framework tools for the dotnet command-line interface.

```
dotnet ef database update
```

ENTITY FRAMEWORK MIGRATIONS

When a project is created, it contains no database. In order to create it together with the all the tables needed, a specific setup procedure must be run. This is done by running the database migration. This part is explained in more detail in Chapter 9.

With the dotnet command-line interface, you can also add references to both NuGet packages (for example `dotnet add package Newtonsoft.Json`) and references to other projects (`dotnet add reference ../lib/lib.csproj`). And of course you can also remove them with the `remove` command.

FIGURE 8-5: Options for the MVC project template

Using Yeoman

Being part of the SDK, the dotnet command-line interface is a very convenient way of creating ASP.NET Core applications, but it doesn't give much flexibility. To solve this problem, the .NET community developed some generators for Yeoman. Yeoman is a general-purpose scaffolding and code generator tool that is widely used in the front-end development community for creating projects for various frameworks (like Angular) using the best-practice folder setup and tool configuration.

First you have to install the Yeoman scaffolding tool. As with all the tools mentioned throughout this book, this one is installed with npm.

```
npm install -g yo
```

You then need to install the official ASP.NET Core generator, still via npm.

```
npm install -g generator-aspnet
```

yo is the command-line tool used to run the generators. To start the tool just type yo in a terminal window.

> **NOTE** *Although Yeoman doesn't strictly depend on them, most generated projects make use of both Bower and Gulp, so if you just jumped to this chapter skipping the Chapters 5 and 6, you might want to install them as well.*

Now you can select which generator to run (if this is your first usage of the tool, you'll only have the just installed aspnet). Figure 8-6 shows the generators selection screen of Yeoman.

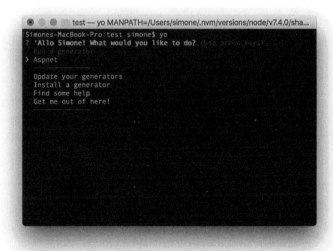

FIGURE 8-6: Yeoman generators selection screen

Once you select `aspnet`, you get prompted with another menu, which lists (Figure 8-7) all the types of ASP.NET Core projects it can generate. (You can launch Yeoman directly to this menu by directly typing `yo aspnet` in the terminal.)

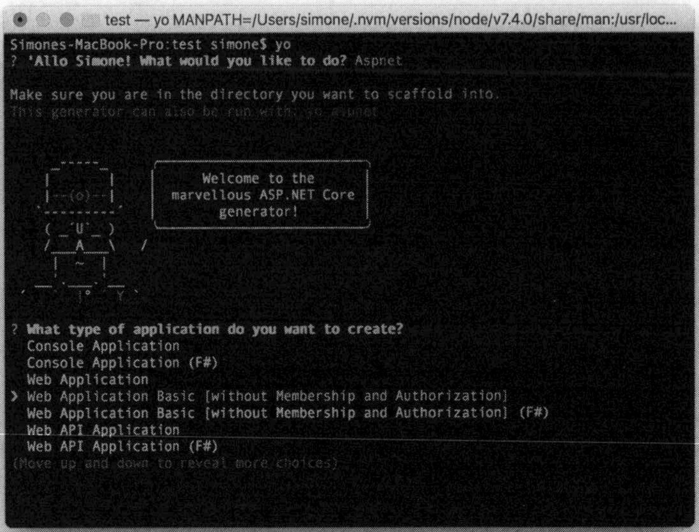

FIGURE 8-7: Yeoman ASP.NET Core generators

Among the available options, you can see Web Application Basic, which refers to the template for an ASP.NET Core application without membership and authorization. If you select this one, you will be asked which UI framework to use. (You have the choice between Bootstrap and Semantic UI.)

Finally, choose which name to give to the application and hit Enter.

On the screen, you can follow the progress of the installation. First, folders and files are created, and then Bower dependencies are retrieved from their repositories. At the end of the process, you can read on the screen how to build and launch the application.

VISUAL STUDIO CODE

Now that that the project is generated, you need a text editor to write some useful code, possibly with IntelliSense and with a way to debug it. For this, Microsoft developed Visual Studio Code, an open-source, text-based, general-purpose IDE.

Setting It Up

Visual Studio Code can be downloaded from `https://code.visualstudio.com/`. Like many other text editors, it can be extended with extensions. One of them is the extension that adds support for C# IntelliSense and debugging of ASP.NET Core applications. In order to install it, open the Extensions pane and type `@recommended`. A list of the recommended extensions will be shown, from which you'll find the one that brings C# support.

When this extension is installed and enabled, open the folder that contains a web application created either via the dotnet command-line interface or by using Yeoman. The C# extension now inspects the file, and it will ask you to add two configuration files that are needed for it to work properly: `launch.json` and `tasks.json`. Then you need to restore the dependencies if you haven't done so already. See Figure 8-8.

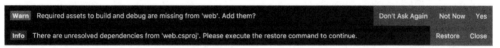

FIGURE 8-8: Warning in Visual Studio Code

Those two files are then saved in the `.vscode` folder, and they contain the configuration for launching and building the application. The right settings are added automatically, so don't worry too much about what's inside for the moment.

> **INSTALLING C# SUPPORT FOR VISUAL STUDIO CODE**
>
> The first time you open a .NET Core project after installing the extension, all native debuggers and runtimes will be installed, so it will be a few minutes before you can start using it. The extension also checks for updates of the debuggers and runtimes every time it starts, so this download will also happen when there is a new update. But don't worry, everything happens behind the scenes.

Development Features in Visual Studio Code

With the proper configuration in place, Visual Studio Code is now a fully-fledged code-based IDE for building .NET Core applications. Now you will have a look at the main features.

IntelliSense

Thanks to the C# extension, Visual Studio Code can provide IntelliSense, code completion, syntax highlighting, and contextual help like the standard Visual Studio does. See Figure 8-9.

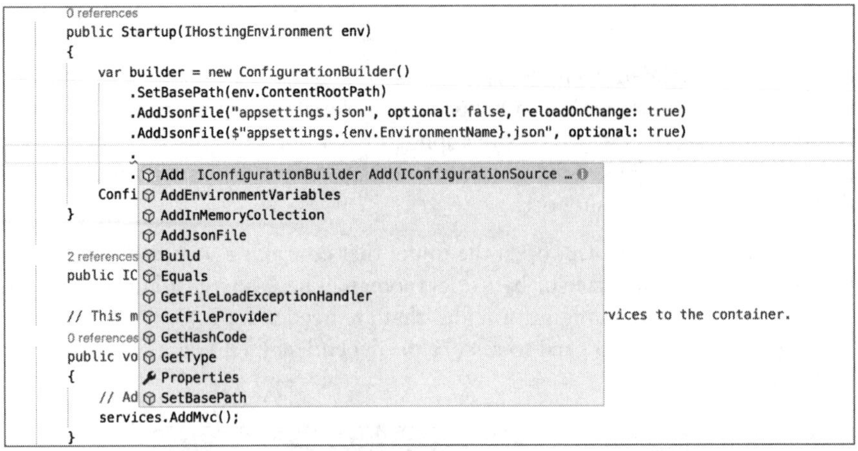

```
0 references
public Startup(IHostingEnvironment env)
{
    var builder = new ConfigurationBuilder()
        .SetBasePath(env.ContentRootPath)
        .AddJsonFile("appsettings.json", optional: false, reloadOnChange: true)
        .AddJsonFile($"appsettings.{env.EnvironmentName}.json", optional: true)
        .
         ⊕ Add    IConfigurationBuilder Add(IConfigurationSource … ⓘ
    Confi ⊕ AddEnvironmentVariables
}         ⊕ AddInMemoryCollection
          ⊕ AddJsonFile
2 references ⊕ Build
public IC ⊕ Equals
          ⊕ GetFileLoadExceptionHandler
// This m ⊕ GetFileProvider                        rvices to the container.
0 references ⊕ GetHashCode
public vo ⊕ GetType
{         🔧 Properties
    // Ad ⊕ SetBasePath
    services.AddMvc();
}
```

FIGURE 8-9: IntelliSense in Visual Studio Code

This is not limited to .NET code, but also applies to JavaScript and Typescript, which are both natively supported by Visual Studio Code, and to many other languages like CSS, HTML, and Sass via their own specific extensions.

Refactoring

Some of the refactoring and code navigation features that you are used to in Visual Studio are also available in Visual Studio Code. You can use features such as Go to Definition, Find All References, Rename Symbol, Peek Definition (shown in Figure 8-10), and so on.

Errors and Suggestions

Just like its big brother Visual Studio, Visual Studio Code can also put a red underline under lines of code that have problems. And in some cases, it can also prompt suggestions on how to fix the error by displaying the light bulb icon. See Figure 8-11.

Visual Studio Code also shows all the problems and errors in the Problem panel, which is activated by clicking on the status bar with the count of errors. See Figure 8-12.

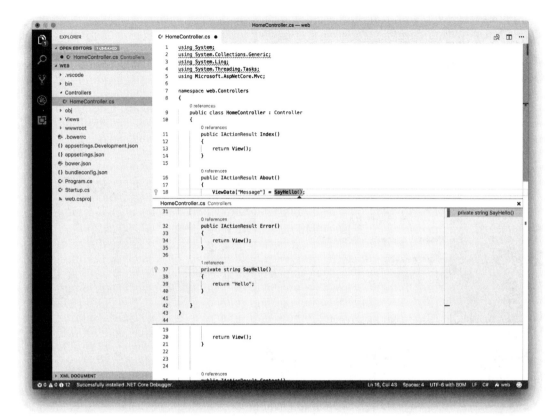

FIGURE 8-10: Peek Definition

Debugging

Probably the most important feature is the capability to debug the code you wrote. Visual Studio Code really shines in this capacity.

Once the two previously mentioned configuration files, `tasks.json` and `launch.json`, are in your folder, debugging.NET applications is as easy as pressing the Run icon in the toolbar and setting a breakpoint in the code. See Figure 8-13.

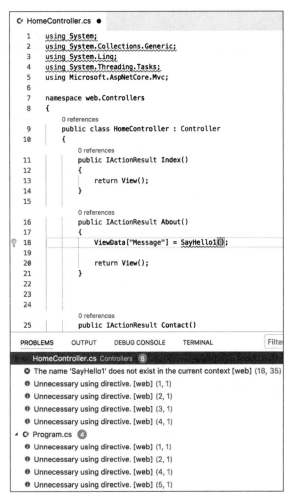

FIGURE 8-11: Error highlighting

FIGURE 8-12: Status Bar with problems count

As with the other features, debugging is also possible for other languages for which extensions have been installed, such as JavaScript, Typescript, or Node.js.

Version Control

Another interesting feature is the integrated support for version control systems. Visual Studio Code ships with git client with a simple UI for the most common features such as commit, sync, pull, and push. It also has a more text-based interface (via the command palette) when more control is needed. But other version control systems are available for download (as extensions) like Visual Studio Team Services, Perforce, and Mercurial. See Figure 8-14.

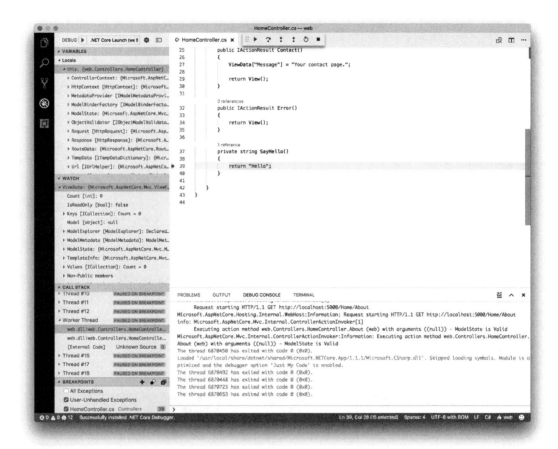

FIGURE 8-13: Debugging ASP.NET Core application

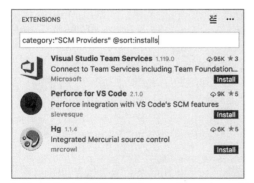

FIGURE 8-14: Additional Source Control providers

The editor also shows some clues directly inside the text, marking new lines and updated lines with different colors.

It also has an integrated file comparison tool that can be used both to show the differences between versions and to compare arbitrary files. See Figure 8-15.

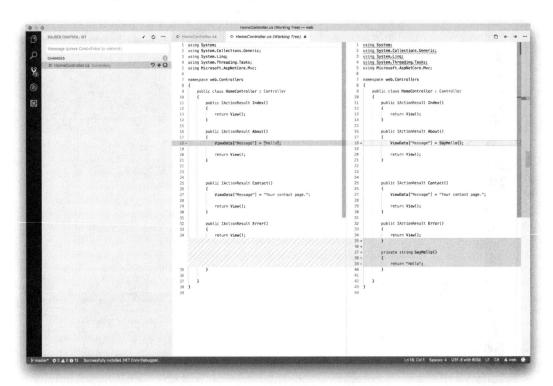

FIGURE 8-15: Diff window

Tasks

Visual Studio Code has support for task runners, so you can run your Gulp and Grunt tasks directly from the command palette. You can also run any other kind of command by specifying it in the tasks.json file, the same that was previously mentioned for setup of the C# extension.

LISTING 8-1: Tasks.json file

```
{
    "version": "0.1.0",
    "command": "dotnet",
    "isShellCommand": true,
    "args": [],
    "tasks": [
```

```
{
    "taskName": "build",
    "args": [
        "${workspaceRoot}/web.csproj"
    ],
    "isBuildCommand": true,
    "problemMatcher": "$msCompile"
}
        ]
    }
```

In Listing 8-1 you see the basic structure of the `tasks.json` file. The command to run is specified in the `command` property, and then you can indicate the tasks that are going to use the specified command. In this case there is only one specified task, that's `taskName` is `build` and that takes the current `.csproj` file as argument. This specific example also instructs Visual Studio Code to use the task as the default build command for the project (`isBuildCommand`) and specifies that the output of the task will be scanned by a "problem matcher," `$mscompile`, to report errors and problems inside the editor and the problems panel.

Other Features

Visual Studio Code contains so many interesting features that describing all of them probably would take over half of the book. Apart from the ones just mentioned, it includes all the features typical to modern text editors. It has an integrated snippets library with auto-expansion so that you can enter code faster. It also has the already mentioned command palette from which you can easily access all the commands provided by the editor and its extensions, even the ones that do not have an explicit menu item. You can also interact with the terminal window directly within Visual Studio Code without opening an external application.

And, more importantly, it's extensible so the support for new languages or features can be easily added if needed. For example, I wrote this book entirely using Visual Studio Code and its support for the Markdown language.

To explore in more detail what you can do with Visual Studio Code, I encourage you to visit the official web site at `code.visualstudio.com`.

OmniSharp

All these features, as far as their support for .NET Core is concerned, are possible thanks to OmniSharp. OmniSharp is a set of OSS projects that work together for bringing .NET development to any text editor.

The base layer is a server that runs Roslyn and analyzes the files of the project that is open inside the editor.

On top of this there is an API (REST-based over HTTP or over pipes) that allows clients (text editors via their extensions) to query the code model to get IntelliSense, parameter information, the references to a variable, or the definition of a method.

At the top layer are all the editor-specific extensions that display the information retrieved from the OmniSharp server in a user-friendly way. The top layer also includes other features that are purely client-side such as code formatting or snippet expansion. It is also the extensions that interact with the debugger to provide all the features needed for debugging your code.

OmniSharp extensions have been developed for the most popular text editors on the market. Apart from Visual Studio Code, there are extensions for Atom, Vim, Sublime, and even Emacs. This means that you can continue using your favorite text editor and still be able to get all the benefit of a rich code-editing experience powered by OmniSharp.

Other IDEs

As mentioned previously, OmniSharp enables developing .NET Core applications also with other text editors, like Atom, Sublime, Vim, and Emacs. But all of these lack the support of the many code refactoring VS plugins that most developers use, like ReSharper and similar tools.

To close this gap, JetBrains, the company behind ReSharper, has decided to expand its line of IDEs. It is working on Project Rider, a fully-fledged IDE based on its IntelliJ platform and that includes all the refactoring features of ReSharper.

It is still a work in progress, but given the popularity of ReSharper among .NET developers and the popularity of their other tools (especially WebStorm for JavaScript development), Rider has a chance of becoming a big player in the market of text-based C# IDEs.

Microsoft has also released a "full" version of Visual Studio that runs on the Mac. If you are interested you can download it at the URL `https://www.visualstudio.com/vs/visual-studio-mac/`.

USING COMMAND-LINE TOOLS

When reading the previous chapters, you might have quickly passed over the parts that were explaining how to use the various front-end tools using the command line. Visual Studio has integrated support for them so you do not have to learn their command-line interface.

When using Visual Studio Core (or your favorite text editor) some of these helping hands might not be available, so you need to start using the command line more than you are used to.

I recommend that you go back to previous chapters of the book and review the part about the command-line usage of the various tools. Table 8-1 provides a short "cheat sheet" with the most common commands you might need.

TABLE 8-1: Useful command-line tools

COMMAND	DESCRIPTION
`npm install <package> --save`	Installs dependencies and saves in local project
`npm update`	Restores all dependencies defined
`bower install <package> --save`	Installs dependencies and saves in local project

COMMAND	DESCRIPTION
`bower install`	Restores all packages
`gulp <taskname>`	Runs the Gulp task
`dotnet restore`	Restores .NET Core dependencies
`dotnet publish`	Publishes a .NET Core project

SUMMARY

It was possible to run ASP.NET on non-Windows machines even before the creation of the CoreCLR, by using Mono, but it was considered more of a toy than something businesses would use for their production environments. And even then, the IDE was not stable enough to allow developers to build the applications directly on their Mac. So the fact of being cross-platform was more about the possibility of running the final software on a Linux box.

With .NET Core and Visual Studio Code, aspects of being cross-platform have also become about developing without using Visual Studio and Windows.

Visual Studio Code is not just for Mac and Linux users. Visual Studio Code also runs on Windows, and many developers are now starting to use it as a replacement of the more resource-hungry Visual Studio. In fact, this chapter could have possibly been named "Developing without Visual Studio."

All the aspects of front-end development have been individually explored, from the server-side part of ASP.NET Core to the client-side with JavaScript and CSS, and from the management of third-party packages and the deployment on the Cloud. It is now time to put everything together and see how to build a simple, yet complete, modern ASP.NET Core web application.

Putting It All Together

WHAT'S IN THIS CHAPTER?

➤ How to use Entity Framework Core

➤ Authenticating users with OAuth

➤ Taking advantage of Visual Studio scaffolding

Throughout the book, you have learned individually all the various technologies and languages needed to develop and deploy modern web applications using ASP.NET Core, but you haven't yet used them all together to build a complete application.

This chapter covers this gap and shows how to use all the technologies together to build (part of) a real-life application. In the process it shows some features of ASP.NET Core that were not covered in previous chapters, like authentication with OAuth (Facebook or Twitter) and data persistence with Entity Framework Core.

WROX.COM CODE DOWNLOADS FOR THIS CHAPTER

The wrox.com code downloads for this chapter are found at `www.wrox.com`. Search for the book's ISBN (978-1-119-18131-6), and you will find the code in the chapter 9 download and individually named according to the names throughout the chapter.

BUILDING A TRIATHLON RACE RESULTS WEB SITE

As you might have guessed from some of the samples in the other chapters, I am into triathlons. Despite the very high quality of web applications that help track training, the sites for race registration and results are mostly stuck 10 years or more in the past, and very few race tracking sites have some kind of live tracking and comparison of performances among different races.

The application used as a sample in this chapter is a very simple version of such a web application.

The full site is made of three main sub-sites:

➤ The back-office, where administrators can create races, enter results, register athletes, and do any kind of manual intervention to the data.

➤ The public site, where users can enroll in races and the public can track the results of athletes and see the final standings of a race.

➤ A set of APIs that can be called by IoT devices like timing mats or GPS trackers to update the results or the position of athletes along the race course.

Obviously, the samples available in this chapter are not implementing the full feature set of the project but are just used to show the development flow and some examples of usage of the technologies shown in the book.

If you are interested in the fully functional triathlon race-tracking site, you can get on my GitHub repository `http://github.com/simonech/TriathlonRaceTracking` and clone the repository.

BUILDING THE BACK-OFFICE SITE

The back-office site is a traditional web application that does not make use of Angular or other single-page application frameworks. It uses Bootstrap to make it easy to style the site and uses the features of ASP.NET Core MVC like tag helpers to simplify the creation of repetitive editing screens.

To build this project you can use the MVC application project template available in the New Project dialog (Figure 9-1). This sets up a project with all the dependencies needed by an MVC project.

The first step is to build the general layout of the back-office, with a menu to access the various areas of the site. The project template already installs Bootstrap, so designing a menu bar for the various functions of the site is an easy task.

The menu will contain the links to the various sections of the back-office: races, athletes, and results. Listing 9-1 shows the master layout for the back-office, including the navigation bar and all the script references added by the project template.

LISTING 9-1: Views/Shared/_Layout.cshtml

```
<!DOCTYPE html>
<html>
<head>
    <meta charset="utf-8" />
    <meta name="viewport" content="width=device-width, initial-scale=1.0" />
    <title>@ViewData["Title"] - TriathlonRaceTracking</title>

    <environment include="Development">
```

```
            <link rel="stylesheet" href="~/lib/bootstrap/dist/css/bootstrap.css" />
            <link rel="stylesheet" href="~/css/site.css" />
        </environment>
        <environment exclude="Development">
            <link rel="stylesheet" href="https://ajax.aspnetcdn.com/ajax/
bootstrap/3.3.7/css/bootstrap.min.css"
                  asp-fallback-href="~/lib/bootstrap/dist/css/bootstrap.min.css"
                  asp-fallback-test-class="sr-only" asp-fallback-test-
property="position" asp-fallback-test-value="absolute" />
            <link rel="stylesheet" href="~/css/site.min.css" asp-append-version="true" />
        </environment>
    </head>
    <body>
        <nav class="navbar navbar-inverse navbar-fixed-top">
            <div class="container">
                <div class="navbar-header">
                    <button type="button" class="navbar-toggle" data-toggle="collapse"
data-target=".navbar-collapse">
                        <span class="sr-only">Toggle navigation</span>
                        <span class="icon-bar"></span>
                        <span class="icon-bar"></span>
                        <span class="icon-bar"></span>
                    </button>
                    <a asp-area="" asp-controller="Home" asp-action="Index"
class="navbar-brand">TriathlonRaceTracking</a>
                </div>
                <div class="navbar-collapse collapse">
                    <ul class="nav navbar-nav">
                        <li class="dropdown">
                            <a href="#" class="dropdown-toggle" data-
toggle="dropdown">Races <span class="caret"></span></a>
                            <ul class="dropdown-menu">
                                <li><a asp-area="" asp-controller="Races" asp-
action="Create">Add Race</a></li>
                                <li><a asp-area="" asp-controller="Races" asp-
action="Index">List Races</a></li>
                            </ul>
                        </li>
                        <li class="dropdown">
                            <a href="#" class="dropdown-toggle" data-
toggle="dropdown">Athletes <span class="caret"></span></a>
                            <ul class="dropdown-menu">
                                <li><a asp-area="" asp-controller="Athletes" asp-
action="Create">Add Athlete</a></li>
                                <li><a asp-area="" asp-controller="Athletes" asp-
action="Index">List Athletes</a></li>
                            </ul>
                        </li>
                        <li><a asp-area="" asp-controller="Results" asp-
action="Index">Results</a></li>
                        <li><a asp-area="" asp-controller="Home" asp-
action="About">About</a></li>
                    </ul>
                </div>
```

```
        </div>
    </nav>
    <div class="container body-content">
        @RenderBody()
        <hr />
        <footer>
            <p>&copy; 2017 - TriathlonRaceTracking</p>
        </footer>
    </div>

    <environment include="Development">
        <script src="~/lib/jquery/dist/jquery.js"></script>
        <script src="~/lib/bootstrap/dist/js/bootstrap.js"></script>
        <script src="~/js/site.js" asp-append-version="true"></script>
    </environment>
    <environment exclude="Development">
        <script src="https://ajax.aspnetcdn.com/ajax/jquery/jquery-2.2.0.min.js"
                asp-fallback-src="~/lib/jquery/dist/jquery.min.js"
                asp-fallback-test="window.jQuery"
                crossorigin="anonymous"
                integrity="sha384-K+ctZQ+LL8q6tP7I94W+qzQsfRV2a+AfHIi9k8z8l9ggpc8X+
Ytst4yBo/hH+8Fk">
        </script>
        <script src="https://ajax.aspnetcdn.com/ajax/bootstrap/3.3.7/bootstrap.min.js"
                asp-fallback-src="~/lib/bootstrap/dist/js/bootstrap.min.js"
                asp-fallback-test="window.jQuery && window.jQuery.fn && window.
jQuery.fn.modal"
                crossorigin="anonymous"
                integrity="sha384-Tc5IQib027qvyjSMfHjOMaLkfuWVxZxUPnCJA7l2mCWNIpG9m
GCD8wGNIcPD7Txa">
        </script>
        <script src="~/js/site.min.js" asp-append-version="true"></script>
    </environment>

    @RenderSection("Scripts", required: false)
</body>
</html>
```

The navigation bar, created using Bootstrap, links directly to the various actions inside the controllers. It does so with the help of the link tag helper, which generates the link controllers' actions just by specifying their name.

```
<a asp-area="" asp-controller="Athletes" asp-action="New">Add Athlete</a>
```

Besides the navigation bar, Listing 9-1 shows the usage of many tag helpers like environment, which is used to render whatever is inside depending on which environment the site runs on, and link, which adds references to JavaScript or CSS files directly from a CDN or locally in case the CDN is down.

As example, you'll implement the screens to list, create, and edit a race. A race is made of a certain number of pieces of textual information and a list of intermediate timing points, each of which might define a fraction of the race. In order to start with the implementation, first you need to set up the database.

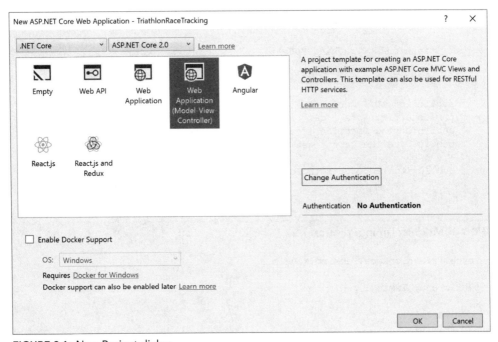

FIGURE 9-1: New Project dialog

Setting Up Entity Framework

There are a variety of options when it comes to data persistence. You can you use an ORM like Entity Framework to connect to a standard SQL database, or you can use a document database. For this sample the simplest solution is using Entity Framework Core (also known as EF Core).

The Object Model

To use Entity Framework Core, the first step is to define the object model of the application without worrying about how the underlying database tables will be created. In this simple scenario you are going to have two classes that have a one-to-many relationship:

➤   A `Race` class, with the main information about a race

➤   A `TimingPoint` class, which specifies where timing mats are located

Listings 9-2 and 9-3 show the two classes.

LISTING 9-2: Models/Race.cs

```csharp
using System;
using System.Collections.Generic;

namespace TriathlonRaceTracking.Models
{
    public class Race
    {
        public int ID { get; set; }
        public string Name { get; set; }
        public string Location { get; set; }
        public DateTime Date { get; set; }

        public ICollection<TimingPoint> TimingPoints { get; set; }
    }
}
```

LISTING 9-3: Models/TimingPoint.cs

```csharp
namespace TriathlonRaceTracking.Models
{
    public enum TimingType
    {
        Start,
        SwimEnd,
        BikeStart,
        BikeEnd,
        RunStart,
        End,
        Intermediate
    }

    public class TimingPoint
    {
        public int ID { get; set; }
        public int RaceID { get; set; }
        public string Name { get; set; }
        public TimingType Type { get; set; }

        public Race Race { get; set; }
    }
}
```

Notice how the one-to-many relationship between the race and its timing points is defined by both adding a `TimingPoint` list to the `Race` object and specifying the `RaceID` and the actual reference to the `Race` object in the `TimingPoint`. A timing point can define either an official start or end of a fraction (the swim, the bike, the run, or the two transitions), or it can be just a lap in the course or any other intermediate point without any meaning in the context of the results. For simplicity, this is implemented as an enumeration in the same file.

The EF Core Context

Once the object model is defined, you need to register the two classes in the Entity Framework context object, which acts as single point of entry for operations on data. Listing 9-4 shows the Entity Framework context for the application.

LISTING 9-4: Data/TriathlonRaceTrackingContext.cs

```
using Microsoft.EntityFrameworkCore;

namespace TriathlonRaceTracking.Data
{
    public class TriathlonRaceTrackingContext : DbContext
    {
        public TriathlonRaceTrackingContext (DbContextOptions<TriathlonRaceTracking
Context> options)
                : base(options)
        {
        }

        public DbSet<TriathlonRaceTracking.Models.Race> Race { get; set; }

        public DbSet<TriathlonRaceTracking.Models.TimingPoint> TimingPoint { get;
set; }
    }
}
```

In addition, the connection string must be specified and passed to the context object inside `ConfigureServices` in the `Startup` class.

```
public void ConfigureServices(IServiceCollection services)
{
  services.AddMvc();

  services.AddDbContext<TriathlonRaceTrackingContext>(
    options =>
            options.UseSqlServer( Configuration.GetConnectionString("TriathlonRace-
TrackingContext")));
}
```

The connection string can be defined in the `appsettings.json` file (Listing 9-5).

LISTING 9-5: appsettings.json

```
{
  "Logging": {
    "IncludeScopes": false,
    "LogLevel": {
```

```
        "Default": "Warning"
      }
    },
    "ConnectionStrings": {
      "TriathlonRaceTrackingContext": "Server=(localdb)\\mssqllocaldb;Database=Triath
    lonRaceTrackingContext-19f1651f-d333-4fe1-9301-e75c84ec0b6e;Trusted_Connection=True
    ;MultipleActiveResultSets=true"
      }
    }
```

The creation of the context class and the changes in the `Startup.cs` and `appsettings.json` files are done automatically the first time you scaffold a controller from the Add Controller dialog in Visual Studio 2017.

Migrations

Now you need a database where EF Core can store the data. By default, EF Core populates the objects of the data model from tables named exactly like the classes, with columns named like the properties. In addition, it expects the ID to be the primary key and everything that represents a relationship (for example `RaceID` of Listing 9-3) to be a foreign key. The easiest way to create the correct tables and keys based on the default mapping conventions is to use a feature called *migrations*. Migrations can be used for the first setup of the database but more importantly later in the development when adding more features that require new tables or properties for existing tables.

To create the baseline migration for the two classes `Race` and `TimingPoint`, you first need to install the `Microsoft.EntityFrameworkCore.Tools` package.

Then you need to run the **Add Migration** command to generate the code to create the database schema (it gets stored in the `Migrations` folder), followed by the **Update Database** command to run this code on the database.

These two commands can be run either inside Visual Studio 2017, the Package Manager Console, or using the `dotnet` command-line tool.

In the first option type the following:

```
PM>Add-Migration Initial
PM>Update-Database
```

If you prefer using the `dotnet` command line, type these lines in the command prompt:

```
>dotnet ef migration Initial
>dotnet ef database update
```

You have just scratched the surface of Entity Framework, a topic that entire books have been written about it. I hope this little introduction helps with the basics needed for building a simple application.

Another interesting feature is the possibility of "seeding" the database with an initial set of data. This is going to be very useful in this sample application for setting up the database for the frontend to work.

Together with adding the initial data, you can also run any pending migration directly in code. Listing 9-6 shows a simple data seed class that adds a race with its timing points.

LISTING 9-6: Models/InitialData.cs

```csharp
using Microsoft.EntityFrameworkCore;
using Microsoft.Extensions.DependencyInjection;
using System;
using System.Collections.Generic;
using System.Linq;
using System.Threading.Tasks;
using TriathlonRaceTracking.Data;

namespace TriathlonRaceTracking.Models
{
    public static class InitialData
    {
        public static async Task InitializeAsync(IServiceProvider service)
        {
            using (var serviceScope = service.CreateScope())
            {
                var scopeServiceProvider = serviceScope.ServiceProvider;
                var db = scopeServiceProvider.GetService<TriathlonRaceTrackingCont
ext>();
                db.Database.Migrate();
                await InsertTestData(db);
            }
        }

        private static async Task InsertTestData(TriathlonRaceTrackingContext
context)
        {
            if(context.Races.Any())
                return;
            var race = new Race { Name="Ironman World Championship
2017",Location="Kona, Hawaii",Date=new DateTime(2017,10,14,7,0,0) };

            var timingPoints = new List<TimingPoint>
            {
                new TimingPoint{ Race=race, Name="Start", Type=TimingType.Start},
                new TimingPoint{ Race=race, Name="Stairs", Type=TimingType.
SwimEnd},
                new TimingPoint{ Race=race, Name="T1 Exit", Type=TimingType.
BikeStart},
                new TimingPoint{ Race=race, Name="Turnaround", Type=TimingType.
Intermediate},
                new TimingPoint{ Race=race, Name="T2 Entrance", Type=TimingType.
BikeEnd},
                new TimingPoint{ Race=race, Name="T2 Exit", Type=TimingType.
RunStart},
                new TimingPoint{ Race=race, Name="End", Type=TimingType.End}
            };

            context.Add(race);
            context.AddRange(timingPoints);
            await context.SaveChangesAsync();
        }
    }
}
```

This code does a very basic check to understand whether the initial data has to be added (if(context.Races.Any())), but in a real-life application probably something more elaborate might be needed.

To launch this procedure, just call the InitializeAsync method from the Configure method in the Startup class.

```
InitialData.InitializeAsync(app.ApplicationServices).Wait();
```

Building CRUD Screens

Now that the database has been configured, it's time to build the controllers and more importantly the views.

Start by creating RacesController. If you use the Add Controller (Figure 9-2 and Figure 9-3) wizard of Visual Studio, the scaffolding engine creates the skeleton code for you to extend and build upon.

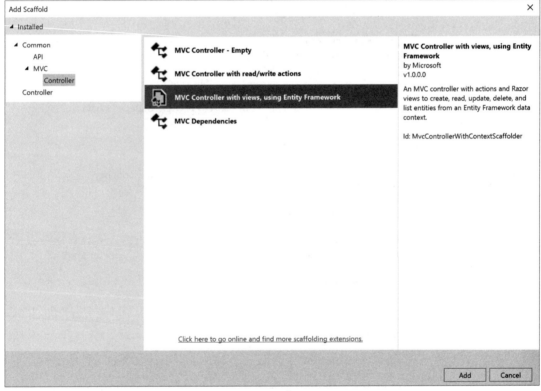

FIGURE 9-2: Add Scaffold... dialog

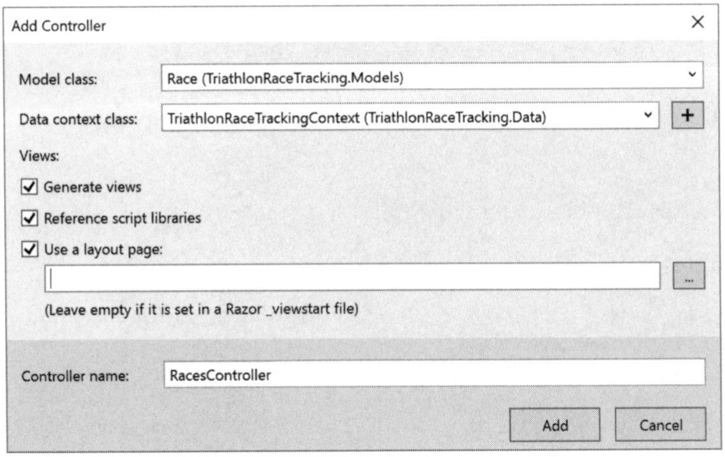

FIGURE 9-3: Add Controller... dialog

> **WARNING** *In this sample, the model coming from Entity Framework is also used as a ViewModel sent to the view. This has been done just to avoid making the code too complex for the sample. In a real production-grade application, you might want to keep the two models separate and map properties from the data model to the ViewModel using mapping libraries like Automapper.*

The next step is to examine the code (both in the controller and in the views) needed to add a new race to the database. This operation uses the standard pattern Post-Redirect-Get to avoid duplication of data in case the user refreshes the page after the form has been submitted:

1. The Create form is rendered in the browser.

2. The user enters data and presses the Submit button.

3. The form is submitted using the POST HTTP method to the controller.

4. The controller checks if the data is valid and does one of the following:

   ➤ If the data is valid, it redirects the user to the subsequent page, in the sample to the Index, which is requested with the GET method.

   ➤ If the data is not valid, the controller just renders the edit form again with the validation errors highlighted.

The Controller

There are two action methods needed for the Create operation. The first simply returns the empty editing form.

```
public IActionResult Create()
```

```
    {
        return View();
    }
```

The second method, still called `Create`, is invoked when the form is submitted with POST.

```
[HttpPost]
[ValidateAntiForgeryToken]
public async Task<IActionResult> Create([Bind("ID,Name,Location,Date")] Race race)
{
    if (ModelState.IsValid)
    {
        _context.Add(race);
        await _context.SaveChangesAsync();
        return RedirectToAction(nameof(Index));
    }
    return View(race);
}
```

The generated code incorporates a lot of the best practices for securing the application. It uses the `ValidateAntiForgeryToken` attribute to check the token added by the form tag helper. This is used to prevent cross-site request forgery (also known as CSRF).

It also uses the `Bind` attribute in the model binding to avoid overposting. This prevents malicious users from tampering with the request, adding properties that were not supposed to be edited via the editing form. This attribute is especially needed when the data model is exposed directly to the views instead of using a specific ViewModel.

The action method then goes on checking the validity of the request, adds the object to the database, and finally redirects to the Index action method, which renders the list of races.

The View

The `Create` view (Listing 9-7) is a bit more interesting than the action method.

LISTING 9-7: Views/Races/Create.cshtml

```
@model TriathlonRaceTracking.Models.Race

@{
    ViewData["Title"] = "Create";
}

<h2>Create</h2>

<h4>Race</h4>
<hr />
<div class="row">
    <div class="col-md-4">
        <form asp-action="Create">
            <div asp-validation-summary="ModelOnly" class="text-danger"></div>
            <div class="form-group">
                <label asp-for="Name" class="control-label"></label>
                <input asp-for="Name" class="form-control" />
```

```
                    <span asp-validation-for="Name" class="text-danger"></span>
                </div>
                <div class="form-group">
                    <label asp-for="Location" class="control-label"></label>
                    <input asp-for="Location" class="form-control" />
                    <span asp-validation-for="Location" class="text-danger"></span>
                </div>
                <div class="form-group">
                    <label asp-for="Date" class="control-label"></label>
                    <input asp-for="Date" class="form-control" />
                    <span asp-validation-for="Date" class="text-danger"></span>
                </div>
                <div class="form-group">
                    <input type="submit" value="Create" class="btn btn-default" />
                </div>
            </form>
        </div>
    </div>

    <div>
        <a asp-action="Index">Back to List</a>
    </div>

    @section Scripts {
        @{await Html.RenderPartialAsync("_ValidationScriptsPartial");}
    }
```

As seen in Chapter 1, ASP.NET Core MVC introduced the tag helpers to make writing views easier. This is an example of the form, label, input, and validation helpers in action. Just by adding the `asp-for` or `asp-validation-for` attributes, the standard HTML tags become aware of the ViewModel and render the values of the properties and, if needed, also the HTML attributes needed for the Bootstrap-based validation framework.

Bootstrap is also used extensively. Notice the `.col-md-4` class name used to instruct the grid to use just 4 out of the 12 columns to render this form (so using only one-third of the width of the page).

The form is styled using Bootstrap classes using the `.form-group` to define individual elements of the form and `.form-control` to identify the actual input field. Finally, also the button is styled using the `btn btn-default` classes from Bootstrap. For more formatting options for forms using Bootstrap, you can refer back to Chapter 4 and Listing 4-6.

BUILDING THE REGISTRATION PAGE

In the back-office someone has created the race. Now it is time for athletes to register for it. For this feature, a user will be able to log in using a social media login like Facebook or Twitter, and once registered they can choose which race to participate in.

You are going to create a new Visual Studio project for this, but you want to keep on using the same Entity Framework data model, so you need to refactor the solution and move all the EF-related classes to a separate Class Library project. Once the project is created and all the content of the Data and Model folders has been moved to the new project, you have to reference the

EntityFrameworkCore and EntityFrameworkCore.SqlServer NuGet packages. This was not needed before because they were part of the mega-package Microsoft.AspNetCore.All used in the ASP.NET Core MVC project. You will also need to configure the appsettings.json file and Startup class the same way they were done for the backoffice project.

Adding social media authentication is easy with ASP.NET Core. You start by creating another project, still as an ASP.NET Core MVC project, and selecting Individual User Accounts as the Authentication mode. This way the project template will add the database entities, controllers, and views to collect and store all the information needed to create a private site where users can register either directly (providing a username and password) or via OAuth providers like Facebook, Twitter, Google, Microsoft, GitHub, and others.

Adding a social login is just a matter of adding the right NuGet package and configuring the authentication provider in the ConfigureService method in the Startup class. For example, to add a Facebook login, add the NuGet package Microsoft.AspNetCore.Authentication.Facebook. Then add the following lines of code in the ConfigureService method:

```
services.AddAuthentication().AddFacebook(facebookOptions =>
{
    facebookOptions.AppId = Configuration["Authentication:Facebook:
AppId"];
    facebookOptions.AppSecret = Configuration["Authentication:Facebook:
AppSecret"];
});
```

Now you have to register a new application on the Facebook developer portal in order to get the AppId and AppSecret needed to authenticate your application with Facebook. Go to the URL https://developers.facebook.com/apps/ and click on the Add a New App button (Figure 9-4).

FIGURE 9-4: Facebook developer portal

Then enter the name of your app and your email address (Figure 9-5).

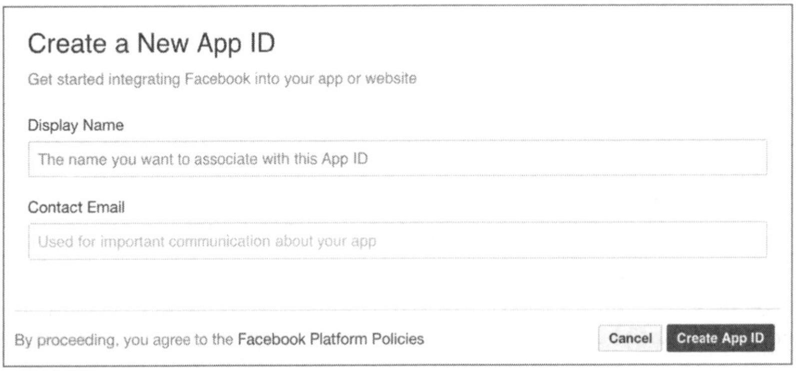

FIGURE 9-5: Create New App ID

And then select Facebook Login as the product to set up (Figure 9-6).

FIGURE 9-6: Select the product to set up

Then skip the wizard that pops up and select Settings from the sidebar on the left. Inside this page enter the absolute URL of the route /signin-facebook. This route has been added by the NuGet package. Leave all the other settings untouched (Figure 9-7).

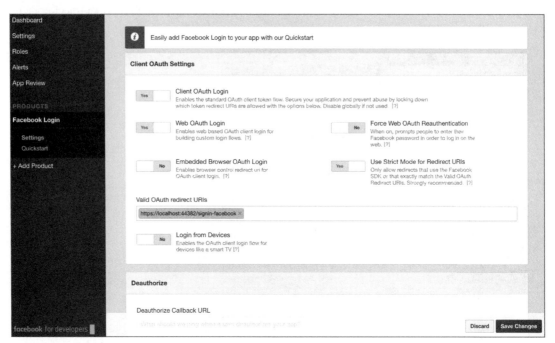

FIGURE 9-7: OAuth Settings page

The last thing is to retrieve the AppId and AppSecrets needed for the application to work. For this go to the Dashboard inside the developer portal (Figure 9-8).

Dashboard

myawesomeapp ○

This app is in development mode and can only be used by app admins, developers and testers [?]

API Version [?]

App ID

v2.10

App Secret

••••••••   Show

FIGURE 9-8: The Dashboard

Now you can save them either in the `appsettings.json` file or using the user secret management. The second option is better because it stores the configuration outside of the application folder (in the user's profile) and avoids the common mistake of storing such sensitive information as the social login key and secrets in the source repositories. Figure 9-9 shows how to open the user secrets file from within Visual Studio via the Manage User Secrets context menu item on the project node inside the Solution Explorer.

FIGURE 9-9: Manage User Secrets menu item

Next type the following configuration (obviously putting in your own values instead of the place-holders) in the `secrets.json` file:

```
{
  "Authentication": {
    "Facebook": {
      "AppId": "myappId",
      "AppSecret": "myappsecret"
    }
  }
}
```

Now launch the project and go to the login page, and you'll see a new button under the text that says "Use another system to log in" (Figure 9-10).

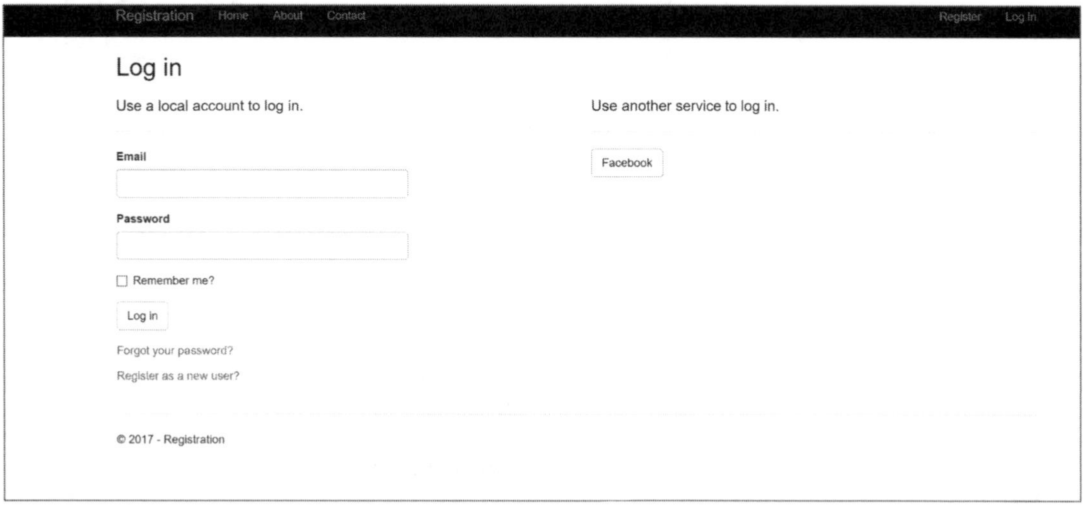

FIGURE 9-10: Login page

At this point, once a user authenticates to your system, you can prompt them with a page to register for a race.

SHOWING REAL-TIME RESULTS

Unlike the previous two sites, where the interaction with the data was relatively simple, showing real-time results requires a more complicated UI. For this purpose, you are going to use Angular coupled with some web APIs to retrieve the data from the database.

Creating the Angular Client-Side Application

For this site, you can use the Angular project template provide by Visual Studio 2017. This sets up a project using the JavaScript services mentioned at the end of Chapter 3 (Figure 9-11).

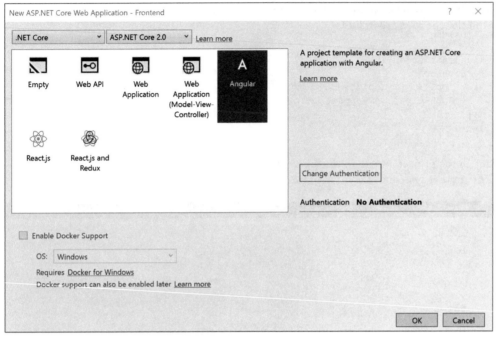

FIGURE 9-11: New Project dialog, Angular

The architecture of this application is going to be very simple. The web service sends the list of athletes with all their timing points to the JavaScript frontend,which will then show them and allow filters to be applied and statistics to be analyzed. As explained in Chapter 3, the frontend is implemented with a specific set of Angular components and services. The final result is shown in Figure 9-12.

As with any non-trivial Angular application, this one is made of a cascade of components.

The root element is the `Results` component, which is responsible for the general layout of the page and for handling the interaction between the child components. Listing 9-8 shows both the TypeScript file and the HTML template file.

LISTING 9-8: Results Component

TEMPLATE FILE

```
<h1>Kona Ironman Top 5 men</h1>
<results-list (selected)=showDetails($event)>Loading athlete list...</results-list>
  You selected: <app-athlete-details [athlete]="selectedAthlete">
</app-athlete-details>
```

TYPESCRIPT FILE

```
import { Component } from '@angular/core';
```

```
import { Athlete } from './athlete';

@Component({
    selector: 'results',
    templateUrl: 'results.component.html'
})
export class ResultsComponent {
    selectedAthlete: Athlete;

    showDetails(selectedAthlete: Athlete) {
        this.selectedAthlete = selectedAthlete;
    }
}
```

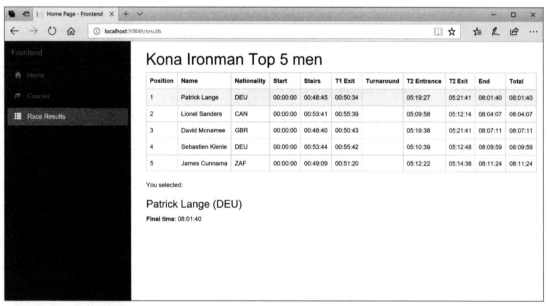

FIGURE 9-12: Results list

This component includes two child components and handles the selected event of the results list in order to show the details of the results list to the user.

The first child component is `results-list`, which builds the table that contains the results list, as shown in Listing 9-9. The table is styled using the `table` class of Bootstrap to make a bordered table with highlighting of the line on which the mouse pointer is.

LISTING 9-9: Results-list.component.html

```
<table class="table table-bordered table-hover">
    <tr>
        <th>Position</th>
        <th>Name</th>
```

```
            <th>Nationality</th>
            <th *ngFor="let point of timingPoints">{{point.name}}</th>
            <th>Total</th>
        </tr>
        <tr app-athlete *ngFor="let athlete of athletes | slice:0:5;let i = index">
            (click)="select(athlete)"
            [athlete]="athlete"
            [timingPoints]="timingPoints"
            [position]="i+1">
        </tr>
    </table>
```

The header of the table is also built dynamically, adding one column per each intermediate point. And obviously, the rows of the table are displayed iterating over the `athletes` property of the component, which contains the list of all athletes participating in the race. Notice the usage of the pipe `slice:0:5` to just show the top five athletes. This last part is the one that requires most of the code. Listing 9-10 shows the TypeScript class that handles this template.

LISTING 9-10: Results-list.component.ts

```typescript
import { Component, Output, EventEmitter, OnInit } from '@angular/core';
import { AthleteService } from './athlete.service';
import { Athlete } from "./athlete";
import { TimingPoint } from "./TimingPoint";
import { Observable } from "rxjs/Observable";


@Component({
    selector: 'results-list',
    templateUrl: 'results-list.component.html'
})
export class ResultsListComponent implements OnInit {
    athletes: Athlete[];
    timingPoints: TimingPoint[];
    @Output() selected = new EventEmitter<Athlete>();
    constructor(private athleteService: AthleteService) { }

    getAthletes() {
        this.athleteService.getAthletes()
            .then(list => {
                for (var i = 0; i < list.length; i++) {
                    var athlete = list[i];
                    athlete.timingValues = new Map<string, string>();
                    for (var j = 0; j < athlete.timings.length; j++) {
                        athlete.timingValues.set(athlete.timings[j].code, athlete.
timings[j].time);
                    }
                }
                this.athletes = list;
            });
    }
```

```
    getTimingPoints() {
        this.athleteService.getTimingPoints()
            .then(list => this.timingPoints = list);
    }

    ngOnInit() {
        this.getAthletes();
        this.getTimingPoints();
    }

    select(selectedAthlete: Athlete) {
        this.selected.emit(selectedAthlete);
    }
}
```

The implementation is very similar to the one shown at the end of Chapter 3. During the `ngOnInit` event, the lists of athletes and intermediate timing points are retrieved by calling an external service (`AthleteService`), which is the one responsible for the actual HTTP request to the web APIs. In the method `getAthletes`, the response coming from the service is processed and a bit elaborated in order to craft the ViewModel needed to easily render the template.

The final element in the graph of components is the one that renders each row of the results list table, and it's shown in Listing 9-11.

LISTING 9-11: Athlete.Component

TEMPLATE FILE

```
<td>{{position}}</td>
<td>{{athlete.name}}</td>
<td>{{athlete.country}}</td>
<td *ngFor="let timing of timingPoints">
    {{athlete.timingValues.get(timing.code)}}
</td>
<td>{{athlete.time}}</td>
```

TYPESCRIPT FILE

```
import { Component, Input } from '@angular/core';
import { Athlete } from './athlete';
import { TimingPoint } from './timingpoint';

@Component({
    selector: 'tr[app-athlete]',
    templateUrl: 'athlete.component.html'
})
export class AthleteComponent {
    @Input() athlete: Athlete;
    @Input() position: string;
    @Input() timingPoints: TimingPoint[];
  constructor() { }
}
```

Also in this case, the template iterates over the list of intermediate points and displays the timing for the athlete at that specific point. The highlighted lines are the ones for which the results coming from the server are manipulated, as will be explored in the upcoming "Building the Web APIs" section.

This component cannot know in which position it is rendered, so, to render the position of the athlete, it has an input parameter called position that is supplied by the parent component.

The final missing piece is the service that actually calls the server. This is pretty simple, as you can see in Listing 9-12.

LISTING 9-12: athlete.service.ts

```
import { Injectable } from '@angular/core';
import { TimingPoint } from './TimingPoint';
import { Athlete } from './athlete';
import { Http, Response } from "@angular/http";
import 'rxjs/add/operator/map';
import 'rxjs/add/operator/toPromise';

@Injectable()
export class AthleteService {
  constructor(private http: Http){}

  getAthletes(){
    return this.http.get('/api/standings')
      .map((r: Response) => <Athlete[]>r.json().data)
      .toPromise();
  }

  getTimingPoints() {
      return this.http.get('/api/timingpoints')
          .map((r: Response) => <TimingPoint[]>r.json())
          .toPromise();
  }
}
```

All that is left to do is to build the web APIs that return the data to the Angular client-side application.

Building the Web APIs

Returning the list of results is a very simple operation. Its only complexity is computing the intermediate time at the various timing points. For this sample, two APIs are made. The first (Listing 9-13) sends the list of all registered timing points to the Angular client, so that it can show them in the header of the results list.

LISTING 9-13: Controllers/TimingPointsController.cs

```
using System.Collections.Generic;
using System.Linq;
using Microsoft.AspNetCore.Mvc;
using Frontend.ViewModels;
using Frontend.Services;

namespace Frontend.Controllers
{
    [Produces("application/json")]
    [Route("api/TimingPoints")]
    public class TimingPointsController : Controller
    {
        private readonly ITimingService _service;

        public TimingPointsController(ITimingService service)
        {
            _service = service;
        }
        [HttpGet]
        public IList<TimingPointDefinition> Get()
        {
            var data = _service.GetTimingPoints(1);

            var model = data.Select(tp => new TimingPointDefinition
            {
                Code = tp.Code,
                Name = tp.Name,
                Order = tp.ID
            }).ToList();

            return model;
        }
    }
}
```

The second web API is used to provide all the athletes that are on the course with a list of all their intermediate timing points. In this case the controller is very basic as it delegates the complex operations of calculating intermediate times to a service, the `TimingService`, injected via DI. Listing 9-14 shows the simple API.

LISTING 9-14: Controllers/StandingsController.cs

```
using Frontend.Services;
using Frontend.ViewModels;
using Microsoft.AspNetCore.Mvc;
using System;
```

```
using System.Collections.Generic;
using System.Linq;
using System.Threading.Tasks;
using TriathlonRaceTracking.Data;

namespace Frontend.Controllers
{
    [Route("api/[controller]")]
    public class StandingsController : Controller
    {

        private readonly ITimingService _service;

        public StandingsController(ITimingService service)
        {
            _service = service;
        }

        [HttpGet]
        public AthletesViewModel Get()
        {
            var data = _service.GetStandings(1);

            var model = new AthletesViewModel(data);
            return model;
        }
    }
}
```

As you can see, not much is going on in Listing 9-14. The actual computation happens in the service (Listing 9-15).

LISTING 9-15: Services/TimingService.cs

```
using Frontend.ViewModels;
using Microsoft.EntityFrameworkCore;
using System;
using System.Collections.Generic;
using System.Linq;
using System.Threading.Tasks;
using TriathlonRaceTracking.Data;
using TriathlonRaceTracking.Models;

namespace Frontend.Services
{
    public class TimingService : ITimingService
    {
        private readonly TriathlonRaceTrackingContext _context;
        public TimingService(TriathlonRaceTrackingContext context)
        {
            _context = context;
        }
```

```csharp
public IList<AthleteViewModel> GetStandings(int raceId)
{
    var data = _context.Registrations
        .Include(r => r.Timings)
            .ThenInclude(t => t.TimingPoint)
        .Include(r => r.Athlete)
        .Where(r => r.RaceID == raceId);

    var result = new List<AthleteViewModel>();
    foreach (var position in data)
    {
        var athleteVM = new AthleteViewModel(position.Athlete.FullName,
position.Athlete.Nationality);
        if (position.Timings.Count == 0)
        {
            athleteVM.Time = "DNS";
        }
        else
        {
            var start = position.Timings.Where(t => t.TimingPoint.Type ==
TimingType.Start).Max(t => t.Time);
            var furthestPosition = GetFurthestPosition(position.Timings);
            athleteVM.Time = TimeFromStart(start, furthestPosition).
ToString();
            athleteVM.Timings = position.Timings.Select(t => new
TimingPointViewModel
            {
                Time = TimeFromStart(start, t),
                Order = (int)t.TimingPoint.Type,
                Name = t.TimingPoint.Name
            }).ToList();
        }

        result.Add(athleteVM);
    }

    return result;

}

private static TimeSpan TimeFromStart(DateTime start, Timing timingPoint)
{
    return timingPoint.Time.Subtract(start);
}

private Timing GetFurthestPosition(List<Timing> timings)
{
    Timing furthest = new Timing() { ID = -1 };
    foreach (var timing in timings)
    {
        if (timing.TimingPointID > furthest. TimingPointID)
            furthest = timing;
    }
    return furthest;
}
```

```
public IQueryable<TimingPoint> GetTimingPoints(int raceId)
{
    return _context.TimingPoints.Where(tp => tp.RaceID == raceId);
}
        }
    }
```

The `GetStandings` method first retrieves all the athletes participating in the race, joining them with all their intermediate timings and as well as their details. Later, it finds the time of each departure (in many races nowadays the start time is different for everyone) and identifies the difference with each intermediate timing to get the various splits. Finally, it returns all the data back to the controller so that it can be sent back to the web browser.

CONNECTING WITH IOT DEVICES

Nobody is going to sit in front of a laptop entering data as soon as an athlete passes from a timing point. This task is left to machines, which can sense when an athlete, who is wearing an RFID chip, crosses a timing mat. This information needs to be sent to the server so that it can show the real-time standing of athletes.

Implementing the full solution that tracks athletes is complicated, but you are just going to create the API that receives the raw data, and you'll later test it by simulating the calls using a REST client emulator.

You do this with an API controller that receives the race number of the athlete and some identifiers for both the race and the timing point, together with the time of the day. Listing 9-16 shows the code for the API.

LISTING 9-16: Controllers/TimingsController.cs

```
using System;
using System.Collections.Generic;
using System.Linq;
using System.Threading.Tasks;
using Microsoft.AspNetCore.Http;
using Microsoft.AspNetCore.Mvc;
using Microsoft.EntityFrameworkCore;
using TriathlonRaceTracking.Data;
using TriathlonRaceTracking.Models;

namespace TriathlonRaceTracking.Controllers
{
    [Produces("application/json")]
    [Route("api/Timings")]
    public class TimingsController : Controller
    {
        private readonly TriathlonRaceTrackingContext _context;

        public TimingsController(TriathlonRaceTrackingContext context)
```

```csharp
        {
            _context = context;
        }


        // GET: api/Timings/5
        [HttpGet("{id}")]
        public async Task<IActionResult> GetTiming([FromRoute] int id)
        {
            if (!ModelState.IsValid)
            {
                return BadRequest(ModelState);
            }

            var timing = await _context.Timings.SingleOrDefaultAsync(m => m.ID ==
id);

            if (timing == null)
            {
                return NotFound();
            }

            return Ok(timing);
        }

        // POST: api/Timings
        [HttpPost]
        public async Task<IActionResult> PostTiming([FromBody] TimingPostModel
model)
        {
            if (!ModelState.IsValid)
            {
                return BadRequest(ModelState);
            }

            var registration = _context.Registrations.SingleOrDefault(r =>
r.BibNumber == model.BibNumber && r.RaceID == model.RaceId);
            var timingPoint = _context.TimingPoints.SingleOrDefault(tp => tp.Code.
Equals(model.TPCode) && tp.RaceID == model.RaceId);

            var timing = new Timing
            {
                RegistrationID=registration.ID,
                TimingPointID=timingPoint.ID,
                Time=model.Time
            };

            _context.Timings.Add(timing);
            await _context.SaveChangesAsync();

            return CreatedAtAction("GetTiming", new { id = timing.ID }, timing);
        }

    }
```

```
public class TimingPostModel
{
    public int BibNumber { get; set; }
    public int RaceId { get; set; }
    public string TPCode { get; set; }
    public DateTime Time { get; set; }
}
}
```

There is nothing particularly complicated here, but there a few noteworthy elements. The most important thing is that the PostTiming method doesn't use a Timing object as an input parameter but as a post model. The reason, apart from avoiding possible over-posting, is because the time-keeping device at a timing point won't know the IDs used in the database but will most likely have some other code and will know the race number of the athlete.

Another element is the usage of CreatedAtAction, which will make the REST API return the 201 HTTP code that is typically used when a new object is created by a REST call.

Since you don't have a time-keeping point to connect to the system, you can test the REST endpoint using any REST client. I like to use Postman, which is available both as a Google Chrome extension and as a standalone application.

You can directly specify the request body in JSON and send the request to the server. The request body must be a JSON representation of the TimingPostModel class, for example:

```
{
    "bibNumber": 1,
    "raceId": 1,
    "time": "2017-10-08T20:49:54.730Z",
    "TPCode": "T1S"
}
```

Postman has the possibility of executing some scripts (in JavaScript) before the execution of the request, so you can replace the hard-coded timestamp with a variable that contains the exact moment in which the request is executed. This makes it easy to test the API without changing the time parameter each time. To do this, just add the following line of code into the Pre-request Script tab:

```
postman.setGlobalVariable('timestampUtcIso8601', (new Date()).toISOString());
```

Then replace the time parameter with the variable {{timestampUtcIso8601}}. Figure 9-13 shows the Postman request builder screen ready to add new timing information to the system.

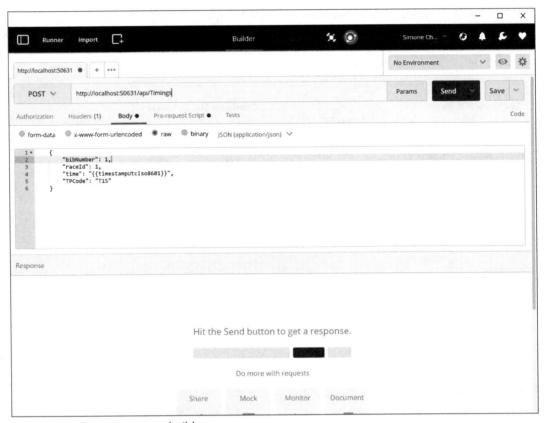

FIGURE 9-13: Postman request builder screen

DEPLOYING

Now that the projects are developed, it is time to publish them to allow triathletes to register online for races. For this purpose you are going to deploy them on Azure.

Chapter 7 contains a step-by-step procedure for deploying the sites, so here I'll skip explaining the steps in detail and just highlight the main points.

You'll start by publishing the back-office site first. When going through the publishing dialogs I recommend creating a Resource Group specific to these sets of applications. In addition to what is shown in Figures 7-12 and 7-13, you must also create a DB server (if needed) and a SQL Database. Figure 9-14 shows the two dialogs that contain the forms to create both the database and the server.

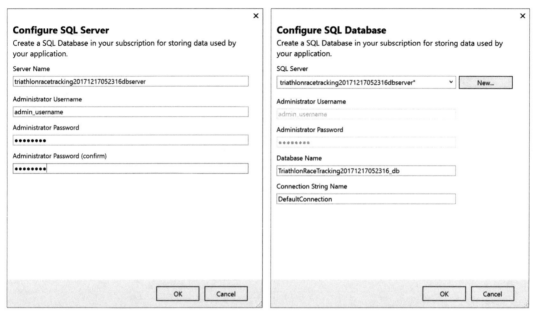

FIGURE 9-14: Server and database creation dialogs

Once the publishing process is complete, there is still one small detail to change. In the dialog for the creation of the database, you left `DefaultConnection` as the name for the connection string. Now you have to go in the Application settings blade on Azure portal (Figure 9-15) and change it to the name used by the application, which is `TriathlonRaceTrackingContext`, as shown in Listing 9-4.

SETTINGS	Connection strings			
≡ Application settings	The connection string values are hidden Show connection string values			
Authentication / Authorization				
Managed service identity	TriathlonRaceTrackingContext	< Hidden for Security >	SQL Database	☐ Slot setting
Backups	Name	Value	SQL Database ⌄	☐ Slot setting

FIGURE 9-15: Connection string settings on the Azure portal

Now just browse to the URL of the Azure app service, and Entity Framework Core will automatically create the tables and fill them with the data specified in the `InitialData.cs` file.

After the back-office, it is time for the Angular-based frontend. Just follow the same procedure as previously, but choose the now existing Resource Group instead of creating a new one. And do not create a SQL Database because the application uses the same database as the back-office.

For this application, the connection string has to be set manually, copying the value of the one set for the back-office.

For the frontend, the publishing takes a bit more time than the back-office because all NPM packages have to be installed, and also webpack, being the application in release mode, has to generate a minified and bundled version of all TypeScript classes used to develop the Angular frontend.

After having deployed the two applications, the Resource Group will contain, as shown in Figure 9-16, five items:

➤ The two web applications

➤ The database server and the database

➤ The App Service Plan

NAME	TYPE	LOCATION	
Frontend20171217060027	App Service	West Europe	•••
TriathlonRaceTracking20171217052316	App Service	West Europe	•••
triathlonracetracking20171217052316dbserver	SQL server	West Europe	•••
TriathlonRaceTracking20171217052316_db	SQL database	West Europe	•••
TriathlonRaceTracking20171217052316Plan	App Service plan	West Europe	•••

FIGURE 9-16: Content of the Resource Group

Now, if you just followed the chapter for testing, remember to delete the resource group to avoid incurring any unexpected expenses.

SUMMARY

This chapter showed how all the technologies explained in the book can (and must) be used together to build a complete solution made of a "classic" ASP.NET Core MVC-based back-office, a more modern single-page application for the frontend, and a REST service.

It also showed how to publish everything on the cloud for it to be accessible by anyone else.

The code in this chapter is just the tip of the iceberg for the application. You can have a look at the complete example on my GitHub repository `http://github.com/simonech/ TriathlonRaceTracking`.

I hope you enjoyed reading the book as much as I enjoyed writing it and that you have learned how to develop ASP.NET Core applications that include a lot of frontend development techniques.

INDEX